100 THINGS UTES FANS SHOULD KNOW & DO BEFORE THEY DIE

Patrick Sheltra

TRIUMPH
BOOKS

Library of Congress Cataloging-in-Publication Data

Sheltra, Patrick.
   100 things Utes fans should know & do before they die / Patrick Sheltra.
      p. cm.
   Includes bibliographical references.
   ISBN 978-1-60078-597-9
   1. Utah Utes (Football team)—History—Miscellanea. 2. University of Utah—Football—History—Miscellanea. I. Title.
   GV958.U73S54 2011
   796.332'6309792258—dc23
                        2011025179

This book is available in quantity at special discounts for your group or organization. For further information, contact:
   Triumph Books
   542 South Dearborn Street
   Suite 750
   Chicago, Illinois 60605
   (312) 939-3330
   Fax (312) 663-3557
   www.triumphbooks.com

Printed in U.S.A.
ISBN: 978-1-60078-597-9
Design by Patricia Frey
All photos courtesy of AP Images unless otherwise noted

For Utes fans everywhere

Contents

Acknowledgments ix

Introduction xiii

1 Big-Time Entry: Utah's Invitation to the Pac-10 1

2 Urban Meyer 3

3 2009 Sugar Bowl Win Against Alabama 7

4 Original BCS Buster 10

5 Alex Smith 13

6 The Holy War 17

7 The MUSS 24

8 Dr. Chris Hill 26

9 Ron McBride 29

10 Classic Finish I: 2008 Texas Christian 33

11 1995 BYU 35

12 Ike Armstrong 38

13 The 2002 Winter Olympics and the Expansion of
Rice-Eccles Stadium 40

14 What is a Ute? 43

15 Hiking Up to Block U 46

16 Larry Wilson 47

17 Yergy's Drive from 55 in the 1993 Holy War 50

18 Bowling Them Over 52

19 Eric Weddle 57

20 "Utah By Five!" 61

21 Fred and Kyle Whittingham 63

22 Bill Marcroft 65

23 Lusk's Dash in the Dusk 68

24 The Eccles Family 71

25 LaVell Edwards 73

26 Swoop 76

27 Dynasty Architect I: Norm Chow 79

28 The Dark Ages 82

29 The Night the Lights Went Out in Laramie 84

30 Joseph B. Wirthlin 87

31 The Lost Championship of 1969 89

32 Utah's 2004 Coaching Staff 92

33 Flat Broke and Busted in Vegas 94

34 Our Cheerleaders Can Beat Up Your Fans 96

35 The Pie 99

36 2008 Holy War 100

37 Dynasty Architect II: George Seifert 103

38 Rivalry Rewind: Utah State and the Battle of the Brothers . . 106

39 Fred Gehrke 107

40 John Mooney 110

41 Brian Johnson 112

42 The Utah Pass 116

43 The 1964 Liberty Bowl 118

44 The "Utah Man Fight Song" Lyrics 121

45 Robert Rice 123

46 Tailgating in the Guardsman Way Lot 125

47 Luther Elliss 127

48 The Rice Bowl: 1988 Holy War 130

49 Utah Traditions, Part I 132

50 Classic Finish II: 1995 Air Force 134

51 How O.J. Simpson Almost Became a Ute 137

52 The Romney Brothers: Utah's First Family of Sports 140

53 How Utah Won the MWC Title with Just Three Points . . . 142

54 The North End Zone 144

55 Utah Sports Bars 146

56 1994 Freedom Bowl 148

57 Good-bye to the Mountain West Conference 150

58 Classic Finish III: 2008 Oregon State 154

59 Polynesian Power 157

60 Holy War Hijinks 159

61 The Dyson Brothers 162

62 Where to Go When the Game Is Over 163

63 Utah's Twin No. 1 Draft Picks 166

64 Utah's First Dynasty: 1928–33 167

65 How a Ute Took Center Stage in the Heidi Game 170

66 The 1989 Holy War 173

67 Utah Traditions, Part II 175

68 Rivalry Rewind: Arizona State 177

69 Steve Odom 179

70 Classic Finish IV: 1990 Minnesota 182

71 Scott Mitchell 184

72 Bruce Woodbury 187

73 Rivalry Rewind: Colorado 190

74 Louie Sakoda 192

75 Wayne Howard 195

76 The Andersons 198

77 Crazy Eights: How Utah Lost the 1994 WAC Title 201

78 Chuck Stobart 203

79 Visit the Charlie Monfort Family Hall of Champions 206

80 Steve Smith 208

81 Mac Speedie 210

82 Erroll Tucker 212

83 Dynasty Architect III: Pokey Allen 215

84 Who Are These Guys? Old-School Utah Coaches 217

85 The Duck 222

86 Rivalry Rewind: Wyoming 224

87 The BYU Players U. Love to Hate 227

88 Mike McCoy 230

89 The Kenneth P. Burbidge Family Academic Center 233

90 1994 Holy War 234

91 Carlisle Indian School Comes to Utah 236

92 Utah Traditions, Part III 239

93 Jordan Gross 240

94 Morgan Scalley 242

95 Dee Glen Smith Center 246

96 Mike Giddings 247

97 Thomas Herrion 251

98 Roy Jefferson 254

99 Classic Finish V: 1972 Arizona 256

100 Steve Marshall's Seven-Touchdown Game Against
Colorado State 259

General Sources 263

Acknowledgments

The inspiration and contributions that were made to make *100 Things Utes Fans Should Know & Do Before They Die* are almost too numerous to mention here, but I'll give it a shot.

Without the success of the Utah program in the 21st century, it is difficult to imagine the demand and interest behind such a book. From the moment Chris Hill settled on Urban Meyer as head coach to Utah's invitation into what is known today as the Pacific-12 Conference, Utah football has been relevant on a national scale. But as one who has lived away from Salt Lake City since graduating from the U. in 1996, I often relied on the powers of technology to keep me connected with Utah football.

With that, a special thanks is first extended to Christopher Evans, operator of Utefans.net, and many of the site's contributors who over the years have engaged my mind and raised my interest in Utah football to the point where I believed there was a void that could be filled by *100 Things Utes Fans Should Know & Do Before They Die*. Sean Reynolds at Block U, Brian Swinney at Scout.com's Inside the Utes, and Tom Cella at Utezone.com—an affiliate of the Rivals network—also deserve thanks for their efforts to bring the pulse of the U. community to fans and alumni both near and far. Without these sites, there would have been an inevitable disconnect from Utah football for this Utah Man. At the same time, Sean, Brian, and Tom earned a lot of credit for helping fuel the growing interest in Utah football.

Adam Miller, whose fascination with Utah football history exceeds even my own, deserves mention for his efforts in putting together the blog "The Greatest Utah Football Games Ever Played." Many of those games are mentioned here in some form, but Adam's blog provides additional insight, color, and background, making it a must-read for any Utah fan. His efforts significantly aided my research, and he wasn't afraid to give me his opinion on topics he believed should be covered in this book.

Several people at the University of Utah aided my research efforts. In no particular order of importance, Liz Abel, Manny Hendrix, and Brett Eden deserve recognition for first addressing, then delivering my requests. Outside of the current U. community, the cooperation of Dick Rosetta, Ron McBride, Bill Marcroft, George Seifert, and Mike Giddings was vital in filling in a lot of holes on events that weren't as well documented during their immersion in the Utah program. Finally, a collective thank-you for those who consented to interviews; their names can be found in the General Sources section at the end of this book. I hope your sentiments toward the finished product are equal to the admiration I have for your contributions to Utah football.

Tom Bast at Triumph Books deserves special recognition for sharing the same vision I had for this book. Triumph Books has published the *100 Things* series for several professional teams, and its collegiate lineup consists of Texas, Oklahoma, Ohio State, Michigan, Notre Dame, Alabama, Auburn, and Georgia. He didn't need to grant Utah entry into such elite territory, but he did. My editors, Adam Motin and Karen O'Brien, were always quick to respond to my questions and concerns, and were a tremendous asset for this first-time book author.

Those who took part in this project are as numerous as those who influenced and guided me during my professional career in print, online, and broadcast media. Within the state of Utah, at the top of that list would be Grant Flygare at Utah Valley Community College (now Utah Valley State College) and Matt Ott at the U.

On a personal note, my decision to attend the University of Utah—an institution without peer and one of which I am proud to call myself an alumnus—would not have been possible if not for my mother, Lonna Johnson, and her decision to move to Salt

Lake City and go back to school at the U. when I was a teenager. Finally, my wife, Roberta, and my three children, Carson, Delaney, and Wyatt, endured many a weekend without my company while I was locked away and working on this book. They are the loves of my life, and I thank them for their patience and support.

Ki-Yi!

Introduction

When it comes to the subject of football at the University of Utah, I have never been shy about sharing my opinion. Those who know me on even the most casual of levels can attest to that. With that in mind, the responsibility of taking the 100 most important things about Utah football—*and ranking them!*—was terrifying. Who am I to make those kinds of distinctions?

However, once I remembered that the number of lists or rankings that gained universal and unanimous agreement are in the vicinity of zero, putting them together for this book became a little bit easier and a lot more enjoyable. The whole point of such rankings is to generate debate, to enlighten, and to entertain. And if you don't believe that to be the case, explain the furor and fascination caused by the weekly Associated Press and coaches' poll rankings over the years. College football, by its very nature of determining which team is best, is controversial.

So if you have a disagreement on the placement of a particular item, guess what? You're right! The who, what, and when of Utah football have different meanings for different people. My best measure of the success of this book won't come from the number of copies sold but from the number of people I encounter who aren't shy in telling me that I put this player too low or rated another game too high. Or as Evan Woodbery wrote in the Auburn version of the *100 Things* series, "Take this book not as a definitive pronouncement...but as a jumping-off point for further discussion and debate."

Notice that the word *greatest* is absent from the book's title. To best appreciate the ground Utah football has covered over the last decade, it's important to remember the countless toe-stubbings, near-misses, and empty off-seasons that followed blowout losses to BYU that the program endured for nearly 30 years. It's important for that period to be documented in this book—not just for perspective's sake, but for the simple fact that there were still some dynamite players and games in that era.

Many of my greatest memories as a sports fan have involved Utah football, and no project in my professional career has been as enjoyable to work on as this one. For you, the reader, I hope this book provides a similar amount of satisfaction.

1 Big-Time Entry: Utah's Invitation to the Pac-10

"When you compete for championships in the Pac-10, you compete for national championships."

—Dr. Chris Hill at a press conference announcing Utah's entry into the Pac-10 Conference

The summer of 2010 was the most anxiously anticipated off-season in the history of Utah football. The Big 10 made its long-awaited expansion from 11 to 12 teams by adding Nebraska, and rumors had been swirling all around Salt Lake City that the Pac-10 would follow suit. While previous Pac-10 leaders had scoffed at the idea of expansion, new Pac-10 president Larry Scott openly talked about the possibility of adding two teams—something the league last did with Arizona and Arizona State in 1978.

Adding to the tension were Texas media outlets—most notably Chip Brown at Orangebloods.com—detailing the Pac-10 and the University of Texas' efforts to create the first super-conference among the Bowl Championship Series conferences. Almost all of those possibilities listed Utah as an afterthought candidate at best.

But on June 16, not long after Texas made its public commitment to keep the Big 12 Conference intact—albeit at 10 teams, for the time being anyway—Scott sent the message every Utah fan had been waiting a lifetime to hear: "Come on board, Utes."

"It raises the opportunity to not have that glass ceiling that is there for teams not in one of the six BCS conferences," Hill said when asked what the invitation's biggest benefit would be for Utah football.

Translation: Utah will never again have to fear going undefeated and being relegated to a non-factor in the national title picture, as was the case during perfect campaigns in 2004 and 2008.

"It's a win-win for us," Coach Kyle Whittingham said. "No question about it. It's a win-win for the university."

In the fall of 2010, Utah's future was further cemented when its new conference leaders decided on a new name for the league, the Pac-12 Conference, and a true geographical North-South setup for divisional play. Utah will compete in the Pac-12 South along with long-ago conference rivals Colorado, Arizona, and Arizona State, plus USC and UCLA. Utah will play those teams every year and four more from the Pac-12 North, which features Stanford, Cal, Oregon, Oregon State, Washington, and Washington State. The conference setup will also feature a championship game between the winners of the two divisions.

Adding to the benefits of the new league were the enhanced bowl opportunities for Utah. As a champion in the Mountain West Conference, and provided it didn't qualify for a BCS bowl game, Utah's bowl destination would be against the Pac-10's No. 5 team in the Las Vegas Bowl. Now should Utah win the Pac-12, it would be headed for the granddaddy of them all—the Rose Bowl.

That possibility was not lost on Pac-10 leaders, who brought along officials from the Rose Bowl to Utah's celebratory press conference.

There will likely be some growing pains. Utah will not be a full partner in revenue sharing until after its third year in the league, which would come in the 2014–15 athletic year. But a separate television contract for the first Pac-12 championship game and additional televised games as the result of expansion reportedly will pay $25 million to the conference. Split 12 ways, Utah's take is just more than $2 million, or nearly double the $1.2 million it received annually from the Mountain West Conference.

As it becomes a full partner in revenue sharing, Utah's revenue will vastly exceed what it received in the MWC. Some estimates say Utah could get as much as $13–$14.5 million per year as a fully vested revenue partner with a new Pac-12 television contract…and that's before BCS bowl and NCAA basketball tournament shares are calculated into the mix.

Utah can ride out the initial financial concessions a little easier knowing it will receive more fan interest, media attention, and marketing opportunities than it would have gotten in its previous conferences as the Utes enjoy their initial season in the Pac-12, traveling to new locales and establishing new rivalries (or in the case of Colorado, Arizona, and Arizona State, reestablishing). There is no more exciting time to be a fan of Utah football as it heads into its initial season in the Pac-12 Conference.

2 Urban Meyer

Urban Meyer's tenure with the Utes lasted all of two seasons. But they were the most glorious, thrilling two years Utah had ever experienced, displaying once and for all the potential that existed in Utah football. At the same time, the foundation Meyer helped build during the 2003–04 seasons was strong enough to endure long after his departure, and without that foundation, it's possible that inclusion in the Pac-12 Conference would remain a fantasy for Utah.

There were periods of greatness in the Utah football program prior to Meyer, but mostly they were significant only for history buffs and the lucky few fans still alive who remembered Ike

Urban Meyer brought an intensity and passion to Utah football that helped carry it to unprecedented heights with back-to-back conference titles in 2003–04 for the first time in 50 years, as well as leading the first team from a non-automatic qualifying conference into a BCS bowl game. (Photo courtesy Tom Smart)

Armstrong's teams from way back when. For the 60 years previous to Meyer's arrival, Utah was a basketball school.

So what factors were in play to help Utah land arguably the best college football coach of his generation?

More than a decade before arriving in Salt Lake City, Utah coaches had crossed paths with Meyer on the recruiting trail when Meyer was a wide receiver coach at Colorado State. His first boss, Earle Bruce, remembered Meyer as a graduate assistant who had worked with Bruce when they were at Ohio State in the mid-1980s. It was Bruce who saved Meyer from the rigors of an 8-to-5 job in order to support his family—Meyer made just $6,000 as an assistant coach at Illinois State—and offered him a job as a receiver coach with a much-needed pay increase.

"My dad is first, Earle is second," Meyer said in a 2009 article in *Sports Illustrated*, talking about the men who have influenced his life.

"I've never seen a coach so deep into [the game]," Bruce said. "Some coaches bitch about the hours you put in, but the guys who like football don't; they only bitch about wasting hours. When it came time to recruit, he brought in more good players than anybody we had there."

Bruce was fired after the 1992 season, and Meyer appeared out of a job. New coach Sonny Lubick—a stark contrast to Meyer's disciplined, tough-love approach—saw something in Meyer and rehired him. Meyer stayed at CSU for another three years.

Next was a five-year stint as the receiver coach at Notre Dame—a dream job for Meyer, who is Catholic. There he became associated with Mike Sanford, who was the quarterback coach under Bob Davie.

"He was constantly coming up with ideas of how to spread out the ball, just for fun," said Sanford, who later would be Meyer's offensive coordinator at Utah. "We'd put together entire game plans that just wouldn't fly in the offense Notre Dame was running."

Meyer's first head coaching job was at Bowling Green, where he inherited a team that went 2–9 and turned it into an 8–3 outfit the following year. A nine-win season followed, and he was hired as the 16th coach in Utah history after the 2002 season.

Having enjoyed her previous trip out west, Shelley Meyer encouraged her husband to consider Utah's offer. Meyer, who had seen Utah's 10-win team in 1994 as a CSU assistant, knew there was potential. "I couldn't see why Utah wasn't winning," he said.

Meyer had previously seen Utah's talent on film and on game day, but there was little else there. Meyer was shocked at how poor

Utah's facilities were, Rice-Eccles Stadium notwithstanding. Fan support was lukewarm, and there wasn't the dedication to conditioning necessary to be a big winner, or at least the dedication Meyer wanted to instill.

As he had done at Bowling Green, Meyer's first workout at Utah consisted of locked doors, trash cans, and an endless sprinting session. "We stared at each other for 45 minutes," running back Marty Johnson said. "We couldn't believe what life was going to be like."

There were some rough patches that first year, but there was nothing to give anyone a reason to believe Meyer wouldn't be a smashing success. Quarterback Brett Elliott went down for the year with a broken collarbone on a failed two-point conversion attempt after leading Utah back from a multiple-score deficit in the fourth quarter at Texas A&M. Utah won five straight with Alex Smith as quarterback but was outclassed in a 47–35 home loss to New Mexico.

The positives were far greater. In Meyer's third game, Utah set a single-game home-attendance record against Cal that still stands today. The following week, with his former team driving for the winning score, Arnold Parker returned a fumble 80 yards for a touchdown as Utah beat Colorado State for the first time since 1994.

The season concluded with a pair of shutouts against BYU and Southern Mississippi in the Liberty Bowl. It was a nice prelude to the 2004 season, in which Utah went 12–0 and became the first team from a non-BCS conference to play in a BCS game. Although Meyer moved on to Florida after the 2004 season, questions about his former program came up often in the 2008 season—Meyer's Gators won the national title, while Utah, which featured some notable Meyer recruits, finished No. 2.

"Utah is not going away now," Meyer said before the media and a room full of Gator fans after the Gators defeated Oklahoma to win the 2008 national championship. "If you go evaluate that program…you keep hearing the words 'BCS conferences.' I can't think of many schools that are better than Utah."

2009 Sugar Bowl Win Against Alabama

To say Utah was an underdog in the 2009 Sugar Bowl against Alabama is an understatement of Terrence Cody–sized proportions. The previous year, Hawaii had crashed the BCS from the Western Athletic Conference and was pummeled by Georgia in the Sugar Bowl. Although Utah and Boise State had registered BCS bowl wins in 2004 and 2006, respectively, many viewed the Hawaii game as a return to the norm—that schools from non-BCS conferences had no business playing in bowl games against traditional powers from major conferences.

Entering the game, No. 4 Alabama had been ranked more weeks at No. 1 than any team in the country, while No. 6 Utah, despite being undefeated, had more than its share of close calls.

So from the moment Las Vegas issued its opening line on the game (Alabama was a 10½-point favorite) to the Fox pregame show when Barry Switzer said not one player on Utah's roster would have been recruited by Alabama coming out of high school, Utah fans were forced to either bite their tongues or debate a skeptical public that insisted this game would be a blowout.

At least they got the blowout part of the equation right.

Utah's 31–17 beating of Alabama was far more decisive than the score indicated. The Crimson Tide offense was never a threat, scoring its lone touchdown on a short field after a Brian Johnson fumble. Its other touchdown came on a Javier Arenas punt return.

Meanwhile, Utah and Johnson shredded the 'Bama defense in opening a 21–0 first-quarter lead.

Utah's defense sacked quarterback John Parker Wilson eight times, intercepted him twice, forced a fumble, and stuffed the vaunted 'Bama ground attack—which only featured a third-round NFL Draft pick in Glen Coffee and 2009 Heisman winner Mark Ingram—to just 31 rushing yards and 208 total yards.

Alabama wanted to be there, fighting back from the early three-TD hole to get within four points at 21–17. But just like it did against Michigan, Air Force, Oregon State, and TCU, Utah remained cool and quickly regained momentum. A 33-yard pass-and-run by Freddie Brown advanced the ball into Crimson Tide territory. Bradon Godfrey caught a key 10-yard pass on third-and-10. And on another third-and-10, Johnson hit David Reed on a curl pattern. Reed slipped a tackle and raced to the end zone untouched to regain Utah's two-possession lead.

Utah would force two Alabama turnovers in the fourth quarter and win going away.

Having listened to a month's worth of dismissal, chagrin, and skepticism, it was now Utah's turn to talk.

"You tell us where to be, when to be there, and we will be there," Utah coach Kyle Whittingham said. "We are the only ones standing right now with an unblemished record."

"Without question we are one of the best teams, if not the best team, in the country," Johnson said.

Perhaps Utah's greatest motivation came from Alabama coach Nick Saban. Maybe Saban was trying to salve his team's wounds after a loss to Florida in the SEC championship game. However, his claim of Alabama being the only team in the country to go undefeated in a "real BCS conference" struck a nerve within the entire Utah program.

It would be one thing to tout SEC supremacy; it was quite another to let clearly inferior leagues like the Big East and Pac-10 (which went 1–7 against the MWC in 2008) piggyback onto Alabama's success. But Saban's words were merely an extension of what the national pundits had been saying all season long: Utah couldn't live up to the week-in, week-out demands of any BCS conference.

"The whole team knew about that," said senior defensive tackle Greg Newman. "We came out here hungry, ready to go. It was no respect, a slap in the face."

In the aftermath, it was nothing but hugs and tenderness.

"Find me anybody else that went undefeated," argued Rick Reilly for *ESPN The Magazine*. "Thirteen-and-zero. Beat four ranked teams. Went to the Deep South and seal-clubbed Alabama in the Sugar Bowl.... So that's it. Utah is the national champion."

John Feinstein begged AP poll voters to reconsider Utah's spot in the polls. "I am writing to urge you—no, implore you—to cast your final ballot of the season with one team and one team only ranked No. 1: the University of Utah."

Many listened but not enough to leapfrog Utah ahead of Florida and former coach Urban Meyer. Still, with 16 first-place votes (as opposed to zero during the regular season), it was good enough for Utah's No. 2 finish in the AP polls. The coaches, apparently oblivious to Utah's undefeated mark and Sugar Bowl Stomp, relegated Utah to No. 4. Nonetheless, both finishes represented Utah's best ranking ever in the polls.

It was a magical season by any standard. And for the Oklahomas and USCs of the world who find no satisfaction in finishing No. 2 in the polls...if any of them carried Utah's 2008 resume, highlighted by four wins against Top 25 teams and two in the Top 10, and no other team finished undefeated, they would end up being ranked at the top.

4 Original BCS Buster

When the Bowl Championship Series, nee Bowl Alliance, was formed in 1996, it effectively created a caste system in college football. There were the privileged teams from the six power conferences at the time—Big East, Big Ten, Big 12, Atlantic Coast, Southeastern, and Pac-10, plus independent Notre Dame. And then there were the ne'er-do-wells, led by the Western Athletic Conference, the Mid-American Conference, Sun Belt, Big West, and Conference USA. In 1998, the breakup of the 16-team WAC led to the formation of the Mountain West Conference, of which Utah was a member. The Big West stopped sanctioning football in 2000, leaving five non-BCS conferences.

The ultimate formation of the BCS was, and remains today, about concentrating money and exposure among the elite programs and their conferences. On the field, it would appear the BCS was formed to keep another team like Brigham Young from winning the national championship, as BYU did in 1984 despite facing a slew of unranked, losing programs on its way to posting the nation's only perfect record.

The bar was set almost impossibly high for teams from non-BCS conferences, and the gap in exposure and financial windfall from TV contracts and bowl appearances grew greater and greater. For any team from a non-automatic-qualifying conference, it must finish in the top six of the BCS standings for entry into a major BCS bowl game—Rose, Sugar, Fiesta, and Orange.

And with a bunch of components slanted against the non-automatic-qualifying schools, like strength of schedule, margin of victory, and quality wins, not to mention the bias routinely exhibited by the poll voters in favor of the bigger conferences, reaching that top-six benchmark seemed like droplets of water to a man dying of thirst. Sure, the access was there, but could any team realistically break through? Until 2004, the highest finish by a non-automatic-qualifying school was 10th, by Tulane in 1998.

Going into the 2004 season, Utah wanted to be that team. It certainly had the talent to be that team, returning 15 of 22 starters and both specialists. It was a team without anything remotely resembling a glaring weakness, plus it had plenty of depth at the skill positions. And 13 players on the roster were either drafted or played in the NFL.

Steve Savoy salted away Utah's first 11–0 season and trip to a major New Year's Day bowl game with this 92-yard touchdown run against BYU in the 2004 Holy War. (Photo courtesy Tom Smart)

"That's what I think of every day when I'm in the weight room—undefeated," junior center Jesse Boone said that off-season. "That's what I'm working for—undefeated season and BCS. Make it so they can't keep us out of the BCS, that's all I can think about.... I don't just mean undefeated, either. I mean just beat teams to where they're just like, 'Wow, who are these guys?'"

Urban Meyer wanted Utah to be that team, but he also knew there were 11 games to go before the Utes could be that team. So he shut down all talk of what could await Utah at the end of the season and got his players to focus solely on next week's opponent.

It took just three plays into the 2004 season for the hype to validate itself when Steve Savoy ran a post route, caught a perfectly delivered ball from Alex Smith for a first down on third-and-18, and finished the play with a 78-yard touchdown reception to kick off a 41–21 rout of Texas A&M.

"Subversives who enjoy seeing the college football establishment squirm have found their team for 2004," wrote Pat Forde for ESPN.com after the game.

The blowouts continued and Utah, ranked 20th in the preseason by the Associated Press, started a steady climb up the polls. Utah bounced between sixth and seventh in the BCS standings, then prior to playing BYU, Utah solidly moved into the No. 6 spot for good. After beating BYU, the gap between Utah and No. 7 Georgia was the largest between adjacent teams in the BCS standings.

The only thing left between Utah and a BCS bowl were the monsters under the bed. Conspiracy theorists were convinced these monsters would never allow a program like Utah's to join the cool kids' club and play in a major bowl game.

In the end, they were partly right. The Utes got their major-bowl-game invitation but hardly an opponent befitting such an occasion. Pittsburgh may have come from a major conference in the Big East, but at 8–3 it had won a four-way tiebreaker for first for the right to get trampled by Utah in the Fiesta Bowl. The Utes, 17½-point favorites, scored touchdowns on five of their first seven possessions and rolled 35–7.

Starting in 2006, the restrictions on non-BCS-conference teams getting into a BCS bowl game have been lessened. Now teams must finish in the top 12 and can gain entry by finishing as low as 16th in the BCS standings, provided they finish ahead of a BCS conference champion. But even in its undefeated 2008 season, Utah didn't need the relaxed conditions, finishing at No. 6.

Since 2004, Boise State, Texas Christian, and Hawaii have all crashed the party and played in a BCS bowl game. It's no longer the insurmountable task it once seemed. But Utah will always carry the distinction of being the original BCS buster.

5 Alex Smith

Who is the greatest Utah player of all time? It's a good question, with plenty of ammunition available for several players. Larry Wilson is the only Ute enshrined in the Pro Football Hall of Fame. Scott Mitchell rewrote the NCAA record book like no other Utah quarterback before or since. And Eric Weddle played—and contributed in big ways—at just about every position on the field save interior lineman.

Those are impressive credentials. But what separates Alex Smith from everyone else are these undeniable facts—no Utah quarterback won a greater percentage of his starts than Smith, and he finished fourth in the Heisman voting in 2004, one of the deepest Heisman fields ever.

Finishing fourth doesn't sound like a big deal, but consider the resumes of the five Heisman finalists who assembled in New York City that year for the award's 70th presentation:

- Matt Leinart, University of Southern California—won 2004 Heisman Trophy
- Adrian Peterson, University of Oklahoma—finished second, the highest finish ever by a freshman
- Jason White, University of Oklahoma—won 2003 Heisman Trophy
- Alex Smith, University of Utah—No. 1 pick in the 2004 NFL Draft
- Reggie Bush, University of Southern California—won 2005 Heisman Trophy

Alex Smith kicked off his spectacular 2004 junior season and eventual Heisman Trophy chase by leading Utah to a 41–21 shellacking of Texas A&M in the season opener. (Photo courtesy Tom Smart)

Three Heisman winners, the top freshman running back of all time, as well as a standout NFL player, and the No. 2 pick in the 2006 NFL Draft. And if those accolades don't knock you over, consider that the regular-season records of the three programs represented was 35–0.

Unlike his Heisman competition—all of whom were either highly touted prep stars and/or experienced early success in their collegiate careers—by comparison, Smith came from the wrong side of the tracks.

Although Smith was a decent high school quarterback at San Diego Helix High School, where he played in the same backfield as Bush and was twice named his league's offensive MVP, Smith had all of two offers—and one of those came largely because his uncle, John L. Smith, was the head coach at Louisville.

The start to his collegiate career was an unqualified disaster. As the sands were rapidly passing through the hourglass of Ron McBride's stint as Utah head coach, Smith was inserted into a game against San Diego State. Utah had lost three straight after a 2–0 start when Smith was put in the game for starter Brett Elliott. He was 2-for-3 in passing, was sacked, and threw an interception that was returned for a touchdown as the Aztecs rolled 36–17.

Smith threw one more pass that season. At season's end, and with a year of eligibility wasted, Smith thought about transferring. But Meyer was hired, and Smith had warmed to the climate in the Utah locker room, so he stuck it out.

Elliott was still the starting quarterback at the beginning of the 2003 season, but Smith saw meaningful snaps in the season-opening victory against Utah State. The following week, Elliott went the distance and led a Utah comeback on the road against Texas A&M. But in trying to run for the tying two-point conversion, Elliott broke his collarbone, ending his season.

Smith was solid if not spectacular as the Utes won his first two starts against Cal and Colorado State. Unleashed against nationally

Alex Smith throws against Wyoming late in the 2004 season, a victory that clinched Utah's second consecutive outright Mountain West Conference championship. (AP Photo/Laramie Daily Boomerang, Michael Smith)

ranked Oregon, Smith threw for 340 yards and a pair of scores as the Utes won 17–13.

"When the bright lights come on at game time, a lot of guys go in one of two directions," said Mississippi State head coach Dan Mullen, who was Smith's quarterback coach for two years at Utah. "They either take it up a step, or they kind of shy away from it. And when the lights went on for [Smith], it was showtime."

In 2004, Smith's trajectory shattered all conceivable expectations. Utah was ranked in the preseason AP and coaches polls for the first time in history, and Smith captained the most devastating offense in Utah history. Utah smashed the 500-point barrier for the only time in school history, averaging 45.3 points per game.

If there were any negatives to Smith's career at Utah, it was that he has no defining moment-in-the-clutch. All of Utah's wins in 2004 were by at least 14 points, and close games in 2003 largely featured heroic plays by the defense. Football, however, remains a team game, and with Smith at the helm, Utah won consecutive conference titles for the first time in 51 years.

6 The Holy War

The name of the annual football game between Utah and Brigham Young University is far from being politically correct, even before the events of September 11 and the U.S. war on terrorism. There are members of the Church of Jesus Christ of Latter-day Saints who abhor the nickname and correctly point out that the rivalry's nickname is a misnomer since a holy war constitutes conflict between two religious groups—an impossible distinction since the majority of Utah's citizens are Mormon. Never mind the affront it poses to veterans of the armed forces, many of whom know what a real war is all about.

While Mormons of all genders, ages, and races practice their faith to varying degrees within the state of Utah, their coexistence with one another doesn't come within a galaxy of, say, Jews and Palestinians.

Whether one views the nickname as appropriate or unfortunate, it will stand in this book for purposes of identification. Utah has had several rivals throughout the program's history and has played Utah State more than any other team. But when one mentions the Holy War, the opponent cannot be mistaken. And besides, the name is unique, setting it apart from rivalries that carry mundane titles, like the Big Game for Stanford-Cal, or where the stakes are for some lifeless object, like a bell or a cup.

Religion plays a huge role in the intensity of the rivalry…the true calling card on the roll call of great college football rivalries. It simply does not exist on this scale anywhere else in major college football. If there are warring factions, they can best be described as such: the University of Utah is the state-run secular school that offers all the same diversions of a typical college campus, while BYU is owned and operated by the LDS Church, and its students must live by a strict Honor Code (which encompasses everything from dress and grooming to sexual habits) or risk expulsion.

The factions carry themselves past their respective campuses. At their most extreme levels, Utah fans characterize BYU fans as nothing but sanctimonious do-gooders who are unflinchingly hypocritical and arrogant, while BYU fans stereotype Utah fans as incorrigible drunks capable of committing all kinds of unspeakable acts against humanity. If the Ute supporter is a practicing Mormon (and there are many of them), then his or her allegiance to the church and God himself is questioned.

Again, those are the extremes. But is it any wonder this rivalry carries all the necessary ingredients of spite and bitterness? Coupled with an amazing run of games that don't get nearly the amount of credit that they should within the collegiate landscape, it is one of the nation's truly great rivalries.

But it wasn't always that way—at least on the field.

For nearly 70 years, this was one of the least-compelling rivalries in the nation. Utah lost only once in the first 33 meetings between the two schools, going 34–2–4[1] from 1922–64. And one of those losses came during World War II, when able-bodied athletes were at a premium, as evidenced by the discontinuation of the rivalry from 1943–45.

BYU finally started a winning streak against Utah, winning three straight from 1965–67. Then Utah followed by winning four straight. While those wins were hard-fought affairs, no one envisioned the dominance BYU would establish in this series when LaVell Edwards was hired in 1972. During the next 20 years, BYU would win 18 of 20 against the hapless Utes, who finished with just eight winning seasons during that time and rarely challenged for Western Athletic Conference crowns.

Looking for true competition between these schools? Save it for basketball season.

Things changed in 1993, when a pair of average teams with glaring holes in the secondary going up against high-powered offenses combined for a 34–31 classic, a Utah victory that came on Chris Yergensen's 55-yard field goal in the final minute. It was Utah's first triumph in Provo since 1971, and if the victory didn't provide enough fuel, Utah players and fans did their part to pour kerosene on the entire affair by trying to tear down the goalposts.

---

1. At the time of this publication, Utah recognized the overall series as 54–34–4 in favor of the Utes, but BYU has it at 51–31–4, refusing to acknowledge six games that were played when the school was known as Brigham Young Academy from its origin in 1875 until 1903, when it officially became Brigham Young University. Never mind that BYU holds true to 1875 as its date of establishment. Maybe BYU refuses to acknowledge its Academy days for fear of having to explain more about its football history, such as dropping the sport entirely in 1898 because it was "a barbarous, brutal exercise not to be dignified by the title of a game." Such trivial debating points make up a good chunk of every great rivalry.

Holy War Results

*1896: Utah 12, Brigham Young Academy 4
*Utah 6, Brigham Young Academy 0
*Brigham Young Academy 8, Utah 6
*1897: Brigham Young Academy 14, Utah 0
*1897: Brigham Young Academy 22, Utah 0
*1898: Utah 5, Brigham Young Academy 0
1922: Utah 49, BYU 0
1923: Utah 15, BYU 0
1924: Utah 35, BYU 6
1925: Utah 27, BYU 0
1926: Utah 40, BYU 7
1927: Utah 20, BYU 0
1928: Utah 0, BYU 0
1929: Utah 45, BYU 13
1930: Utah 34, BYU 7
1931: Utah 43, BYU 0
1932: Utah 29, BYU 0
1933: Utah 21, BYU 6
1934: Utah 43, BYU 0
1935: Utah 32, BYU 0
1936: Utah 18, BYU 0
1937: Utah 14, BYU 0
1938: Utah 7, BYU 7
1939: Utah 35, BYU 13
1940: Utah 12, BYU 6
1941: Utah 6, BYU 6
1942: BYU 12, Utah 7
1943-45: No game
1946: Utah 35, BYU 6
1947: Utah 28, BYU 6
1948: Utah 30, BYU 0
1949: Utah 38, BYU 0
1950: Utah 28, BYU 28
1951: Utah 7, BYU 6

1952: Utah 34, BYU 6
1953: Utah 33, BYU 32
1954: Utah 12, BYU 7
1955: Utah 41, BYU 9
1956: Utah 41, BYU 6
1957: Utah 27, BYU 0
1958: BYU 14, Utah 7
1959: Utah 20, BYU 8
1960: Utah 17, BYU 0
1961: Utah 21, BYU 20
1962: Utah 35, BYU 20
1963: Utah 15, BYU 6
1964: Utah 47, BYU 13
1965: BYU 25, Utah 20
1966: BYU 35, Utah 13
1967: BYU 17, Utah 13
1968: Utah 30, BYU 21
1969: Utah 16, BYU 6
1970: Utah 14, BYU 13
1971: Utah 17, BYU 15
1972: BYU 16, Utah 7
1973: BYU 46, Utah 22
1974: BYU 48, Utah 20
1975: BYU 51, Utah 20
1976: BYU 34, Utah 12
1977: BYU 38, Utah 8
1978: Utah 23, BYU 22
1979: BYU 27, Utah 0
1980: BYU 56, Utah 6
1981: BYU 56, Utah 28
1982: BYU 17, Utah 12
1983: BYU 55, Utah 7
1984: BYU 24, Utah 14
1985: BYU 38, Utah 28
1986: BYU 35, Utah 21
1987: BYU 21, Utah 18

1988: Utah 57, BYU 28
1989: BYU 70, Utah 31
1990: BYU 45, Utah 22
1991: BYU 48, Utah 17
1992: BYU 31, Utah 22
1993: Utah 34, BYU 31
1994: Utah 34, BYU 31
1995: Utah 34, BYU 17
1996: BYU 37, Utah 17
1997: Utah 20, BYU 14
1998: BYU 26, Utah 24
1999: Utah 20, BYU 17
2000: BYU 34, Utah 27
2001: BYU 24, Utah 21
2002: Utah 13, BYU 6
2003: Utah 3, BYU 0
2004: Utah 52, BYU 21
2005: Utah 41, BYU 34 (OT)
2006: BYU 33, Utah 31
2007: BYU 17, Utah 10
2008: Utah 48, BYU 24
2009: BYU 26, Utah 23 (OT)
2010: Utah 17, BYU 16

*At the time of this publication, Utah recognized the overall series as 54–34–4 in favor of the Utes, but BYU has it at 51–31–4, refusing to acknowledge six games that were played when it went by Brigham Young Academy from its origin in 1875 until 1903, when it officially became Brigham Young University. Never mind that BYU holds true to 1875 as its date of establishment. Maybe BYU refuses to acknowledge its Academy days for fear of having to explain more about its football history, such as dropping the sport entirely in 1898 because it was "A barbarous, brutal exercise not to be dignified by the title of a game." Such trivial debating points make up a good chunk of every great rivalry.

BYU players quickly intervened, the Utah faction backed down, and Lenny Gomes issued his memorable quote about the "low-life losers" over at Utah.

Two significantly better teams took the field in Salt Lake City a year later, but the final score again was Utah 34, BYU 31. Utah would make it three straight victories in the series with a 34–17 pounding of BYU in Provo for the program's first conference title in 30 years, but BYU rebounded in 1996 by trouncing the Utes in Salt Lake City en route to a school-record 14-win season.

Since then, the teams have met 14 times, with 12 games being decided by a touchdown or less. Utah has the rare blowouts, capping undefeated regular seasons in 2004 and 2008 with lopsided wins, while BYU has a healthy edge in heart-stopping victories. Five times deep into the fourth quarter, BYU was one play away from certain defeat yet rallied in the most soul-crushing fashion to win. Or in the case of the 1998 game, when Ryan Kaneshiro doinked a relatively easy field goal on the final play of the game that would have given Utah a victory, you could have watched the Utes stub their collective toes.

There were some who claimed that with Utah's move to the Pac-10 and BYU's move to independent status, the time was right for a break in the rivalry. The atmosphere surrounding the rivalry was too intense, and both sides could use a break from one another. What those people tend to forget is that it has always been an intense rivalry. Always. Those first intense moments didn't even revolve around a football game—it revolved around baseball and track.

The event was "not the success that it should have been," according to one account, because the competing teams treated each other so "discourteously." After several arguments over individual scores, the academy was declared the winner in track and field by a margin of four points. The final score of the baseball game was never fully resolved because when the University of Utah team scored three runs on what the academy team claimed was a foul ball, a brawl broke out. The umpires decided to grant the runs, tying the score, and then called the game a draw.

There have been far fewer fists clenched and punches thrown over the years, but that doesn't diminish from the animosity and ill will created by the rivalry—especially when it comes time for the Holy War.

7 The MUSS

"There's something about the MUSS and Utah playing at home."
—ESPN college football analyst Kirk Herbstreit during ESPN *Gameday's* broadcast at Rice-Eccles Stadium before the 2010 game against TCU

Never mind that TCU made a mockery of Herbstreit's prediction of a Utah victory with a 47–7 thrashing of the No. 5 Utes. That a national sports personality thought Utah's student section could provide the boost needed to upset the fourth-ranked Horned Frogs would have been seen not even a decade prior as pure folly by Utah followers.

Herbstreit's ringing endorsement of the MUSS—the University of Utah's student fan club for football, as well as men's basketball and women's soccer, volleyball, and gymnastics—was probably the only highlight of an otherwise dreary and embarrassing day for the Utah football program, which saw its BCS bowl hopes go up in smoke. That loss, however, won't deter future members from joining the MUSS, whose numbers are growing every year.

The MUSS (Mighty Utah Student Section) has been an emotional and vocal force behind Utah's resurgence in football with 6,000 active members and room for more. (Photo courtesy Tom Smart)

Founded in 2002—a year before Urban Meyer arrived with his own brand of enthusiasm—MUSS membership was modest at first, numbering around 600 students in its first year. In just two years, ESPN.com named it one of the five top student sections in the nation. It has since grown to more than 6,000 students, and their impact on games has not gone unnoticed by key figures within the program.

"It starts with those guys," said Coach Kyle Whittingham about the MUSS before Utah's 2010 season opener against Pittsburgh. "They're one of the best student sections in the country. It just keeps getting bigger and better each and every year."

There are several aspects that make the MUSS one of the best student sections in the country, says Michael Rueckert, a MUSS board member.

"The way it's grown, it's become the cool thing to do," Rueckert said. "That's what all the students want to do. They want to be at the games on Saturdays. The way it's organized, the traditions that have grown, there are students that take pride in…being one of the best student sections in the country.

"We're kind of like the athletic department for the MUSS. We recruit members and promote traditions," he added. "We're connected with the team and the athletic department. There's a game-day atmosphere committee and committees for communications, tailgating, and marketing. Each of those committees is in charge of their own area, and the whole goal is to get more students involved in creating a better game-day atmosphere."

The benefits of such a strong student section are obvious on game day but also for the future of the football program, as well. It's not a coincidence that Utah home attendance has consistently been at or better than 100 percent capacity since the first MUSS members graduated in 2006. And when Rice-Eccles Stadium eventually expands to be more in line with the capacity of the remaining Pac-12 Conference stadiums, it will be done in part to meet the demand and enthusiasm for the program that has been created by younger alumni.

8 Dr. Chris Hill

The Utah athletic department, and not just the football program, has made a living off uncovering diamonds in the rough—players and coaches who reached their full potential in the environment provided by the athletic department and the university as a whole.

The person largely responsible for creating that environment arrived at Utah as an unfinished product himself. But in the nearly 40 years since he arrived in Utah as a graduate assistant basketball coach to Bill Foster in 1973, Dr. Chris Hill has played the biggest role in transitioning Utah athletics into the force it is today.

Unlike the many coaches and players who have come and gone during his time—whether it be for professional riches or, quite frankly, better jobs—Hill has seen to it that there is no better place for him professionally than in Salt Lake City.

Unlike mentor Bill Foster, who justified his move to Duke with a Final Four and national runner-up appearance in 1978, Hill turned down the Blue Devils' offer to become athletics director in 1998. In 2004, he rejected Washington's overtures. And those are just the offers that were made public.

"There are a lot of things people don't know about opportunities I had on the East Coast," said Hill, a Rutgers University alumnus. "There were some things that were never public."

Don't expect Hill to reveal which schools were after him. Hill's ability to keep sensitive issues from getting into the public arena is just one reason why he has been as successful as he has been while athletic director at Utah.

There are no guarantees Hill will remain at Utah until retirement—he is originally from New Jersey, carries a faint "Joisey" dialect in his voice, and will gladly talk about what he loves about the East Coast—but he has given every indication thus far that he will stay put. Getting into the Pac-10 certainly ensured Hill would be around a lot longer.

"If we didn't get into the Pac-12, I would have been simply bored," Hill said. "And that may have made me do something else. But now there are big challenges. As I like to tell people, I got a new job without having to interview and without having to move. And that's pretty good in this day and age."

Hill's impact extends far beyond football. Virtually every sport at Utah, save for the basketball program, competes in facilities that did not exist, either structurally or in their current state, when Hill became athletic director in 1987. The biggest coup landed by Hill was the renovation and expansion of Rice Stadium, helped significantly by a $10 million gift from the George S. and Dolores Dore Eccles Foundation.

The cost of the project totaled $50 million, with $8 million supplied by the International Olympic Committee toward the hosting of the 2002 Winter Olympics. Rice-Eccles Stadium thus became only the second college football stadium in the country to host the Opening and Closing Ceremonies of an Olympic Games.

While Hill's work in fundraising (he was the director of the Crimson Club prior to being named athletics director) and facilities is noteworthy, it is his knack for hiring successful coaches that has earned him widespread acclaim.

Hill's first home-run hire was on the basketball side with Ball State's Rick Majerus, who took a basketball program that had languished for a good chunk of the 1980s and turned it into a national power in the 1990s, capped by a Final Four and national runner-up appearance in 1998, as well as numerous NBA lottery picks.

After the 1989 season, Hill hired Ron McBride, a man Hill had known for years under previous Utah coaching regimes, to replace Jim Fassel.

How good were those two hires? Utah, along with Syracuse, was one of just two Division I Football Bowl Subdivision (FBS) programs not to make a coaching change in either football or basketball for the entire decade of the 1990s.

"I thought he could bring in players [who] were tough and that we would get some pride back into the program," Hill said in explaining the hiring of McBride.

Hill called the decision to fire McBride after the 2002 season "about as difficult as it gets." McBride was immensely popular with his players, fans, and the media. But Hill's decision was justified by many as an unqualified slam-dunk when he hired Urban Meyer, who led Utah to back-to-back conference crowns for the first time in 50 years in the 2003–04 seasons.

How did a coach from the Mid-American Conference catch Hill's attention?

"You're always looking around and talking to other athletic directors," Hill said. "When someone hires somebody, I always call and ask, 'Who else were you looking at?' [Meyer] kept rising on the list, I kept getting good feedback from people, and he had the energy and personality to help us make a step and grow the interest in the program."

Hill has done pretty well for a guy who viewed Utah as a place in which he could further his career, rather than have it serve as a final destination.

"I never thought I would be here more than four to six years," Hill said. "Now I'm in my 24th year as athletic director. I was close to going other places…but this has such an opportunity to grow, and it's been fun."

9 Ron McBride

"Utah was a soft program, an underachieving program, and a program that was going nowhere. Their expectations weren't that high. When they hired me they said, 'Well, if you cannot embarrass us against BYU and be in about the middle of the league and be respectable, you can stay here as long as you want.' The bar was low. The expectations were they just didn't want to get embarrassed on Saturday."

—Ron McBride in 2008 as Weber State's
head coach, leading up to his return to Utah
for his first game there since being fired

As things turned out, Ron McBride was a victim of his own success. Consider the circumstances surrounding his firing at the end of the 2002 season. Utah had just finished a 5–6 season by beating its hated rival and were ranked fifth in the eight-team Mountain West Conference—near the middle and ahead of BYU, which finished seventh—its worst conference finish in more than three decades.

There are alumni, fans, and boosters these days who will put a "For Sale" sign in your lawn for just one losing season, much less the two Utah had in McBride's final three years. In Salt Lake City, however, where the passion for college football at the time had always taken a backseat to the basketball program and the NBA's Utah Jazz, there were many who just weren't right with firing the program's second-winningest coach.

Utah wouldn't be the first program to kick a good coach to the curb in hopes of finding someone better. Was this a case of a program creating expectations it couldn't come close to attaining?

Fortunately, with the hiring of Urban Meyer, everyone associated with the program never had to live under that assumption. The dividends from the Meyer hire were immediate and bountiful. At the same time, it is impossible to ignore McBride's impact on those teams. McBride recruited many of the players that made up the 2003–04 Meyer teams. McBride was one of the first coaches to recognize the talent that existed in the Polynesian communities, a community he had been recruiting since his days at Gavilan Junior College in the 1960s. And instead of struggling to adapt to the Mormon church's insistence that all young men serve a two-year church mission, McBride embraced it.

"I already knew the mistakes that Fassel and Stobart made and things that weren't embraced by Wayne," said McBride from his offices at Weber State University, where he is currently the head coach. "If you're going to be successful in Utah, you have to take [Mormon] kids and their missions. Most of the coaches who worked at Utah never took that factor seriously."

"Utah was a sleeping giant, but it needed to be handled correctly," McBride said. "Everything was there for it to be successful. But there were a lot of things that needed to be done to make it a tough program, a hard-nosed program."

McBride knew he had to make a break from tradition and find a spot where he could take his team for preseason camp, a spot that would be "conducive to making our players tough." For several years, until Utah changed its academic calendar from a quarter system to a semester system, McBride and his program set up shop in Price, Utah, which was known as Camp Carbon and located in the middle of Utah's mining industry. McBride believed his players could get a better understanding of the benefits of hard work from people far less fortunate than a collegiate scholarship athlete.

"That alone really helped make the players tougher and more committed. To isolate them down there for 15 days…made it pretty ideal. The people down there were excellent. We had barbecues, dinners with the townspeople, and we would be part of the community during the time we were down there.

"All these people work hard for a living. Some of them don't have jobs, some of them do have jobs; a lot of them were coal miners and had to scrape by."

The defense reaped immediate rewards from McBride's emphasis on toughness. Although Utah only went 4–7 in McBride's first year, the defense gave up 176 fewer points than the 1989 team. Another key factor was the arrival of Fred Whittingham as defensive coordinator, a longtime BYU assistant coach who was coming off a stint with the Oakland Raiders.

Each year, there were encouraging signs that McBride was leading the Utes out of the wilderness. In 1991, the Utes had a winning record. The following year saw Utah receive its first bowl invitation since the 1964 Liberty Bowl. The 1993 edition defeated BYU in Provo for the first time since 1971 and received consecutive bowl invites for the first time ever. The national breakthrough came in 1994 when Utah finished 10–2 and ranked 8th in the final Associated Press poll after beating Arizona in the Freedom Bowl.

McBride led Utah to shared conference titles in 1995 and 1999, earning both with wins against BYU in Provo, but the lack of an outright crown and another season like 1994 were testing the patience of some. McBride recalls an increasing number of clashes with the athletic department over player eligibility and bowl selections, concluding that the administration was looking for reasons to make a change.

The bottom fell out with a six-game losing streak in 2002. Although Utah rebounded to win its final three games, McBride was fired rather than accept athletic director Chris Hill's offer of a reassignment within the athletic department. McBride had always found jobs through the recommendations of his peers, and the only job he ever officially applied for was the Utah job. It was also the only position from which he was fired.

The ending wasn't pretty, but McBride remains a loyal Ute.

"Absolutely I'm a Utah Man," McBride said. "If I had my wish list, I'd like to retire as an employee of the University of Utah, but that's no big deal. But the players I coached are the ones who built the legacy there. I'm proud of what the coaches and players did because it was a lot of hard work to get to the point where it was a respected program."

10 Classic Finish I: 2008 Texas Christian

Rice-Eccles Stadium has seen its share of amazing performances, heart-stopping finishes, and bitter defeats. But no game forced Utah fans, coaches, and players alike through the widest range of emotions as did a November 6, 2008, showdown against No. 10 Texas Christian University.

When the clock reached triple zeroes after TCU quarterback Andy Dalton's desperation pass was hauled in by Utah safety Robert Johnson, Utah was again on the brink of another perfect season and an appearance in a BCS bowl game for the second time in five years.

The Horned Frogs entered the game ranked one spot higher in spite of carrying a loss to Oklahoma. After a shaky first quarter against the Sooners, the TCU defense shut down Oklahoma's high-powered offense, which later in the year would score 60 or more points in an NCAA-record five consecutive games. Additionally, TCU had previously ended BYU's streak of 16 straight wins, the nation's longest at the time, with a 32–7 blowout in Fort Worth.

Utah owned narrow victories against Michigan and Oregon State, but TCU's feats trumped those of Utah's in the eyes of odds-makers, who made the Frogs a slight favorite as the teams kicked off on a cold Thursday night in Salt Lake City.

By the middle of the first quarter, everything was in store for a TCU rout. The Frogs scored on their first two drives to take a 10–0 lead and had outgained Utah 136–20 to that point.

Utah would get on the board with a field goal late in the first quarter from Louie Sakoda. The second quarter belonged entirely to Utah, as the defense repeatedly came up with big plays. Paul

Kruger sacked Dalton to knock TCU out of field-goal range on one drive, and Sean Smith's interception and long return set up Sakoda's second field goal just before halftime.

"No one panicked. We just hung in there," Kyle Whittingham said. "Nothing came easy, but the guys toughed it out and they came up with big plays each time we needed them."

"I told the guys, 'Stay in it. We're going to have a chance to win it late,'" quarterback Brian Johnson said.

The score remained 10–6 midway through the fourth quarter when TCU was poised to add to its lead, but Ross Evans' 26-yard field goal bounced off the left upright.

Utah's offense responded by going three-and-out, punting the ball with 5:33 left in the game. To make matters worse, any elation left over from the Evans miss was completely sucked out of the stadium when Sakoda's punt traveled only 28 yards, giving TCU the ball at the Utah 48.

Six plays later, Evans lined up for a 35-yard field goal, but he pushed it right. How many more suggestions did Utah need from the football gods that this game was there for the taking?

Johnson got to work, completing three straight passes to open the drive, the third going to Brent Casteel for 22 yards into TCU territory. The Rice-Eccles Stadium crowd of 45,666—the second-largest crowd in school history—came to life.

Just as importantly, TCU started to panic. A pass-interference penalty moved the ball to the TCU 31. Two plays later, on third-and-5, Utah went for the kill shot—a corner-post route to Casteel, the same play that had set up the game-winning field goal against Oregon State just five weeks prior.

Johnson just missed, overthrowing a wide-open Casteel by a foot.

"Oh, would you want to have that one back, Brian Johnson?" said Dan Fouts, who was doing color commentary for a national audience on *CBS College Sports*.

There was no time to reflect on the near-miss. Even though Utah had two timeouts remaining, Johnson and the Utah offense huddled up for the biggest down in school history. The snap came a split-second before the play clock expired, and TCU blitzed safety Steven Hodge off the right edge.

Johnson fired the ball just inches away from Hodge's arms, who flew into the air to knock down the ball. As Johnson threw, Freddie Brown cut to his left and, coming out of his break, caught the ball for 11 yards and a first down.

Now it was Utah, which had gotten off the canvas more than once in this game, who was poised to deliver the knockout blow. It came two plays later when Johnson hit Brown on a slant pattern with 48 seconds left and a 13–10 Utah lead.

"It's like he has no pulse. He just stays calm in those situations," Johnson said of Brown, who finished with nine receptions for 105 yards.

The same could have been said of Johnson, whose heroics marked the third game-winning, fourth-quarter drive of the season.

11 1995 BYU

"I came here six years ago, and this is what I wanted. I wanted to win the WAC title, and I wanted to win it against BYU at BYU."

—Ron McBride after a 34–17 victory in the 1995 Holy War

Winning the WAC wasn't supposed to happen in 1995...not after the 1994 season, in which Utah won the most games in school history, won its first bowl game in 30 years, and finished with top-10 rankings in both major polls.

Not when the 1995 season saw Utah begin the season with only six returning starters—the fewest in all of Division I-A.

Not when the starting quarterback stumbled badly out of the gate and was replaced by a quarterback who had to walk on at a junior college, of all places, and was more known for being the nephew of someone famous rather than for his own ability.

A drop-off was inevitable. Or was it?

Because there was Utah, after a 34–17 stomp-the-mud-hole-dry victory against its heated rival that was nowhere as close as the final score indicated, on top of the WAC. At that moment, the Utes held the tiebreaker over Air Force, both with 5–2 marks. Yes, Colorado State and BYU would win the following week to create a four-way tie for the WAC title. Yes, Utah was passed over for a bowl game.

Yet all of that paled in comparison to the big picture—the Utes had finally showed some staying power. And they did it emphatically, with conviction…and on their hated rival's turf, to boot.

There were Holy Wars when more was riding on the line for Utah. There were Holy Wars with more unbelievable finishes. That the placement of this game is as high as it is—not just in the annals of the rivalry, but in the program's entire history—is certain to raise debate among Ute fans.

But when one looks at how one-sided this rivalry had become since LaVell Edwards began his coaching tenure at BYU in 1972, the 1995 Holy War has to rank as the most unlikely outcome in the rivalry's history. It signaled the end of Utah's days as a pushover. The program's Dark Ages were officially over. The program was still years away and another head coach from being nationally relevant. But for the first time in decades, Utah football was actually relevant in its own state.

If one could go back to the period leading up to the 1995 season, Utah fans were riding high over their newfound "dominance" over BYU. Conversely, it would have been easy to dismiss the 1993 and 1994 victories as flukes. That they were both wins with the identical score of 34–31 was the first sign. BYU's pass defense was uncommonly bad in 1993, while Utah's offense was spectacular, and it took a miracle kick to win. The 1994 outcome was between two evenly matched teams, with Utah's home field trumping BYU's tradition.

Certainly, 1995 would be, in the eyes of the BYU program, a return to normalcy…of domination in the Holy War…of a return for Utah to its rightful place in the conference standings, which was far below BYU.

Not in 1995. Utah stormed to a 27–3 lead after three quarters and controlled the ball for 40:47. And freshman running back Chris Fu'amatu Ma'afala—the difficulty in pronouncing his name exceeded only by the ability needed to bring him down in the open field—ran for 104 yards and two scores on 28 carries.

Mike Fouts—he of the cannon arm, scattershot decision-making ability, and NFL Hall of Fame QB Dan Fouts' bloodlines—threw for 275 yards and a pair of scores on 21 of 31 passing with no interceptions. Utah converted a whopping 15 of 22 third-down conversions.

On defense, Utah picked off BYU quarterback Steve Sarkisian four times and held BYU to 50 yards rushing.

Veteran *Deseret News* columnist Brad Rock immediately captured what this victory meant to the Utah program.

"The Utes left the field with the bearing of a team that feels it has arrived…. It seemed as though the Utes had grown into something to take seriously. Storming the goal posts is for when you're not supposed to win. Nowadays they don't even stick around to argue."

And who could argue? Utah football had finally emerged as a viable, consistent threat.

12 Ike Armstrong

As ABC's broadcast of the 2005 Fiesta Bowl neared its conclusion, with a 35–7 Utah victory against Pittsburgh well in hand, viewers were treated to a trivia item at the bottom of the screen, one that probably would have stumped a good number of Utah fans.

The item explained that the victory marked Utah's fourth perfect season. Quick, raise your hand if you knew Utah had recorded even one perfect season prior to 2004, much less three.

All were the result of head coach Ike Armstrong, "Old Kickapoo," Utah's only member of the College Football Hall of Fame. Ike led the U to perfect seasons three times in his first six seasons on the job in 1926 and 1929–30. Two additional times, in 1928 and 1941, Utah went without a loss but finished with two ties in each season.

Coaches, even those as accomplished as Armstrong, are often a superstitious bunch, and Ike was no different, as explained by one of his players, halfback Delmar "Swede" Larson.

"Ike never varied his pregame ritual at home," Larson said. "On game day, the squad would gather at the cafeteria for tea and toast. Then we'd walk across campus and stop under a specific tree. There Ike would name his starting lineup, and that lineup would run one play. But Ike always took his quarterbacks to the stadium and walked them over the field, telling him just what plays he wanted called in specific situations."

Marwin "Marvin" Jonas, a center and one of Utah's first All-American players, told of numbers Ike didn't want to see on his players.

"He never allowed a No. 1 or No. 13 on a jersey, and the captain had to sleep in the No. 7 lower berth on the train and stay in a hotel room that had a No. 7 in the room number."

On the field and in formations and play-calling, Old Kickapoo was as traditional as they came. Everyone on Utah's schedule knew of Armstrong's preference for the single-wing attack, and he had its tendencies mapped out. But Utah won on execution and fundamentals and only rarely through the trickery of the forward pass, whose use had yet to become anywhere near as sophisticated as today's passing attacks. But when the T formation sprouted up, largely because rule changes had increased the significance of the quarterback position, Armstrong evolved his offense to match the times.

Armstrong did what he could to make Utah more than an Intermountain West act, scheduling games against the Western powers of the time, including USC, Washington, UCLA, Oregon, Texas A&M, and Oregon State. He even took a team to Hawaii in 1926—no small feat given the only way his team could get there was by boat.

Armstrong excelled in football from the very beginning, making the varsity team as an eighth grader at Seymour High in Iowa. From there, he went to Drake University, where he was a fullback on a Bulldogs team that went 7–0 in his senior season. He stayed on at Drake to coach the freshman team for three years before beginning his career at Utah in 1925. He coached the football, basketball, and track teams, but he turned over the basketball duties to Vadal Peterson after compiling a 9–18 record in three seasons.

Basketball wasn't Armstrong's cup of tea, but football obviously was. His record at Utah was 141–55–15, for a winning percentage of .702. Only Urban Meyer and Kyle Whittingham have won a greater percentage of games at Utah. But Meyer was here for only two seasons; Whittingham could catch Armstrong late in the 2018 season at the earliest, provided he maintains his current pace of 9.5 wins per year.

Armstrong stalked the Utah sidelines for a quarter-century, serving as athletic director in addition to his coaching duties.

In 1947, as part of Salt Lake City's centennial celebration, he brought the NCAA track and field championships to campus. In 1949, Armstrong said good-bye to Utah and moved closer to his Midwestern roots by becoming athletic director at the University of Minnesota. And in 1957, Armstrong was inducted into the College Football Hall of Fame. He died in 1983 at the age of 88.

13 The 2002 Winter Olympics and the Expansion of Rice-Eccles Stadium

Speaking purely from a football standpoint, the biggest gain for the University of Utah with Salt Lake City's selection to host the 2002 Winter Olympics was the upgrade that was needed for Rice Stadium to host the Games' Opening and Closing Ceremonies.

Built in 1927 and known as Ute Stadium until Robert Rice kicked in $1 million for a 1972 renovation and expansion, the stadium was more than showing its age as the 1990s commenced. Contrary to popular opinion, the Winter Games didn't provide the impetus for plans to renovate Rice Stadium. But it did provide the urgency to finally get something done. Hosting the rest of the world for one of the planet's biggest sporting events can have that effect on a community.

Chris Hill likes to get all Dickensian when asked about the impact the 2002 Winter Olympics had on the University of Utah and its athletic program.

"It was the best of times, and it was the worst of times," Hill said. "[The International Olympic Committee] gave us $7.5–$8 million for the stadium, but it cost us $52 million. So we're out there raising money, but everyone thinks the Olympics paid for it."

And the money from the IOC didn't arrive until the Games were played in 2002. Meanwhile, the stadium was essentially torn down and rebuilt all in the off-season prior to the 1998 season.

"It was a much more difficult financial situation than anyone ever knew," Hill said. "Those that understood everything, it gave us tremendous momentum to build the stadium. It was difficult [to raise money] because the perception was the [IOC] paid for it. It was good because everybody said, 'This has got to happen.'"

The Eccles family stepped up to the plate first, donating $10 million through foundation and individual gifts. The athletic department and university raised another $22 million, and the remaining $10 million were acquired through bond measures.

"Our stadium was falling apart. We had to do something," Hill said. "The Olympics far outweighed any downside. It built momentum and put a spotlight on how the stadium was woefully

The 2002 Winter Olympics and the Expansion of Rice-Eccles Stadium. Neither rain nor sleet nor snow slowed down progress on the renovation and expansion of Rice-Eccles Stadium after the 1998 season. (Photo courtesy Tom Smart)

A view from the southwest stands at Rice-Eccles Stadium, with Block U. easily visible in the distance. (Photo courtesy Tom Smart)

inadequate and falling apart. The Olympics gave us visibility and helped the image of our city when it came to recruiting."

Today, Rice-Eccles Stadium is a highly visible landmark at the U, with its expanded press box and luxury seating areas standing 14 stories high and dominating the campus skyline. It is easily seen several miles west of campus in downtown Salt Lake City.

Several improvements have been made to keep the stadium current with the times. In 2003, a $1.6 million donation was made by Larry H. and Gail Miller—the since-deceased owner of the Utah Jazz and his wife—for a video display system and new scoreboards. Utah Sports Properties installed a 200-foot LED board along the north end zone at a cost of $500,000. In 2009, a new field turf playing surface was installed. And reminders of the Olympics are still in place with the Olympic Cauldron Park, located just outside the south gates of the stadium. Rice-Eccles Stadium, along with the Los Angeles Coliseum, are the only full-time college football stadiums in use today that have hosted the Opening and Closing Ceremonies of the Olympics.

It took some time for Rice-Eccles Stadium to reach capacity-crowd status on a consistent basis, but seven of the stadium's 10 biggest crowds have come from 2008 to the present. The biggest crowd, however, came in Urban Meyer's second home game as Utah's coach, when 46,768 attended the Utes' 31–24 victory against Cal in 2003.

With the increased excitement over joining the Pac-12 Conference, highlighted by more high-profile opponents, it stands to reason that Rice-Eccles Stadium, which will be the new league's second-smallest stadium, isn't done expanding. The corners of the south end zone appear to be prime areas for growth, as well as the possibility of a second deck on the stadium's east side. Whatever future plans may hold, Rice-Eccles Stadium is the crown jewel of Utah's athletic programs and a constant reminder of a time when it hosted the world for one of the largest spectacles in sports.

14 What is a Ute?

Vincent LaGuardia Gambini: "Is it possible the two yoots…"
>Judge Chamberlain Haller: "The two… The two what? What was that word?"
>Gambini: "Uh, what word?"
>Judge Haller: "Two what?"
>Gambini: "What?"

Judge Haller: "Did you say 'Yoots'?"
Gambini: "Yeah, two Yoots."
Judge Haller: "What is a Yoot?"
Gambini: "Oh, excuse me, your honor. The two Yooo-ths."
—Joe Pesci (Gambini) and Fred
Gwynne (Haller) in *My Cousin Vinny*

Long before Utah crashed the BCS and put the Utes on the national map, the film *My Cousin Vinny* forced many a Utah fan into countless explanations to those outside the state of Utah as to just exactly what a Ute was—even if "Ute" was merely Brooklyn-ese for "youth," which was what was clearly being talked about in the movie.

That hasn't stopped anyone—especially Utah's rivals in the Mountain West Conference—from running with the film as a friendly way of poking fun at Utah's program. For instance, at San Diego State basketball games, the exact video of the above exchange has been shown on its Jumbotron as Utah players take the floor.

So just exactly what is a Ute?

In short, it is a Native American who is a member of the Ute Tribe. Tribal membership across four reservations numbers around 7,000 people. In the native Ute language, "Ute" means "Land of the Sun," although other definitions exist, such as "People of the Mountains." And one doesn't need to be majoring in linguistics to recognize that the state of Utah derived its name from the word "Ute." The Northern Utes are most closely affiliated with the U, and their reservation, the Uintah and Ouray, is where about 3,000 members live.

In 2005, the NCAA listed Utah among 18 universities that used American Indian nicknames, mascots, or imagery in a "hostile" or "abusive" matter. Schools that maintained a presence on that list would not be allowed to use their nicknames in NCAA-sanctioned postseason competition, nor would they be allowed to host post-season events—a significant matter given the Jon M. Huntsman Center has hosted the third-most number of games all-time in the NCAA men's basketball tournament, as well as nine national finals meets in women's gymnastics.

The inclusion of Utah on this list was puzzling at first glance, given Utah's repeated efforts to be sensitive toward Native Americans, and not just members of the Ute Tribe. Until 1972, the nickname Utes and Redskins were used interchangeably by the school and media when it referenced the athletic teams at the U. The university did away with an Indian warrior mascot and feathered headbands for the cheerleaders, among other Indian-influenced traditions. All that remains today is the drum and feather logo and the nickname, and the former is slowly being phased out in favor of a red block U.

All of that is fine with the Ute Tribe, which has repeatedly given the athletic program and the university permission to use the Ute name. A letter from the Uintah and Ouray Tribal Business Committee was presented to the NCAA as part of the U's appeal to the NCAA, and it repeated its consent for the university to use the name. Written permission by the Ute Tribe for continued use of the nickname was instrumental in the NCAA taking the U off its list of offenders shortly after it was compiled.

The relationship between the Ute Tribe and the university has been beneficial to both sides. The U has furthered the educational goals of tribal members by sponsoring a wide number of programs and providing financial aid and scholarships for tribal members. The successes of various sports teams are essentially a source of free advertising, prompting others to inquire and educate themselves about the Ute Tribe and its traditions.

It sure beats having Vinny Gambini as an unofficial spokesperson.

45

15 Hiking Up to Block U

With its location on the east bench of Salt Lake City, several buildings that make up the University of Utah campus are visible to the trained eye for several miles. For sports fans, the most recognizable structures are the obvious ones—the silver dome-shaped roof of the Jon M. Huntsman Center, as well as Rice-Eccles Stadium.

Those facilities, however, are incapable of sending a long-distance message of a Utah victory like the Block U, whose lights flash intermittently after a Utah win and burn steady after a loss. Even from an airplane, the lights of the Block U are visible as the plane descends into Salt Lake City International Airport some 12 miles away from Mount Van Cott where the Block U is located.

Mountainside letters are a tradition of the American West, and Block U was one of the first recorded instances of a university getting behind such a project. The only recorded instance that predates Block U is the University of California at Berkeley's Big C, which appeared just weeks before Block U was built in 1905.

The Block U—which is also a registered trademark of the University of Utah—sits nearly one mile above sea level at 5,249 feet. From the letter's baseline to the tops of the serifs, it would stand more than 100 feet tall if placed upright. Originally, the spot for Block U was chosen by students as a place to paint their graduating class year, but school officials wanted something more permanent. Originally built with a limestone base, Block U was converted to a cement base in 1907. Lights and erosion control measures came later.

For a long time, there were no official caretakers for Block U, which was victimized by vandalism, often by the school's Greek fraternities. In 2001, Block U got a much-needed coat of white paint to help alleviate the vandalism and address complaints by neighboring homeowners that the monument had turned into an eyesore.

In 2006, U alumna Sue Christensen led a fundraising campaign called "Renew the U" that would keep Block U properly maintained. At a cost of $400,000, the improvements included new lights and a wireless control system that originates from the Merrill Engineering Building, 240 flush-mounted light fixtures that alternate between white and red lights, a dimmer feature that allows the lights to burn at varying intensities, and an improved drainage barrier above Block U and a drainage system. An official lighting ceremony was held during halftime of Utah's 2006 game against TCU, a game that Utah won 20–7.

Don't be intimidated by Block U's mountain presence. It's an easy drive to a trail that marks the start of a relatively short walk up to Block U. Also, since Block U has a physical address—1635 New Bedford Drive—simply use an online map site or GPS to get accurate directions from wherever you are in Salt Lake City. Just be respectful of the neighborhood and the people who live there, and follow the instructions on where parking is allowed.

16 Larry Wilson

Maybe Steve Smith can supply such a challenge someday, but until his enshrinement and bronze likeness appear in Canton's corridors, Larry Wilson is the only Ute who could ever lay claim on the title of most decorated NFL player who came from Utah.

Consider this: Utah players have combined for 14 Associated Press All-Pro selections. Wilson is responsible for five of them. And

Pro Bowl honors? Wilson takes up eight of 28 such honors. Most importantly, Wilson is Utah's lone entry in the Pro Football Hall of Fame.

Wilson was a 1956 graduate of Rigby High School in Idaho, where he earned 14 letters in four different sports. At Utah, he set or tied five records in his senior year of 1959, including single-season marks for touchdowns (13) and points (84) and the career mark for touchdowns (20). His five rushing touchdowns and 32 points against Arizona remain single-game records to this day.

Wilson's offensive prowess was never on display after being drafted in the seventh round by the St. Louis Cardinals in the 1960 NFL draft because he was switched to defensive back and then safety after just two days at running back. Today's players might balk at such a move, but for Wilson, who played both ways at Utah, it was a seamless transition.

"I preferred defense anyway because that is my kind of football," Wilson said. "I was just excited about the chance to play and meet the players on the team."

What Wilson forgot to mention was his enthusiasm in "meeting" his opponent, usually the quarterback on a well-timed safety blitz. Many have erroneously described Wilson as the inventor of the safety blitz, but to say he turned a risky defensive call into a dependable weapon is gospel truth. Defensive coordinators learned that blitzing from such unorthodox positions, when used properly, could allow them to bring blitzes from any point on the field.

The NFL didn't keep sack totals then, so Wilson's effectiveness as a blitzer can be measured only by those who played against him. But the league did keep interception numbers, and Wilson was without peer at his position with 52 picks, with a career-best 10 in 1966, and including a seven-game stretch in which he had at least one. And the year before, against Pittsburgh and with casts around his two broken hands, Wilson had one interception.

For 43 years, Larry Wilson was with the Cardinals organization, including time as a scout, assistant coach, general manager, vice president, and even interim head coach for three games in the 1979 season. (He went 2–1.) He followed the franchise from St. Louis after it relocated to Phoenix for the 1988 season.

Yet there was a time when it appeared Wilson would return to his alma mater as head coach. Local media repeatedly brought up Wilson's name as a candidate to replace Mike Giddings after the 1967 season—probably prematurely, since Wilson was still a star NFL player—but the job went to Bill Meek, who emerged ahead of Rod Rust to earn the job. In 1973, after Meek left, the job was Wilson's for the asking.

"I've always wanted to come back [to Utah]," Wilson said. "And so has my wife [Dee Ann]. I guess my home is here."

"At this late hour, it's a good guess Wilson will get the job," wrote Hack Miller of the *Deseret News*.

The quick announcement didn't come as more candidates interviewed for the job. Among them was Jim Hanifan, who ironically enough was hired by St. Louis as head coach after Wilson's three-game interim stint but had also been an assistant at Utah under Giddings and Meek. Several other candidates with strong Utah ties as either players or assistant coaches were Lynn Stiles, Chet Franklin, and Pete Riehlman.

Still, on January 23, 1974, the *Deseret News* ran on the front page of its sports section, "Wilson Looms as Utah's Choice," with an announcement of a press conference the following day. But before the press conference, Wilson informed athletic director James R. "Bud" Jack of his decision to remove his name from consideration.

What happened? Miller speculated the school's process for choosing a head coach—a method which Democratic Party bosses would've thought was too politically charged—left Wilson slighted. "Red tape started to strangle the program," Miller wrote. Utah football was a different galaxy from the world Wilson experienced in the NFL, and he possibly came to the conclusion he couldn't do what he wanted at Utah with the limited resources offered by the school.

Two days later, Tom Lovat, an assistant under Meek who was retained by Jack for recruiting purposes, was hired as head coach. "I don't know what took them so long," Lovat said at his initial press conference, referring to the time Utah had wasted in the selection process. While other programs—most notably BYU and Utah State—had staffs in place that were out recruiting, Utah football was withering on the vine. It would take nearly two decades for the Utes to catch up.

17 Yergy's Drive from 55 in the 1993 Holy War

With one swing of his right leg, Chris Yergensen went from possibly the most-doubted player in recent Utah history to a legend. Instantly he went from being the guy stuck with the check to everyone wanting to buy him a drink.

While it would take another two years for a Utah victory against BYU to signify true staying power to the Ute football program, Yergensen's 55-yard field goal with 25 seconds to play in Provo put a tire-screeching stop to the turbo-fueled dominance of the Holy War by BYU.

"I finally got one for you," Yergensen told Ron McBride as the two embraced after the game. "Finally I can hug you on good terms after a game."

Yergensen's career wasn't chock full of inexplicable misses. He ended his career with the most field goals in school history, surpassed since only by Louie Sakoda. Just one—a 20-yarder in the previous year's Copper Bowl against Washington State with more than three minutes to go in the game—could be deemed a costly miss.

Forget for a moment that had Yergensen made the kick, it would have only tied the game in an era where there was no overtime in college football. Forget that Washington State's offense shredded the Utah defense for 636 yards and could've opened up things in a tie game rather than play just to protect the lead. Forget that Utah's defense couldn't get a stop and get the ball back in plenty of time for another score. Yergensen was the goat.

And at a time when Utah bowl invites were as rare as Halley's Comet flashing across the sky, Utah fans were left to lament how things would have been different had the team had a dependable kicker. McBride refused to speak to Yergensen for months.

"He'd saunter into the weight room and say hi to everyone but me," Yergensen said. "But that's how he is. He's a lineman, a smash-mouth Marine kind of coach."

Against BYU, it only got worse. Yergensen was already going through a miserable day at Cougar Stadium, missing an extra point and two of three field-goal attempts.

So as Utah marched downfield but were still too far away to think touchdown, Yergensen prepared himself for the biggest kick of his career. He might have been the only person in the stadium who didn't see it that way.

"No athlete is sitting there thinking about that stuff," he said from his Northern California home, where he has a kicking school in addition to his duties as a junior high history teacher. "But after it's over, you say it's good to get that one."

"It's a different feeling in November. It's cold, and the field is all mud," he added. "I don't know many guys who are sitting there saying, 'Yeah, I hope it does come down to me.' Your chances aren't the same there as they are when its 87 degrees at UCLA."

After making his kick, Yergensen ran in a dead sprint toward the opposite end zone, crossed midfield, and veered toward his bench, where he was mobbed by his teammates. But once he kicked off and BYU got the ball again, terror struck him.

"After I made the kick, I'm thinking about how we did this tremendous thing only to watch BYU march down and score," he said. "I was sitting on the sidelines unsettled, thinking, 'Please let it end. Let's pull this thing out.'"

The Utah defense, which sacked BYU quarterback John Walsh four times and picked him off five more times, wouldn't allow it. The son of a Utah assistant coach even managed to retrieve the ball that Yergensen sent well above the crossbar and down the middle of the uprights, a keepsake that comes in handy given his current surroundings.

"I like to bring up a lot of that stuff with my BYU supporters who live around here," said Yergensen, who lives in El Dorado Hills, California. He once had the younger brother of star BYU receiver Austin Collie as a student in one of his classes. "I can't escape the BYU-Utah rivalry. It's a weird little circle. But it's all good."

18 Bowling Them Over

It is a streak that lasted 13 seasons and covered three head coaches. Among its victims are four programs that have won national championships since 1976.

The streak in question is Utah's bowl game win streak, which ended at nine wins after losing to No. 10 Boise State in the Las Vegas Bowl on December 22, 2010. Only Florida State, which

Utah's Bowl Record

Year	Bowl	Opponent	Score	W–L
1938	Sun	New Mexico	26–0	W
1964	Liberty	West Virginia	32–6	W
1992	Copper	Washington State	31–28	L
1993	Freedom	USC	28–21	L
1994	Freedom	Arizona	16–13	W
1996	Copper	Wisconsin	38–10	L
1999	Las Vegas	Fresno State	17–16	W
2001	Las Vegas	USC	10–6	W
2003	Liberty	Southern Mississippi	17–0	W
2005	Fiesta	Pittsburgh	35–7	W
2005	Emerald	Georgia Tech	38–10	W
2006	Armed Forces	Tulsa	25–13	W
2007	Poinsettia	Navy	35–32	W
2009	Sugar	Alabama	31–17	W
2009	Poinsettia	Cal	37–27	W
2010	Las Vegas	Boise State	26–3	L

won 11 straight as part of a 14-game unbeaten bowl streak, had a longer streak.

With only six bowl appearances prior to the beginning of the streak, which began with a 17–16 victory against Fresno State in the 1999 Las Vegas Bowl, the win streak has made up a significant portion of Utah's nation-best .750 winning percentage in bowl games. To break it down, Utah has won 12 of 16 bowl games in its history.

Just as impressive is Utah's dominance during these bowl games, especially on the defensive side of the ball. Only once has an opponent cracked 30 points (2007 Poinsettia Bowl vs. Navy), and only one other time has a team cracked 20 points (2009 Poinsettia Bowl vs. Cal). Yet even with those games thrown into the mix, Utah's defense has given up an average of just 14.2 points per game.

Utah Bowl Heroes

Rushing
Mike Anderson set a Las Vegas Bowl and single-game Utah record with 254 yards rushing while adding a pair of touchdowns in a 17–16 victory against Fresno State in the 1999 Las Vegas Bowl.

Ron Coleman starred in college football's first-ever indoor game, gaining 154 yards and a score on 15 carries in defeating West Virginia in the 1964 Liberty Bowl, which was played at the Atlantic City (New Jersey) Convention Center.

Receiving
Travis LaTendresse hauled in four touchdowns and 214 receiving yards—both single-game bowl records at Utah—in a 2005 pasting of Georgia Tech in the Emerald Bowl. LaTendresse's yard total is second all-time at Utah, and the most ever against a Football Bowl Subdivision opponent. His 16 catches also rank second all-time in a single game.

Paris Warren's 15 catches against Pittsburgh in the Fiesta Bowl are the third-most ever in a game at Utah, and his 198 yards rank fifth all-time. Warren scored two touchdowns in that game, among them one of the most memorable of the year when Alex Smith threw in the flat to Steve Savoy, who then pitched it back to Warren sweeping around the edge for an 18-yard touchdown.

Freddie Brown didn't get into the end zone against Alabama in the 2009 Sugar Bowl, but his 12 catches (sixth-best single-game mark at Utah) for 125 yards were game highs.

Passing
It was tough to build on the success of his first start—a 34–31 overtime victory against BYU—but **Brett Ratliff** did just that against Georgia Tech in the Emerald Bowl, tossing for 381 yards and four scores on 30-of-41 passing.

While Ratliff broke his mark for passing yards in a bowl game, **Alex Smith's** 29-of-37 passing for a 78 percent completion mark remains a Utah bowl record. Smith also ran for 68 yards on 15 carries and threw for four touchdowns against the Panthers.

Special teams

Louie Sakoda's four field goals are a Utah bowl record and helped defeat Tulsa in the 2006 Armed Forces Bowl. The sophomore was good on kicks from 45, 39, 41, and 34 yards. He also averaged 47.3 yards on three punts.

Cletus Truhe had a forgettable game up to the point he lined up for a 33-yard field goal against Fresno State with 5:07 to play. He had already had two kicks blocked, one of which was returned for a touchdown to open the scoring. But this kick went through the uprights, sparking Utah's nine-game bowl winning streak, a streak that covered 13 years.

Defense

Utah's defense, led by **Sheldon Deckart** (six tackles, two sacks), put up a tremendous effort against USC in the 2001 Las Vegas Bowl, sacking Carson Palmer eight times while holding Troy to just one rushing yard.

Steve Fifita was defensive MVP of the 2005 Fiesta Bowl, leading a nine-sack effort against Pittsburgh's Tyler Palko with three sacks of his own.

Stevenson Sylvester got Utah's upset of Alabama in the 2009 Sugar Bowl off to a rousing start with a sack that ended the Tide's first possession. He added two more, as well as a fumble recovery. The following year, he capped his collegiate career and Utah's win against Cal in the Poinsettia Bowl with a 27-yard interception return for a score.

Utah's defense has been especially harsh to opposing quarterbacks. One year prior to winning the Heisman Trophy, Carson Palmer hit the deck five times in the 2001 Las Vegas Bowl, a 10–6 Ute victory. Tyler Palko ate the Sun Devil Stadium turf nine times in the 2005 Fiesta Bowl. And in the biggest upset in program history, Alabama's John Parker Wilson ended his college career by being sandblasted to the Louisiana Superdome turf eight times in the 2009 Sugar Bowl.

Speaking of the Sugar Bowl, a common excuse from both Alabama fans and BCS apologists alike for Utah's 31–17 beat down of the Crimson Tide was that Alabama, after suffering a deflating loss to Florida in the SEC title game that cost it a spot in the BCS title game, wasn't inspired to face Utah. Deflation has never been an issue for the Utes, who have rebounded from four crushing losses to BYU late in the year only to get up and dominate their bowl opponent.

Whether riding an undefeated high or getting off the deck after a loss to its most hated rival, Utah has found a way to excel in bowl games. Yet Coach Kyle Whittingham insists there's no magic formula in play.

"It's the work ethic of our players," Whittingham said after Utah defeated Cal 37–27 in the 2009 Poinsettia Bowl. "We don't have any secret, magic way of practicing for bowl games. It's how our guys go about their business. It's their work ethic and focus. They understand a bowl game is a reward for a good season but also a chance to win another ballgame."

19 Eric Weddle

Eric Weddle was a man of many duties during his time at the U from 2003–06. But there's only one word needed to describe what Weddle meant to Utah as a football player. He was a throwback, a relic from days long past when players were required to master positions on both sides of the ball. And his class and character came through at one key moment to remind everyone that there are things more important than winning.

In his senior campaign, Weddle's role was almost unlimited. He played every position in the defensive backfield, held the ball on field goals and extra points, and took snaps out of the Wildcat formation. In the 2006 Holy War, he threw for a touchdown pass that sparked Utah's comeback from an early 14–0 hole.

In his junior season, he was Utah's top punt returner. By the end of the 2006 campaign, he was Utah's equivalent of a closer in baseball—entrusted to gain four yards a pop to move the chains, milk the clock, and seal victories.

His teammates needed a locker room in which to get dressed, but Weddle needed just a phone booth. No player before—and almost certainly no player since—will ever be as versatile for Utah as Weddle was during his senior season. He was as close to Superman on the gridiron as anyone will ever see.

Weddle's list of honors is also impressive. He was Utah's third consensus All-American behind Luther Elliss and Jordan Gross. Twice he was named Mountain West Conference Defensive Player of the Year. And Weddle was far from a late bloomer, starting all four years and without the benefit of a redshirt year. His 18 interceptions are second all-time behind Harold Lusk.

Eric Weddle rushes over to provide help from his safety spot to pick off a pass and end a scoring threat against BYU in the 2004 Holy War. (AP Photo/Douglas C. Pizac)

There are many moments from Weddle's senior year that capture the essence of his worth to the Utes, as well as an example in sportsmanship that all players should strive for. Against San Diego State, he scored on back-to-back plays from scrimmage—a Utah first and a rarity at any level—when he scored an offensive touchdown out of the Wildcat, then returned an interception for the second score on the Aztecs' ensuing possession. The total elapsed time between scores was just 32 seconds.

And in his final collegiate game, a 25–13 victory against Tulsa in the Armed Forces Bowl, Weddle tacked on the game-clinching score by carrying seven times on eight Utah plays for 35 yards. Weddle likely could have had a touchdown on the final play of his Utah career, but with nothing but green grass ahead of him, he benevolently took a knee after intercepting Tulsa quarterback Paul Smith.

But it was in the previous game against rival Brigham Young when Weddle took sportsmanship to another level.

Weddle had not lost to BYU in three previous Holy Wars, and he was one play from making it a clean sweep. But BYU quarterback John Beck scrambled to extend the final play of the game and threw across the field to a wide-open Jonny Harline in the end zone for a 33–31 victory. While most players would have sulked, hung their heads, or gotten angry, Weddle's response was completely different. Some would say, in the world of win-at-all-costs, that it was completely out of character.

"For whatever reason, I felt it in me to go up to him and say, 'Hey man, I feel horrible right now, but I am happy for you,'" Weddle said. "Obviously I would go back and win that game a thousand times, but it was his shining moment. I can appreciate and respect a guy who puts it all on the line and does whatever he can to help his team win. I see myself as that guy."

"I have been in games like that, to go down to the wire and lose. You know he was sick inside. Not everybody has character like that," Beck said. "People don't understand how much high-caliber athletes invest to get those wins, and when it doesn't happen, it hurts. He walked up at a moment when it hurt and was a person of high character. That is the mark of a champion on and off the field. To be honest, if I would have lost that game, I don't know if I would have walked up to say great job."

"Sometimes you got to be the bigger man," Weddle said.

Whether intercepting passes or showing respect for the opposition, there has been no bigger man at Utah than Eric Weddle.

Although he made his mark on defense, Eric Weddle was entrusted on offense with the ball in his hands in a variety of ways as a senior in 2006, often as a quarterback out of the Wildcat and running plays to chew up clock, move the sticks, and close out victories. (Photo courtesy Tom Smart)

20 "Utah By Five!"

One, two, three, four, Barberi.

Tom Barberi and the number five are permanently linked in Utah lore. It's part of his email address, and even Barberi has said, "I'll have it on my headstone."

So just exactly how did "Utah By Five!" become, as Barberi put it, "the clarion call for Utah fans" for more than 30 years?

As KALL 700's longtime morning show host in the day when the station's format was news talk, not sports talk like it is today, Barberi had to juggle his interaction with several people—one person did traffic, another did weather. And Bill Howard, who was the voice of the Utes through the 1969 season and thereafter for the ABA's Utah Stars, did the sports updates.

"I loved Bill dearly—he was the stadium announcer for the Green Bay Packers under Vince Lombardi [before moving to Salt Lake City in 1965]," Barberi said. "He had some great stories to tell. But one day at the end of the sportscast, he asked me, 'Do you have a prediction on this game?' And without thinking, I blurted out, 'Five!'

"The spread of five in football is darn near impossible to hit. You've got to have a strange set of circumstances to get to that margin. So Bill says, 'Five?' And I say, 'Utah by five, trust me.' So that became the running gag all season long. People took it to heart, and it became the clarion call for Utah fans—'Utah By Five.'"

What started as a wild, goofy prediction became a weekly staple. Howard would ask Barberi for a prediction, and the response was always the same: "Utah by five. Trust me."

Utah By Five...For Real!

Utah has won 227 games since the 1979 season. Just seven have been decided by five points. Tom Barberi was right. It is a tough margin to hit.

1979: Utah 21, CSU 16
1989: Utah 50, UTEP 45
1991: Utah 12, USU 7
1991: Utah 21, CSU 16
1997: Utah 15, New Mexico 10
2002: Utah 23, Wyoming 18
2010: Utah 28, Air Force 23

The prediction went far beyond a radio broadcast. It became its own line of merchandise, with bumper stickers, license plate frames, coffee mugs, and T-shirts.

Barberi left KALL when the station was sold several times in the 2000s. He is still a contributor in the Salt Lake City broadcast media scene, although he calls himself semi-retired—"A way of saying I can't find a job," Barberi cracked. His daughter Gina has continued the family legacy in radio broadcasting as a co-host of the "Radio From Hell" morning show on X-96 in Salt Lake City, a program that has been lauded for both its ratings and content for more than two decades.

But if Gina really wants to follow in her old man's shoes, she needs to come up with a catchy slogan involving Utah sports that will last for decades.

21 Fred and Kyle Whittingham

Before they became respected then beloved by the University of Utah program at large, Fred and Kyle Whittingham were the enemies. There are several figures associated with Brigham Young University's football program who draw more universal ire from Utah fans, but the two Whittinghams wore and bled blue for such an extensive period during BYU's place as a national power that the two men were simply guilty by association.

Today, the contributions of father and son to the Utah program are so significant that while their BYU days are more than just footnotes when telling the story of the Whittinghams, their roots have been long forgotten by even older Utah fans.

Fred's background is as colorful as it is unconventional. Given up for adoption when he was still an infant, Fred was a brawler and a truant who once stole a car and went on cross-country excursions that would make Jack Kerouac—another fellow New Englander—blush. But Fred excelled on the football field, and when University of Rhode Island coach Harold Kopp was hired as BYU's head coach in 1956, Kopp brought Fred with him to Provo.

It wasn't a good fit for Fred, who was expelled from BYU after two years and finished his career at Cal Poly–San Luis Obispo, but not before surviving a team plane crash that killed 14 people. In the NFL, Fred earned the nickname "Mad Dog" for his ferocious, hell-bent ways, both on and off the gridiron, where he starred on several teams in the 1960s. But before he left BYU, he met his wife-to-be Nancy. They married while both were enrolled at BYU. This was part of the softening process Fred would experience later in life, when he converted to Mormonism and put away his wild side.

Fred's oldest son, Kyle, enjoyed a more traditional childhood in an upper-crust Provo neighborhood while his father was an assistant coach at BYU, first as linebacker coach and then as defensive coordinator. As a player, Kyle starred at Provo High, then started at middle linebacker at BYU in the 1980–81 seasons. While he didn't literally marry the girl next door, Kyle came awfully close—his future wife, Jamie Daniels, lived just four houses down the street.

After the 1981 season, Fred left BYU for a job with the Los Angeles Rams and coached in the pro ranks until Ron McBride offered him the defensive coordinator position in 1992 at Utah. Kyle didn't have the pro playing career his father did, but he did get into coaching, first as a graduate assistant at BYU, then at College of Eastern Utah, a junior college in Price. A six-year stint at Idaho State followed, and in 1994, Fred hired Kyle as a linebacker coach.

"Blood is thicker than water," Kyle said of his decision to coach at his alma mater's biggest rival. "It was a very easy transition for me when the opportunity presented itself to come on board because of my father already having been here."

Defense has rarely been an issue since the Whittinghams have been around, and the schemes Utah runs are almost identical from the day Fred took control of the defense, adjusting for some tinkering to adapt to today's spread offenses.

Fred left Utah for the Oakland Raiders after the 1994 season, and Kyle was promoted to defensive coordinator. The son returned the favor to his father in 1998, when Fred came back to Utah as the linebacker coach. Fred left the program, and football, for good after the 2000 season.

In 2003, Fred died as a result of complications for back surgery. Three weeks later, Utah went down to Provo and shut out BYU 3–0 to clinch its first outright conference crown since 1957, and Urban Meyer presented Kyle with the game ball. It was the first time BYU had been shut out in 361 games, going all the way back to 1975.

Opportunity has presented itself for Kyle at various programs over the years, and that interest has risen since he became head coach. Many coaches believe it's paramount to move around and become immersed in varying philosophies under different head coaches, but Kyle has always maintained that he is "not a grass-is-always-greener kind of guy."

"I've been fortunate to have had the opportunity to be at one place for as long as I have," Kyle said. "From a lot of different points of view, it's been a big blessing. There have been opportunities that have presented themselves over the course of my career here, [but] none that were attractive enough to cause me to want to leave. I have stability for my family, and [Utah] is a great place to work. Plus, this is home for me—my wife, my siblings, my mom still reside here. The Salt Lake area is a great place to raise a family."

22 Bill Marcroft

Bill Marcroft didn't want to step down as the Voice of the Utes following the 2004 season. But with changes in ownership at KALL 700, a certain change in job responsibilities, plus a promise he made to his son, Marcroft has no regrets about how his career ended…especially since his final game was the biggest game ever played by Utah to date.

Marcroft called it a career after the 2005 Fiesta Bowl, having come to the realization that new owners at the longtime radio home of Utah athletics were going in a direction of which he wanted no part.

"The problem I had with [new ownership] is that I had stated unequivocally that I would not do sports talk shows," Marcroft said. "It's the bane of sports broadcasting. That's the lowest you could get. They wanted their play-by-play guy to be the sports talk guy on the radio, and that was something that was antithetical to me."

"Oh yeah, I thought I'd be like Johnny Most [the longtime Boston Celtics announcer] and be doing it in my 80s," Marcroft said. "I mentioned to my son a long time ago I would retire when the Utes went to the Final Four and we won the Holiday Bowl. My son reminded me of that statement, so I stuck with my decision."

Basketball made good on the first goal in 1998, and football obliterated Marcroft's initial hope—the Holiday Bowl is where the WAC champion went bowling prior to the dissolution of the 16-team Western Athletic Conference in 1999.

Those were semi-lofty goals for Marcroft during most of his affiliation with Utah athletics. He began in 1966 as a color commentator for Bill Howard, who preceded Marcroft behind the microphone in doing play-by-play. He left in 1969 to take a job as the radio voice of the San Diego Rockets, an NBA expansion team that later moved to Houston.

Marcroft was much better the second time around as a radio broadcaster. His first assignment, which came in Africa when he was in the military, was a broadcast of a game made up of U.S. troops inside the soccer stadium in Tripoli, Libya.

"I failed so miserably at it," Marcroft said. "I was so bad at it I decided I could never do play-by-play. When [television station] KUTV asked me to do it [for Utah games], I refused."

So Howard took the job, and Marcroft handled the less-demanding task of color commentary. When Marcroft took over in 1969, it was an exceptional period in Utah athletics—the Special Events Center, since renamed after Jon M. Huntsman, was in its first year of existence for Utah basketball, and expansion plans were in the works for Ute Stadium, soon to be Rice Stadium.

Before Marcroft became the Voice of the Utes, however, did you know that his first assignment doing play-by-play for a college football game was at BYU? When Utah wasn't the visiting team?

Lord have mercy.

"A station in El Paso wanted to televise the [1966] BYU-UTEP game…. They called here and were looking for a broadcaster to the ballgame, and they hired me," Marcroft said. "They didn't really have a sports play-by-play person, so a station in El Paso sent their sports guy, who was also their news director, and he did color with me."

"The station manager called at halftime, and BYU [which won 53–33] was just kicking butt. He called and told his employee to tell me to say something about UTEP," Marcroft said. "He thought I was prejudicial to BYU, and I told him if there was anything that was misinterpreted, it was that. But BYU was playing extremely well."

Marcroft never missed a football game, although anyone who listened to his broadcast of Utah-BYU for the 1992–93 WAC crown could clearly tell Marcroft was struggling. With a temperature of 106 degrees and a complete inability to get up and down the steps at the Huntsman Center, Marcroft went to the emergency room after the game. A trip to a doctor before the game had included a diagnosis of pneumonia. Marcroft was given a shot and sent on his way, but the second trip revealed Marcroft had Legionnaires' disease.

"The doctors [at LDS Hospital] saved my life," said Marcroft, who missed two regular-season games and two more in the WAC Tournament before coming back for the NCAA Tournament.

During a game against Houston in 1978, a bout with food poisoning almost pulled Marcroft away from the microphone, but he kept his voice in tip-top shape with a never-ending supply of lemons.

The ending could have been bitter, and with three broadcasters in as many seasons following Marcroft's retirement, the U hasn't come close to establishing a long-term voice for the athletics program the way Marcroft was for more than 30 years.

"I didn't realize how important [my job] was to certain individuals and groups until they came out of the woodwork at my retirement party," Marcroft said. "Everybody came from everywhere, and the feeling to me was that it was more than just retiring…. This career had an influence on a lot of people."

23 Lusk's Dash in the Dusk

The one-word superlative used to describe the Utah–Colorado State matchup on October 22, 1994, had yet to be invented. At the time, it was only the biggest game ever for either program, both of which were undefeated and ranked in the top 20.

Just as important, it was a sign the WAC was coming of age. For once, the conference could showcase that it was more than BYU. This was the latest point in the season where two undefeated WAC teams had met. And these teams stressed defense, which was often the last thing that came to mind when looking at the history of the WAC. Just three years previously, BYU and San Diego State played the highest-scoring tie in Division I-A history at 52–52. Even the Arena Football League looked at the WAC and figured defense was an afterthought.

Hughes Stadium's capacity today is 32,500 seats. Temporary seating pushed Hughes' capacity to a school-record 39,107. ABC broadcast the game regionally, with Brent Musburger and Dick Vermeil doing the broadcast. Even *Sports Illustrated's* S.L. Price was

Utah–Colorado State: A Look Back

Despite playing Colorado State more often than any other school other than Utah State, Brigham Young, and Wyoming, it would be a bit of an overstatement to say that Utah shared a storied history with Colorado State. After all, how can teams share history in a rivalry when little of historical significance had ever developed?

That's not to say Utah–Colorado State wasn't a great regional rivalry, especially in the early days of the two schools' football programs. Between 1915 and 1934, the Redskins and Aggies—the original nickname for both schools—combined to win 16 Rocky Mountain Athletic Conference championships.

But relevance on a national scale? For nearly a century, the closest this game ever came to national relevance was in 1946, when Utah improved to 7–0 with a 13–0 victory over CSU. In the next Associated Press poll, Utah entered the rankings at No. 18. A 13–7 loss the following week to Idaho made quick work of Utah's appearance in the polls, and it would be 48 years before the writers would again think so fondly of Utah.

Modest as it was, at least Utah had token appearances in the polls (Utah finished the 1964 season ranked No. 14 in the coaches poll). Colorado State (or Colorado Agricultural as it was originally known) couldn't even make that claim. Until the 1994 season, the Aggies/Rams had never been ranked. The Rams proved they would be a contender early in the season by denying BYU coach Lavell Edwards in his first shot at 200 career wins, in Provo no less. Three weeks later, CSU shot up in the polls with a victory at No. 4. Arizona. CSU would remain a few spots ahead of Utah in the polls until the two teams met midway through the season.

in town. Never before had either program drawn as much attention as it did on this day.

Everything was in place for the hype to consume one or both teams and lead to a dud of a game. Those fortunate enough to witness the game in person or on television were treated to a classic—a first half dominated by defense, followed by a second half that was the Wacky WAC at its high-flying, scoreboard-exploding best.

From scrimmage, Colorado State dominated. The Rams outgained Utah 470–295 while blocking two punts and recovering three Ute fumbles. Utah also had 14 penalties for 117 yards. Normally, that would be enough for most teams to win.

Utah countered with more big plays. It earned a safety on CSU's opening possession when quarterback Anthoney Hill stepped out of bounds fielding a high snap over his head. It hit the blocked-kick trifecta, getting through to block a punt, PAT, and field goal. And when the Utah offense absolutely had to have a drive that resulted in points, quarterback Mike McCoy engineered a 70-yard, 14-play drive capped by an 8-yard fade pattern to Curtis Marsh for a 38–31 lead.

"I thought that stuff was behind us," McCoy said of the wild second half. "But it was something that just...came up and happened."

With shadows beginning to engulf the playing field, CSU responded by driving to the Utah 10-yard line with less than a minute to go but facing fourth-and-goal from the 8. The call, remembered a receivers coach for CSU by the name of Urban Meyer, was Trio Bunch Y Go 55 Y. Hill, a fine dual-threat quarterback before the term became commonplace in the era of spread-option offenses, rolled to his left and threw to wide receiver Matt Phillips.

Neither saw sophomore free safety Harold Lusk break on the ball five yards deep into the end zone. No Ram had a prayer of tackling Lusk, and the converted quarterback didn't stop doing his Deion Sanders high-step until he reached the section of Hughes that seated the delirious Utah fans.

"All of the Colorado State fans back where I picked off the ball, they went dead silent," Lusk said. "My sideline is jumping and screaming, and as I went, each section of the stadium went silent. I heard Coach Mac yell, 'Go down! Go down!' But as I crossed the 50, he started running after me, yelling, 'Go! Go! Go!'

"All I thought was, 'I'm going to score. I'm going to score. I'm not falling down.'"

Thanks to 19 career interceptions, Lusk remains Utah's all-time leader in that category, with one more than Eric Weddle. He also gained more yards off interception returns than any other Ute defender. But it is the result of one play that defined Harold Lusk's career at Utah.

24 The Eccles Family

Whether you're talking athletics or academics, it is impossible to escape the Eccles name as one makes a visit to the University of Utah. There's the Spencer F. and Cleone P. Eccles Health Sciences Education Building on the grounds of the medical school campus. And the business school is officially known as the David Eccles School of Business. As one of the leaders in the field of genetics research, the University of Utah is also home to the Eccles Institute of Genetics. Aspiring members of the media can hone their broadcasting chops in the Dolores Dore Eccles Broadcast Center, and the George S. Eccles Legacy Bridge, which connected the U campus to the Olympic Village for the 2002 Winter Games, is a constant reminder of the Olympic presence at the U.

Football, however, is where the Eccles name gets the most recognition nationally, thanks to Rice-Eccles Stadium. A generous $10 million gift provided by the Eccles family spearheaded efforts for the stadium's $52 million renovation in time for the Olympics.

Cross the street at 500 South and Guardsman Way, and there's the George S. Eccles Tennis Center, which is connected to the Dee Glen Smith football complex. A 2004 addition, which included an indoor practice facility and also houses the Monfort Hall of Champions, bears the name of Spencer Eccles.

Before he became chairman and chief executive officer of the largest banking organization in the Intermountain West, First Security Corporation, Spencer "Spence" Eccles was an All-American skier on some great Utah teams in the 1950s. He is also the president or trustee of several family foundations that bear the Eccles name, most notably of the George S. and Dolores Dore Eccles Foundation.

It was Spence's competitive spirit that drove him to make the deal on March 31, 2004, when he approached athletic director Chris Hill with a $2 million donation for a new practice facility—a facility promised to Urban Meyer when he was hired as head coach in 2003.

The catch? Hill and the athletic department had to raise $2 million to match Eccles' donation, plus another $2 million to cover the remaining cost of the facility. And those donations had to be secured by Memorial Day so the project could be completed before the end of the 2004 season when the weather often turns nasty in Salt Lake City. Eccles' gift toward renovating the football stadium was made in a similar manner—$5 million up front and another $5 million "made in a challenge fashion" by Eccles to spur other donations.

"This is exciting," Hill said. "This is the last piece of the puzzle as far as facilities are concerned for a lot of our programs—which obviously includes football."

Football isn't the only sport that uses the Spence Eccles Field House. The baseball, softball, and soccer teams all make use of the facility, as well. It is a huge improvement over the inflatable bubble used by previous Utah teams, which deflated on more than one occasion, wasn't big enough to handle the entire team at once, and whose playing surface caused numerous injuries.

"With the addition of our new indoor facility, there is no question Utah is firmly entrenched in the 'haves,'" Meyer said shortly before the 2004 season began.

Meyer never had full use of the facility because he left for Florida after the 2004 season, but his foresight into the necessity of such a facility was vital for Utah football. And all along the way, just like so many other university projects, the Eccles family was there to provide help above and beyond what anyone would expect.

25 LaVell Edwards

As heated as the rivalry is between Utah and BYU, the programs at the two schools have been helped immensely by contributions from the rival school. With that in mind, it is impossible to dismiss the contributions, indirectly or otherwise, that were made by LaVell Edwards, the College Football Hall of Fame coach who led BYU to the 1984 National Championship—the first honor ever attained by a team in the Rocky Mountain states.

Edwards was at BYU long enough to coach against six different Utah coaches, and he had his way with the first five in compiling a 19–2 record against Utah from 1972–92. It wasn't until Ron McBride showed up and turned the tables on the rivalry, making it into one of the most competitive in the nation, before Edwards' and BYU's stranglehold was loosened.

A pair of 34–31 games led to a series of humorous commercials by a local bank in the mid-1990s that shed light on the respect and admiration the two coaches had for each other and the job they were doing at their respective programs. What many fans don't realize is LaVell Edwards played a significant role in one instance of advancing McBride's career.

But first, here's a little bit of background. McBride came to Utah for the first time as offensive coordinator for Wayne Howard's staff in 1977, but McBride had a hefty background in coaching the offensive line. After Howard left, he had stipulated that all of his assistant coaches should keep their jobs. McBride coached for a year under Chuck Stobart, a situation McBride said "had to be a little uncomfortable for Stobart. He comes in by himself, basically with one guy, and the rest were holdover staff, so that's tough for any head coach."

The uneasiness, understandably, went both ways, and some assistants left after that first year. McBride had planned on staying at Utah and was getting ready to enter spring practice, but Wisconsin head coach Dave McClain, who had just lost his own offensive line coach, made a visit west in search of a replacement.

McBride recalled, "Dave came out and talked to LaVell Edwards and asked him, 'Who's the best offensive line coach in this area?' And LaVell said he should look at this guy from Utah."

This was in 1982, more than a decade before the first 34–31 game.

That was how McBride got most of his coaching jobs. The only job he officially applied for was the Utah job in 1990. His connections within the game were numerous.

Edwards' rise in the coaching ranks came almost by accident.

"I still wonder sometimes why I was chosen to be the head coach," Edwards said in his 1980 biography. "My credentials weren't very impressive. A lot of people in football believe that in order to be a successful coach on the major college level, you have to move around a lot, becoming exposed to a variety of different programs and people. My eight years at Granite High with a mediocre win-loss record couldn't have excited many people."

Edwards later explained the only reason he was brought on to BYU's staff in the first place was that he was the only coach in the area that ran the single-wing formation on offense, a formation former BYU coach Hal Mitchell brought with him to BYU in 1961.

"Ironically, the only reason I got the job was because I may have been the only Mormon in the world coaching the single wing.

"I didn't have the usual background for becoming a head coach, but the people in the administration and athletic department knew me well, they liked me, and they thought I could do the job. They believed in me. That's how I got the job."

"It wasn't a matter of whether or not I was going to be fired but a matter of when I was going to be fired," Edwards said. "In the prior 47 years, BYU averaged about three wins a year."

The firing never came, and Edwards' knack for hiring exceptional assistant coaches was on display from the start, although his original choice for offensive coordinator, Don Rydalch, had to decline after being injured in a serious car accident. Rydalch was a quarterback at, you guessed it, Utah, where he was an all-conference performer in 1952.

Instead, Edwards hired Dewey Warren from Tennessee to be offensive coordinator, the first of many great offensive minds at BYU who were willing to adhere to Edwards' newfound philosophy of pass, pass, and pass some more. Two years after taking the job, Edwards was successful in hiring another Utah alum, Norm Chow, as a graduate assistant in 1974. Chow was promoted to full-time coach in 1976 and offensive coordinator in 1982.

On the defensive side of the ball, Fred Whittingham joined the staff, first as linebacker coach, then as defensive coordinator in 1979. By now, it should be easy to connect the dots to realize the impact of those hires. Of course, some of Edwards' players have gone on to be successful coaches at Utah, most notably Kyle

Whittingham, but also Aaron Roderick and Kalani Sitake, the offensive and defensive coordinators during the 2009–10 seasons.

Even though Edwards is retired and McBride is at Weber State, they are often together at local charity functions. In 2010, they shared extensive time and laughter in a television studio for the recording of *Red Blood, Blue Blood: The Rivalry*. Together, Edwards and McBride created a bond that is unlikely to be matched by future head coaches at Utah and BYU.

26 Swoop

Until 1972, Utah's sports teams were interchangeably known as the Utes and the Redskins. To address concerns by Native Americans over the stereotypes such racially charged nicknames perpetuated, the school dropped usage of the word "Redskins" that year, and the media followed the school's request. On a side note, the Special Events Center, now the Jon M. Huntsman Center and built in 1969 for the basketball team, was dubbed "the Wigwam" by the school and local media, and that term, too, was dropped.

It's only natural then that the one great struggle the U had within the athletic program was finding a suitable mascot. For years, after the Crimson Warrior was discontinued in the mid-1980s, Utah was the only program in the Western Athletic Conference without a live mascot at sporting events.

A decade later, Bruce Woodbury, Utah's sports information director at the time, was part of a committee to find a new mascot, a process that was anything but easy.

"We couldn't find one. We went through all the animals," Woodbury said. "Finally, we came up with the red-tailed hawk

Swoop gets ready to lead Utah players onto the field. (Photo courtesy Tom Smart)

because it's indigenous to Utah and related to the Indians. That was a tough deal because everything we came up with, somebody [else] had [it] or nobody liked [it]."

Woodbury doesn't remember the exact person who first brought up the red-tailed hawk, but this much is certain. In 1996, Swoop was born, and he has become a fixture at Utah sporting events ever since...not that his arrival was universally hailed as a stroke of marketing genius or anything.

"We used to have one fan who really hated it," Woodbury said. "[He] called it a chicken."

Swoop came along at the height of Utah's modern-day success in basketball, and ESPN wanted to do a commercial promotion for its college basketball broadcasts, a promotion that involved Utah coach Rick Majerus and Swoop. The two were just one of several coach-mascot combinations asked to participate in the promotion.

ESPN asked Woodbury about the mascot, realized the connection between a hawk and a Ute was very thin, and simply replied to Woodbury to "just bring Coach Majerus."

Today, Swoop is "a lot more accepted than it used to be," Woodbury said. It also helps that there are people today at the U who fully understand the significance of the mascot and take pride in Swoop's identity. Robert Gramse, who donned Swoop's outfit for the 2007–08 football seasons and today is the cheerleading coach at the U, knows what he wants when auditioning Swoop wannabes.

"Swoop is someone outgoing, someone who can create new skits and new ideas to help entertain the crowd," Gramse said. "Someone who's not afraid to be around a lot of people. Someone who's okay with having their identity hidden and not getting credit for all that they do."

Swoop is no different than most of the football players in that he, too, is on scholarship and must maintain full-time student status in order to suit up. And just like the players, Swoop needs to be physically fit. Unlike the players, Swoop wouldn't dare to take off his headgear in public.

"Swoop puts the suit on and runs two or three hours per day," Gramse said in explaining the mascot's preseason conditioning drills. "When you're in the suit for four to five hours straight, he's got to get used to wearing the suit and having it on. Swoop has to be in shape and be able to meet the physical demands of being a mascot."

And of course, there's the creative side of things. As a representative of the school, Swoop also needs to appeal to people of all ages.

"You can basically get away with doing anything you want to anybody if it makes people laugh," Gramse said. "We try and come up with the craziest ways to make people laugh. Whether it's pouring water on someone, shooting them with Silly String, harassing the other team's fans—that sort of stuff—those are the funny times. It's seeing how much you can get away with while in uniform."

Even though Swoop's true identity isn't revealed until his tenure is over, there are still plenty of benefits to being Swoop. Of course, there's the aforementioned scholarship. As the football program's official sportswear provider, there's plenty of Under Armor apparel to be had. Swoop travels to every road football game and several basketball games each year.

But one of the best perks, Gramse said, isn't always associated with sports—especially when it involves younger fans who need someone to brighten their day.

"We do appearances at Primary Children's Hospital," Gramse said. "You have experiences where you're going in, and these kids don't have much or they're having a hard time with what they're dealing with there. You go in and make them smile, make them laugh. Those appearances are the hidden rewards that people don't see.... As the mascot, you know you've made a difference for them."

27 Dynasty Architect I: Norm Chow

Norm Chow has never been about taking a conventional route to the University of Utah, either as a high school player choosing a college or returning to his alma mater as offensive coordinator in 2011 to assist with Utah's transition into the Pac-12 Conference.

"Back then, the coaches went to Hawaii, and we didn't take a visit.... They just offered a scholarship," said Chow, reflecting on his recruitment coming out of the Punahou School in Honolulu. "So I had a scholarship offer from Utah and BYU. I had never been to Utah before, but my brother was living in Boise at the time and encouraged me to take the scholarship [to Utah], and I left the islands. We took Utah up on the offer sight unseen, and we visited my brother in Boise and he drove us down."

"I met my wife here, got two degrees from here," Chow said. "I made lifelong friends here, and it was a nice experience. This is like a dream for me, to be able to go full circle. Hopefully this will be the last [job], and we can make this thing work."

In between his time as a player, which saw Chow earn first team All–Western Athletic Conference honors as a senior in 1967, Chow developed a well-earned reputation as an offensive mastermind and quarterback developer extraordinaire. Among his pupils are three Heisman trophy winners—Ty Detmer, Carson Palmer, and Matt Leinart—and his USC offense allowed a fourth player, Reggie Bush, to walk away with college football's most coveted award. He was also the offensive coordinator for three national-championship-winning teams with BYU (1984) and USC (2003–04).

With a one-year stint at North Carolina State, Chow put a young freshman named Philip Rivers on the fast track to succeed in the college game and eventually become a first-round pick of the New York Giants who then traded him to the San Diego Chargers.

Mike Giddings, whom Chow played under for two seasons, never saw Chow's development into one of the most respected offensive minds coming.

"I'd like to say I did and all that, but I didn't have anything to do with that," Giddings said. "You have to give credit to LaVell [Edwards] and Norm himself.

"We ran the ball more than we passed it," Giddings added. "In those days, our quarterbacks managed the game. With Norm at BYU, his quarterbacks didn't manage the game—they won the game, and that would be the difference."

"I think it depends on who your quarterback is," Chow said. "I think Coach Giddings is right. A lot of times you have a guy you just want to stay in there, but other times you have guys you feel can take the game a long way, and I was blessed to have quarterbacks who had that capability. Philip Rivers, Carson Palmer, Ty Detmer—those guys were brought in to win games no matter who the coach was."

Chow got into coaching after his career in the Canadian Football League was cut short by injury, first at Waialua High in his native Hawaii, then as a graduate assistant at BYU prior to the 1973 season. Edwards had become head coach the year prior, and his throw-throw philosophy on offense was just starting to take effect.

"I was extremely lucky in my career," Chow said. "The [coaching] staffs at that time went from eight to nine, or seven to eight, so I wasn't hired to replace someone. I was hired as an additional coach, and the spot that was open was a receivers coach and the coordinator was Doug Scovil. He was the one who put that whole deal together, throwing the football."

And throwing the football like BYU did often resulted in one-sided victories against his alma mater. It was just business, insisted Chow, who worked his way up the ladder at BYU before earning play-calling duties in 1982. He was officially given the title of offensive coordinator in 1996.

"It was just another game on the schedule, if you will," Chow said. "I do remember once the bus got to their stadium and people started rocking the bus a little bit and LaVell turned to the team and said, 'What do you expect from Norm's alma mater?' It was a rivalry and it was fun to be a part of, and little did we know that someday we'd end up back here."

28 The Dark Ages

This book contends that the Dark Ages ended with Utah's victory in the 1995 Holy War, a victory which earned the Utes a share of the Western Athletic Conference title during a year that the history of the program indicated would be a rebuilding year. Others will claim earlier dates—Ron McBride's hiring, either of the 34–31 Holy Wars, or even Urban Meyer's arrival in 2003. Whatever one's perception is of the history of the Utah program, it has undergone swift and remarkable changes during the past 15 years or so.

There wasn't a whole lot to cheer about for nearly two decades from the mid-1970s to the mid-1990s. There were moments, like the Rice Bowl and the 1981 season, when Utah entered the Holy War in sole possession of first place in the conference. But Utah football rarely entered the month of October with big dreams for the rest of the year. Too often, it was a time to celebrate the beginning of basketball practice.

About the only thing more amazing than the length of Utah's stay in football wilderness was the suddenness with which it arrived. In 1973, Utah scored its biggest win against a ranked foe, defeating Arizona State 36–31. It needed only to beat BYU to clinch no worse than a co-championship and a spot in the Fiesta Bowl. Instead, BYU rolled 46–22, and Coach Bill Meek left after the season.

In 1974, Utah sunk to the depths of major college football by going 1–10. To show it wasn't a fluke, the Utes went 1–10 the following year as well, and Tom Lovat was fired as coach after three years and a 5–28 mark.

How did the Utah program go from holding its bowl destiny in its own hands to being one of the worst, if not the worst, teams in college football in less than a year?

Retired *Salt Lake Tribune* sports editor Dick Rosetta offers up three mistakes Utah made that caused its prolonged stay in mediocrity.

"Bill Meek wasn't technically fired. He wanted too much money at the time...and it was more than the U could handle. He hadn't done a bad job. This was one of the first big mistakes the University of Utah made in football. See, they wanted Larry Wilson, and when those negotiations fell through, they were left hanging right at the last second, and so they had to dip into the assistant coaching staff and they picked Tom Lovat.

"Tom Lovat was a great guy, but he was just barely out of the high school coaching ranks. He coached at Hillcrest High back in the day. That was the first mistake, but it's easy to say now because he only won five games in three years.

"The second mistake wasn't necessarily bringing in Wayne Howard...but the pressure got to Wayne basically, and he pretty much left. That brings me to the second mistake...and that was firing Chuck Stobart."

Really? A Utah coach who seemingly found new and imaginative ways to lose games on a regular basis should have been retained? But Rosetta gives the explanation for why Stobart was fired.

"Chuck was a no-nonsense football coach and he didn't have the 'downtown' charisma, and working with all the high rollers was essentially why he got fired. He was fired after a winning season.

"The third mistake they made was hiring Jim Fassel. They hired a guy with no head coaching experience whose only claim to fame was that he had coached John Elway at Stanford. He was the quarterbacks coach there and [that] was one of the main ways he got the job.

"We'll light up the scoreboard, which was what BYU was doing. We'll catch up with BYU. We'll show them. So Jim goes 8–4 with Stubby's personnel in '85. With his own personnel, picked to win the WAC, but here again, playing with Fassel's offense-only mentality, he got [Scott] Mitchell and forsook any semblance of defense.

"I remember talking to the defensive coaches, and they told me they were taking the best players off of defense and putting them on offense. Because Jim wanted to light up the scoreboard.

"If you wanted to roll [those mistakes] into one, you could see what developed—Utah got caught, in the old expression, with its pants down. When LaVell Edwards took over as football coach, BYU was almost a figment of someone's imagination, that they could possibly be a threat to University of Utah football.

"Maybe [BYU] didn't get lucky, but a fortuitous thing happened. LaVell thought, 'Well, we'll throw the football. Now the chinks [in Utah's armor] are beginning to show.... And as BYU comes up, Utah is going down. It took about 20 years to start the recovery process, and that was the hiring of Ron McBride."

29 The Night the Lights Went Out in Laramie

As Utah was rolling toward its first BCS-busting season in 2004, ABC added the Utes' game against Wyoming in Laramie to its broadcast schedule. For both schools, appearing on a major network was a big deal—it was just the 10th such appearance for Utah since 1981—even if it was just a regional telecast and wouldn't be broadcast back to those in the Eastern and Central time zones without the help of a satellite dish. As an added bonus, former Utes great Jamal Anderson was scheduled to do color commentary for ABC.

But more important were the events of earlier in the day that made this more than just another game for Utah. Aside from the obvious—the chance to improve to 10–0—Wisconsin, the team Utah was chasing for the coveted No. 6 spot in the BCS rankings—lost earlier in the day to Michigan State. A Utah victory was certain to move Utah into the top 6 and position it to become the first school from a non-BCS conference to qualify for a BCS game, provided it defeated BYU the following week. And speaking of BYU, its loss to New Mexico earlier in the day opened the door for Utah to clinch the Mountain West Conference title outright by beating the Cowboys.

In hindsight, it's easy to point to two events that would turn ABaC's broadcast into a complete fiasco and leave Utah players, coaches, and officials with a "What do we do now?" mode of thought. There have been more memorable games in Utah history, but no broadcast provided as many behind-the-scenes stories worth telling than Utah-Wyoming.

First, the date of the game, November 13, coupled with the prime-time start, meant the game would be played in Laramie's brutal cold. Temperature at kickoff was 28 degrees, but winds from the south exceeding 20 mph put the wind chill at 15 degrees.

And with few night games being played at Laramie, it's not like Wyoming has a manual on what to do if, say, the lights went out—which is exactly what happened about 20 minutes before the scheduled kickoff time of 5:00 pm MST. A blown fuse caused a transformer to burn out, delaying the game's start by 1 hour, 39 minutes.

"ABC hooked in their truck and everything else, and they blew out a transformer. It controlled only so many lights, so they had to bring in a backup generator," legendary voice of the Utes Bill Marcroft said. "Laramie is fairly isolated, a lot of TV stations elected not to do games out of there, because it's so difficult—you have to drive everything in to do it. There's nothing available for you to purchase in the area. Like there is in [Salt Lake City], if a network wanted to do a game, they could hire a truck here. We have them in the area."

According to Bill Riley, the subject of moving the game was brought up with Urban Meyer, and he insisted that the game be played that night, no matter how late it began. Riley also remembered talking with offensive coordinator Mike Sanford in a dark, cold press box, wondering what was going to happen next. Eventually, enough of the lights came on to allow the game to be played.

Trouble was, KTVX/Channel 4 in Salt Lake City, uncertain if the game would be played, went to ABC's national feed of *Harry Potter*. Football fans across Utah were incensed and wanted to find out why the game wasn't being televised. One of their first targets was KALL 700, which was unfortunate for producer Zealand Youngman, who was in Salt Lake City and had to deal with the onslaught of complaints, which he relayed to his broadcast team.

"I tried to use what we're doing on the air and be as informative as possible, so I inadvertently used Wes Ruff's private number at the station—it went right to his desk," Marcroft said. "I couldn't remember the switchboard number for Channel 4, but Wes' number I knew. It took a while for me, and a couple of lunches before I placated Wes—he was really incensed."

Riley, today's radio voice of the Utes, had just joined the Utah broadcast team in midseason after being with KSL and being involved with coverage of rival BYU on the Cougars' flag-ship station, vividly remembers Marcroft's judgment lapse—with a slight twist.

"I'm waving my arms saying, 'No, no no Bill!' I'm not saying it on the air, but I'm waving my arms. Bill gives the number out over the air and he looks over at me and on the air says, 'What's wrong Bill Riley? I'm just giving people Wes Ruff's contact number.' But

I don't know if Bill realized at the time he was giving out Wes' cell phone number and not the station line. The switchboard at Channel 4, that blew up as well because they had so many telephone calls."

The game didn't produce anywhere near as much drama. Utah led 31–7 at halftime en route to a 45–28 victory. And with Utah's move to the Pac-12 Conference, it's unlikely the two teams will meet anytime soon in the near future. But for those involved with the program, the 2004 visit to Laramie will burn bright in their minds. Even if the lights didn't do likewise.

30 Joseph B. Wirthlin

Joseph B. "Speedy" Wirthlin wasn't the first apostle of the Church of Jesus Christ of Latter-day Saints to play football for the U. He's not even the highest-ranking LDS Church leader to have played football at the U. In 1894, David McKay played for the U long before he became better known as President David O. McKay while serving as a general authority in the church for more than 60 years.

Time to be frank—it's not always easy for non-Mormons to adjust to living in predominantly Mormon Utah. While there is a lesser percentage of Mormons in Salt Lake City than there is across most of the state, the Church's influence cannot be ignored. Its world headquarters occupy what was for the longest time the tallest building in the state. One is rarely more than a few blocks from a Mormon chapel. For first-time visitors to Salt Lake City, the tour isn't complete without a trip to Temple Square and other historical Mormon sites.

At the same time, the relationship between Wirthlin and Urban Meyer offers a good example of how Mormons and non-Mormons alike can put aside whatever social, political, or religious differences that may exist between them and still be friends.

Wirthlin played under Ike Armstrong and lettered for three years from 1936–38. And while Wirthlin's devotion to his Utes remained strong through the years, very little about Wirthlin the football fan was known prior to the arrival of Meyer in 2003.

Meyer, a Catholic eager to understand some of the workings of the Mormon faith—likely including the effect of some of his players serving two-year missions would have on his program— quickly developed a bond with Wirthlin once Meyer found out he had an ally at the highest levels of LDS Church leadership.

"[The relationship] really got a lot of traction when [Meyer] got here," said Crimson Club chairperson Blake Strong. "He wanted to know Joseph Wirthlin."

"Coach Meyer would ask Dad about the Church—and Dad would ask Coach Meyer about football," Joseph B. Wirthlin Jr. said. "He would always talk about his U of U coach Ike Armstrong and the things he learned as a young man: character, strength, and conviction." The discussions would last hours as the Wirthlins—Joseph Sr. and his wife Elisa—were frequent dinner guests at the Meyers.

The friendship stayed strong after Meyer left for Florida, and Wirthlin even attended a Gator contest in 2005 against Vanderbilt. New Utah coach Kyle Whittingham picked up where Meyer left off, and Wirthlin maintained his grandfather-like status in the program.

"Quietly, which was his way, he became the team's inspirational leader—the Utes' Yoda," wrote *Deseret News* columnist Lee Benson shortly after Wirthlin's death.

"We just enjoyed having him around the team," Whittingham said. "He was very gentle, kind, and had a grandfather-type of demeanor.... 'Genuine' is the word I would use for him."

Sadly, Wirthlin wasn't around for the final chapter of Utah's perfect 2008 season. Nine days after Utah defeated BYU to clinch a spot in a BCS bowl, Wirthlin died at the age of 91. His influence on the program was not lost, however, and when Utah took the field against Alabama in the Sugar Bowl, Utah helmets had a "JBW" decal affixed to them.

A more lasting tribute was established shortly after Wirthlin's death when the athletic department created the Elder Joseph B. Wirthlin Family Scholarship. Whittingham and Meyer were among the initial donors to the scholarship fund. Wirthlin's No. 4 jersey was retired in 2003.

31 The Lost Championship of 1969

It's a question that still eats away at members of Utah's 1969 team:

How could a team with just one loss that also beat the other one-loss team in a league where no one went undefeated fail to be at least conference co-champions?

That was the fate of the 1969 Utah team, which defeated Arizona State 24–23 in Salt Lake City yet didn't receive any hardware for the trophy case by virtue of ASU having the benefit of an additional conference game against a woebegone opponent.

First things first: Arizona State deserves its spot in the record books as champions of the 1969 Western Athletic Conference. But it deserves some company at the top. At the very least, the 1969 Utah team is in need of some long overdue recognition and the acclaim befitting a team that should have been awarded no worse than co-champion status.

"We should have been," agreed Ray Groth, Utah's starting senior quarterback that season, when asked if his team should have been at least co-champions. "In this day and age, they probably would have done it. But all the hype was for Arizona State at the time."

"That was a hell of a team," reflected defensive back Gary Barker, a three-year letterman from 1968–70. "It's like they say today, it's not always the most talented team that wins but the best *team*. We had a lot of camaraderie, maturity, togetherness, and willingness. We fought together."

Especially on defense. Utah's stop unit in 1969 gave up just 107 points in 10 games. Only the 1964 Liberty Bowl champions gave up fewer points in the two-platoon era. Since 1969, no defensive unit at Utah has come within a touchdown of that mark.

Utah had won just 7-of-21 games in the previous two seasons, so a 28–17 loss to an Oregon team that ended up 5–5–1 probably wasn't surprising, especially since the Ducks featured Dan Fouts at quarterback and a sophomore receiver playing in his first varsity game named Bobby Moore, who would later achieve fame in the NFL and as broadcaster Ahmad Rashad.

What was surprising was the seven-win streak that followed the season-opening loss. A pair of blowout victories over San Jose State and Texas–El Paso preceded one of the program's biggest wins of the decade—a 24–23 nailbiter against Arizona State.

"I think every guy has his game, and that, for me, was my pinnacle," said Groth, who is the head football coach at Tooele High School in Utah. "I played fairly well, and we came from behind. I remember calling a couple of plays that worked out for us. It was great—they had all the hype, the speed. Frank Kush was the head coach, and for Utah to come up and beat them was a phenomenal win for us."

Utah passed two more stiff tests, beating Oregon State (the same Beaver squad that crushed ASU 30–7) in Portland by a 7–3 margin, when Clint Harden relieved Groth and led the Redskins to the go-ahead score in the fourth quarter. Then they took two-time WAC champ Wyoming to the woodshed in a 34–10 victory. Two road games remained—at Arizona and BYU. If they won both, then Utah would be the undisputed WAC champions, and they would be headed for a bowl game, almost certainly the Sun Bowl, where the team would have played Nebraska.

Alas, Utah stubbed its toe against the Wildcats, losing 17–16 on a last-minute field goal that featured Sun Bowl representatives in attendance. Utah rebounded to beat BYU 16–6 in the season finale to finish 8–2, but the shiny fancy stuff—a conference title, a meaningful bowl bid, and possible ranking in the polls—was gone.

"We went down there just a little overconfident. We knew the Sun Bowl representatives were there. I think we just went in a little flat, maybe not respecting Arizona that much. I'm my hardest critic, and I didn't play well," Groth said.

"The coaching staff didn't do well in prepping us and getting us up—the significance of that game. We win that game, we get to go to the Sun Bowl. I don't think they even mentioned it. When I look back on it, this is one of the most important games Utah had played in years. Maybe that was their thing, approach each game one game at a time…. But on the other hand, fire us up a little bit and define what's ahead of us. That's my take."

There was a bowl invite on the table—the Pasadena Bowl—a lower-level bowl that featured teams on the level of what is today known as the Football Championship Series. Utah's opponent would have been San Diego State before it made the jump to Division I-A status. But it wasn't what Utah players had set their sights on, and a team vote the day after the BYU game saw Utah players reject the bid.

"No disrespect to San Diego State," said Groth, who voted against accepting the bid, "but at the time, they were kind of a I-AA university. The feeling was, if you're going to do it, do it right. It didn't feel like it was the right thing for the University of Utah."

32 Utah's 2004 Coaching Staff

It's a fun debate Utah fans like to have, and it's also a fair question. Which Utah team was better, 2004 or 2008?

The most obvious—and celebrated—similarities are well-documented. Both teams went undefeated, finished in the top five in both major polls, and stomped big-name programs in bowl games. Both teams featured quarterbacks who are 1–2 in the U record books for most wins as a starter. And both teams featured a bevy of NFL draft picks.

One area in which the 2004 team is clearly superior—although there is plenty of time for this 2008 unit to make up the gap—is in the resumes of each year's respective coaching staff. Consider the following members of Utah's 2004 staff:

Urban Meyer, head coach: Meyer won two national titles at Florida from 2006–10, three BCS bowl games, and two SEC championships. He is currently retired, but no one would be surprised if Meyer donned a headset again.

Kyle Whittingham, defensive coordinator: Whittingham led Utah to a 13–0 mark and a No. 2 national ranking in 2008. He also won the AFCA and Paul "Bear" Bryant Coach of the Year honors.

Mike Sanford, offensive coordinator: Hired by Nevada–Las Vegas after the 2004 season as head coach, Sanford was fired after posting a 16–43 mark in five seasons. He is currently the offensive coordinator at Louisville, and in 2010 he helped get the Cardinals to a bowl game for the first time since 2006.

Dan Mullen, quarterback coach: Mullen followed Meyer to Florida and was the offensive coordinator for Chris Leak and Tim

Tebow, two quarterbacks who won national titles. Mullen was hired by Mississippi State for the 2009 season and is 14–11 in two seasons, including a 9–4 mark in 2010, the Bulldogs' best season in a decade. His offensive line coach at MSU is John Hevesy, another assistant at Utah in 2004.

Gary Anderson, defensive line: The only member of the 2004 staff who was an assistant on the 2008 staff, Anderson was hired as the head coach at Utah State prior to the 2009 season. Anderson is 8–16 thus far in two years with the Aggies. Anderson actually left Utah following the 2002 season for the head coaching job at FCS Southern Utah. Although he got off to a good start there, going 4–7 after inheriting a team that won just one game, Anderson came back to the U because he recognized the opportunity that existed to work with a dynamic staff that was poised to lead the Utes to a breakout season.

With the exception of Meyer, not a single coach from the 2004 staff was out of college football as the 2010 season ended, and several more assistants have been linked to head coaching vacancies. Billy Gonzales (wide receiver coach, now at LSU) and Chuck Heater (defensive back coach) followed Meyer to Florida before taking the job as defensive coordinator at Temple. Both Gonzales and Heater have thrived in the ultra-competitive SEC, and both men appear destined to become head coaches in the future.

As for the 2008 staff, offensive coordinator Andy Ludwig holds the same position at San Diego State, while offensive line coach Charlie Dickey moved closer to his Kansas home and holds the same position at Kansas State. There are plenty of young, up-and-coming coaches currently on Utah's staff, but if they are to gain head-coaching experience, it's going to have to come with another program as long as Whittingham is around.

33 Flat Broke and Busted in Vegas

If there are lessons to be learned in defeat, then Utah's 27–0 loss to Nevada–Las Vegas in the fourth game of the 2007 season is worthy of its own teacher's manual. Not only had Utah never lost to the Rebels in eight games in the history of the Mountain West Conference, it had never even been tested. The average margin of victory for Utah in those games was nearly three touchdowns, and the U had never won by less than double digits. Add three games when the teams played in different conferences, and Utah had won 11 straight.

So watching Utah crush UNLV was as certain as death, taxes, or the house advantage at any Vegas casino.

After an injury-riddled start that saw Utah begin a disappointing 0–2, it appeared everything was back on track after a resounding 44–6 thrashing of No. 8 UCLA at Rice-Eccles Stadium. Presumably the Rebels, along with head coach and former Utah offensive coordinator Mike Sanford, would show up to Sam Boyd Stadium, roll over before halftime, and the Utes would even their record at 2–2.

In a city where there's no such thing as a sure bet, it was only fitting that Utah's history in Las Vegas was altered in the most unimaginable way possible. After a couple of so-so seasons in 2005–06, was this Kyle Whittingham's Waterloo in terms of his head coaching career? Would the bottom fall out entirely on Utah's season?

Even Whittingham was baffled by this turn of events.

"I've been coaching 21 years, and this is the toughest team to figure out that I've ever been part of…how we can be so up and down. As well as we played last week [against UCLA], we played that poorly today.

"It's perplexing, but it's my job to figure it out. That's the bottom line," Whittingham said.

Brian Johnson, who had been sidelined since the season-opener against Oregon State with a separated shoulder, relieved Tommy Grady at halftime. That was Bad Omen No. 1 because Grady had looked so good against UCLA, but he was so ineffective against the Rebels that he had to be pulled for a player who wasn't anywhere close to being 100 percent.

Nonetheless, Utah took the second-half kickoff and marched down the field, looking to cut into the Rebels' 13–0 halftime lead. Then Bad Omen No. 2 struck—on fourth-and-goal from the 1-yard line, Johnson ran into running back Darrell Mack, hit the turf, and turned over the ball on downs.

Utah turned over the ball four times, went 1-for-5 on fourth down, and couldn't tackle Frank Summers, who ran for 190 yards and two touchdowns on 29 carries. He also caught a 29-yard pass for another score.

"You can't be a great team one week and mediocre at best the next week," said Johnson, who called the loss embarrassing. "Guys have got to step up and find a way."

Utah found its way quickly, winning seven straight games and eight of nine to end the season. Only a last-second loss to BYU kept Utah from winning 10 games—something no one thought Utah would come close to doing after losing to UNLV, which wouldn't win another game the rest of the year. With a 9–4 mark, Utah had built up plenty of momentum for the next year.

34 Our Cheerleaders Can Beat Up Your Fans

Like any great rivalry, sometimes the intensity surrounding the Holy War can be too much to handle for some fans. Sporting events have emotions attached to them that turn otherwise sensible people into stark-raving lunatics. Haven't we all been there at least once (hopefully for a very brief moment) while watching our favorite teams? Spectator sports would lose a lot of their appeal if they were insipid affairs without the high brought on by victory or the dreariness that comes with a crushing defeat.

With that in mind, it's still hard to imagine the events of the 1999 Holy War without shaking your head and asking, "What were these guys thinking?"

Here's how it all started. Utah quarterback T.D. Croshaw had just connected with tight end Donny Utu for a 4-yard touchdown and a 20–10 fourth-quarter lead. As is customary, Utah cheerleaders ran onto their side of the field with giant flags that spelled out "U-T-A-H."

Brandon Perry, a BYU fan just days away from entering the Missionary Training Center and beginning his two-year stint as a Mormon missionary, was either looking to get out of going on a mission or he simply lost his mind, because he jumped out of the stands and tackled one of the male Ute cheerleaders who was carrying one of the flags.

What happened then is a moment that makes Utah fans smile and BYU fans cringe. The cheerleader, Billy Priddis, gained an advantage on Perry, much like a wrestler does on his opponent, landing several blows to Perry's body and head before being pulled away by security. No one condemned Priddis' clear act of self-defense, although BYU's athletic director, Val Hale, initially reacted by banning visiting teams from carrying flags such as the one Priddis was carrying.

If this were a boxing match, it would be scored Priddis, KO 1. While Utah fans reveled in one of their own putting a BYU fan in his rightful place, Priddis refused to speak publicly about the incident until the week leading up to the 2010 game.

"I wish [the incident] never would have happened," Priddis told the *Deseret News*. "Whenever I go back to Utah, I can hardly walk the campus without someone recognizing me…. It happens more often than I would like."

Utah cheerleaders do what they do best during a 2006 game. (Photo courtesy Tom Smart)

Priddis wants you to know he's not some kind of sociopath. Like Perry, Priddis later served a Mormon mission; he's now married with five kids, and he remains active in his church. And he talked freely about the incident because he wanted a forum for the Lindon [Utah] Police Department Wives Service Project, a charitable venture geared toward raising essentials for orphans in Afghanistan, where Captain Priddis served with the 82nd Sustainment Brigade.

Serving his country abroad during wartime helped Priddis gain better perspective of the meaning of a sporting event—even one involving bitter rivals.

"The only thing I would change is that I wish that the fans would just relax and realize it's just a football game. Enjoy it and have a good time," Priddis said.

Hale mistakenly thought Priddis attacked an usher, so Hale's initial reaction to ban flags was a decision made largely in the heat of the moment. He eventually reconsidered and allowed Utah to carry its flags in the corner of LaVell Edwards Stadium where visiting fans are seated.

"This game brings out the worst of emotions. I worry for those kids' safety," said Hale, who is now the vice president of university relations at nearby Utah Valley State University in Orem. "It has always bothered me that when flags get run up and down, it's like target practice. So we're going to use some sense and keep the Utah flags in front of Utah fans and BYU flags in front of BYU fans."

But there's one more reversal. After serving his mission, Priddis enrolled in an Air Force ROTC program. He did so, however, at BYU and not the U. Don't let that one decision confuse you about which team Priddis cheers for when the two teams meet. He still remains a Utah fan to this day.

"You might as well ask me if I still breathe," Priddis laughed.

35 The Pie

It's an easy mistake to make, so consider yourself warned. To get the true experience of eating at The Pie, don't head to the U along 1300 South, see the signs for the store's delivery and carry-out location, and figure you've arrived. You haven't—not yet anyway.

Continue north to the next stoplight at 200 South, make a right, and look for the large sign for the University Pharmacy. Park along the street and take the set of steps that go down to the pharmacy's basement, and now you can say you've arrived at the epicenter for Utah's best pizza, or for that matter some of the best pizza found in the country. It's dark inside, and when it's busy—which it often is at lunchtime and on weekends—finding a seat can take some time since The Pie seats only about 70 people. You can get The Pie's delicious pizza at one of four other Utah locations and enjoy many of the same experiences, but a trip to The Pie's original home is a must.

The Pie, located at 1320 E. 200 South, opened in 1965 as Bimbos in the Cellar, one of Salt Lake City's first pizza and pasta restaurants. Back then, one could order a 14-inch pizza for just $2.20. Open six days a week, Bimbo's was closed on Sundays because the room was used as a church meetinghouse. In fact, the seats in Bimbo's were actually wooden church pews.

In 1980, the Palmer family turned it into a pizza parlor. The brick walls are covered with scribbled names and other messages left by its patrons. It's open until 3:00 AM on weekends, and it serves beer, plays host to live music acts, and is a traditional college hangout spot. Its Ogden location is in close proximity to Weber State University.

In 2004, The Pie made its first foray outside of collegiate campuses with a delivery and carryout location in suburban Midvale, and it was promptly overwhelmed by customers who remembered The Pie from their college days and were excited about a location that was more centrally located in Salt Lake County. The Midvale location expanded, and another location in south Salt Lake County in South Jordan opened in 2005. That location is The Pie's largest, with indoor seating on two floors for 120 people, in addition to an outdoor patio area that seats 50.

The Pie—whose logo is the symbol for the Greek letter pi—consistently wins local awards and honors for its pizza, and CitySearch.com once listed The Pie as the seventh-best pizza establishment in the country. If you can't make it to Salt Lake City, you can have The Pie delivered to you anywhere in the United States. But if you're in town and near campus, it's as necessary as it is enjoyable to have at least one meal at The Pie.

36 2008 Holy War

In 2004, Utah quickly established itself as the premier non-BCS team in the country. In 2008, the Utes had to bide their time while their rival to the south was hyped as the next BCS Buster.

Raising the stakes was BYU coach Bronco Mendenhall's slogan for the season: "Quest for Perfection." Utah followers cried hubris on the part of Mendenhall and BYU's athletic program for fueling the hype; the company line from BYU backers claimed it was only a natural progression after back-to-back 11–2 seasons.

In the end, Mendenhall might as well have been on Utah's payroll. After Utah completed a 12–0 regular season with a 48–24

Darrell Mack (6) and Matt Asiata combined to form a sledgehammer ground attack in Utah's undefeated 2008 season. (AP Photo/Douglas C. Pizac)

shellacking of the Cougars, it was a slogan that looked much better on the Utes than it ever could have on BYU. As far as the regular season was concerned, it was the ultimate triumph of substance over style.

The Holy War was a complete reversal as the Utah defense forced six BYU turnovers—all on behalf of quarterback Max Hall with five interceptions and a fumble—and dominated the second half to claim the MWC title outright and earn a Sugar Bowl bid against Alabama.

The final score screams blowout and the fourth quarter was dominated entirely by Utah, but to BYU's credit, it showed up to play. After surrendering a field goal on the opening drive, Austin Collie ran the ensuing kickoff 70 yards to the Utah 30. The Utah defense stiffened and forced a BYU field goal to tie the score at 3–3.

Utah scored touchdowns on its next two possessions—a 16-yard pass from Brian Johnson to Brent Casteel and a 5-yard run by Matt Asiata. BYU fought back, tying the score at 17 on a pair of Harvey Unga touchdown runs from 23 and 2 yards out.

With just less than two minutes left before halftime, Louie Sakoda's 35-yard field goal regained the lead for Utah. BYU drove into Utah territory, hoping to get points before the half, but Hall threw to an area of the field with no BYU receiver in sight, and Joe Dale ran it back to the Utah 41. To make matters worse for Hall, he also picked up an unsportsmanlike conduct penalty, moving the ball into BYU territory with 36 seconds left.

Not content to get another field goal, Utah took one crack at the end zone and David Reed hauled in Johnson's 32-yard bomb for a 10-point halftime lead. But again, BYU came back on Hall's 11-yard TD run on its first possession of the second half.

All that score did was mark the beginning of the end for BYU and Hall, whose final five series ended interception, fumble, interception, interception, interception.

Utah cashed in with touchdowns on the middle three turnovers, first with an 8-yard Johnson-to-Casteel pass, then with an Asiata 4-yard pass to Chris Joppru out of the cleverly named Asiata Formation (known everywhere else as the Wildcat) and a 1-yard pass from Johnson (30 of 36 passing, 303 yards, four touchdowns) to Colt Sampson with 2:48 to play.

All that was left was for the clock to run out and for the predictable rush of humanity onto the Rice-Eccles Stadium field for the third time in what was the most memorable of Utah seasons.

37 Dynasty Architect II: George Seifert

George Seifert wasn't a star at the University of Utah when he played there from 1959–62. He wasn't even a highly sought recruit as a high school player in San Francisco; in fact, he was headed to Cal Poly–San Luis Obispo before a previous pledge's last-minute decision not to come to Utah opened the door for Seifert, who had never even visited the campus prior to enrolling.

"You're not dealing with an illustrious athlete at Utah, that's for sure," said Seifert, who played end and guard.

It took some time for Seifert, a zoology major at Utah, to get his traction in the coaching ranks. Before he was a two-time winner of the Super Bowl as the San Francisco 49ers head coach, Seifert's head coaching career consisted of a start-up program at Westminster College—not even a couple of miles down 1300 South from the University of Utah—as well as a disastrous stint at Cornell in which he went 3–15 from 1975–76.

"I learned I wasn't ready to be a head coach," Seifert laughed.

Fortunately, there were far more pleasant and professionally worthwhile experiences for Seifert. After coaching Westminster to a 3–3 mark in 1965 while working on his master's degree at Utah, Seifert followed Utah coach Ray Nagel to Iowa as a graduate assistant for the 1966 season. Nagel also brought along Lynn Stiles—Seifert's roommate, teammate, and the person most responsible for Seifert's decision to become a coach—as a full-time coach. Stops followed at Oregon and Stanford for Seifert, who coached defensive backs. He was also an assistant coach on freshman teams at Oregon and in Utah's 1964 Liberty Bowl–winning season.

"Each experience that I had was part of my foundation, working with Jerry Frei at Oregon and Jack Christiansen at Stanford, and then certainly Bill [Walsh].

"He was the one who had the most impact when I went back to Stanford [where I was] learning so much more and getting a better feel for being a head coach," Seifert said. "I needed some tutoring."

Stanford went 17–7 in Seifert's first two years before Walsh was hired as head coach of the 49ers. At that time, Seifert was insistent on following his mentor into the pro ranks.

"It was one of the most crushing moments in my life," Seifert said. "I stayed at Stanford for a year, and I was miserable the whole time. It was then that I decided I would do everything I could to get into professional football."

Seifert joined Walsh for the 49ers' first Super Bowl season in 1981 as the defensive back coach, and he was promoted to defensive coordinator in 1983. The following year, Seifert's defense drew widespread praise for how it shut down the Miami Dolphins' passing attack and quarterback Dan Marino, who set the league on fire by throwing an NFL-record 48 touchdown passes that year. The 49ers won Super Bowl XIX going away, and Seifert became a hot commodity, getting inquiries from Indianapolis and Green Bay about being their head coach. Seifert stayed put and enjoyed a reunion of sorts with Stiles, who joined the 49ers as a special teams coach in 1987—and Seifert won a third Super Bowl as an assistant coach. His loyalty to San Francisco paid off when it named him Walsh's successor after the 1988 season.

Seifert and the 49ers repeated as Super Bowl champions in 1989 and were on their way to another appearance in the 1990 season when Joe Montana was knocked out of the NFC title game against the New York Giants, who rallied in the fourth quarter to advance to the title game.

It was the beginning of the toughest time of Seifert's career as 49ers head coach. An elbow injury sidelined Montana for almost all of the 1991 and 1992 seasons, but by the time he regained his health, Steve Young had supplanted Montana as the starting quarterback. With Young being five years younger, San Francisco had a decision to make that was easy on logic but difficult on emotion.

"I can't say if there's any closer relationship between Steve and I because I was the coach who made that change," Seifert said. "We had some fun jabbing each other with regard to the BYU-Utah football game, but I think that was coming more from me than even Steve."

It was quite a journey for Seifert, one that began with his decision to attend Utah without ever having visited the school.

"I really didn't know anything about Utah. My mother took me to the Greyhound bus depot in downtown San Francisco, and the next thing I knew, the bus driver was saying, 'Welcome to Utah' as the sun was rising and we're in the Salt Flats and I thought, 'What did I get myself into?' That was my first experience with Utah. But once I was picked up and taken to campus, it's a beautiful place and a great school."

38 Rivalry Rewind: Utah State and the Battle of the Brothers

Utah's biggest rival today is unquestionably Brigham Young University. But for the first 60 or so years of the program's existence, it was Utah State, formerly known as Utah State Agricultural College. It was Utah State that often filled the date of the season finale, and the Aggies offered more competition than BYU. Although Utah still holds a dominant 77–28–4 mark, the Aggies won 10 games against Utah prior to World War II as opposed to just three ties for BYU.

Utah State hasn't filled the last spot on Utah's schedule or been played after the Holy War since 1968. In 2010, the two schools didn't play for the first time since 1943. Restoring this game on an annual basis remains a dicey proposition due to Utah's entry into the Pac-12 Conference since they have just three non-conference dates available on the schedule, although the two sides inked a four-year deal that begins in the 2012 season.

The two schools will always have a geographical link, and for now, with the hiring of Gary Anderson from his defensive coordinator post at Utah in 2008, there is a strong tie to Utah's past. The only long-term guaranteed matchup between the two schools is on the recruiting trails. The schools have already decided to discontinue their annual matchup in basketball, so it's not impossible to envision a day where the football squads will decide likewise.

Nonetheless, there are still some great games and moments that have been provided by this series. Here are the most notable:

1960: Utah 6, Utah State 0. This was the pinnacle of Utah State football. With Merlin Olsen on the defensive line and head coach John Ralston on the sidelines, USU entered the game undefeated and ranked 16th in the Associated Press poll, but Bud Scalley—father of future Ute star Morgan Scalley—ran 12 yards for the game's only score late in the fourth quarter. Defensively, Utah held Tommy Larscheid, the nation's second-leading rusher, to just 19 yards on 14 carries.

1996: Utah State 20, Utah 17; 1997: Utah State 21, Utah 14. The Utes had won eight straight and 11 of the last 12 before the Aggies pulled off not one but two upsets to start promising Utah campaigns on sour notes. Especially bitter was the 1996 opener, with Utah returning a significant chunk of last year's WAC co-championship team. John L. Smith, who later coached at Louisville and Michigan State, brought an attacking defense that held Chris Fuamatu-Ma'afala to just 49 yards on 14 carries. Dan Pulsipher's miss from 44 yards with 1:32 left sealed defeat.

2008: Utah 58, Utah State 10. Utah set a rivalry record for points scored and, like the perfect 2004 team, equaled the largest margin of victory in the series. While the point total is impressive, it was the Utah defense that shined. Paul Kruger had four sacks, and only a last-minute drive by USU got the Aggies above 100 total yards. If not for an interception and a fumble on special teams, this game likely would have been a shutout.

39 Fred Gehrke

Football is a physical game. It can be violent, brutal, and ruthless.

Fred Gehrke majored in art during his collegiate playing career at Utah, and he played for a decade in the NFL. Yet with such a striking contrast in two completely different pursuits was born one of the greatest innovators in the history of the sport.

Gehrke grew up in Salt Lake City in the 1930s, and he lettered in football, diving, and track and field while at Utah. Although he went undrafted, Gehrke fought his way to a roster spot with the NFL's Cleveland Rams for the 1940 campaign.

The U.S. entered World War II the following year, and Gehrke went to the West Coast, working for Northrup Aircraft as a technical illustrator in the engineering department. (Gehrke failed his war physical due to a knee injury.) On the side, Gehrke played for a series of teams in the Pacific Coast League.

In time for the 1945 season, Gehrke rejoined the Rams, and he led the league in yards per carry and punt return average. The Rams won the NFL title, but with legendary coach Paul Brown leading a new entry in the All-America Football Conference, Rams owner Dan Reeves was given permission to move the team west.

Two years later, inspiration struck. Or maybe it was desperation—desperation to add some style to the drabness of a football player's uniform.

"My gosh, I loved the game," Gehrke said. "But those gosh-awful helmets we used to wear? At best, you'd have to call them dull."

Gehrke got out his brush, painted the brown leather blue, and added the classic ram horns to the sides. He did likewise for the helmets of his 75 teammates, too. Instantly an identity was made, one soon copied by every team in the league. In 1972, the Pro Football Hall of Fame honored Gehrke with the first Daniel F. Reeves Memorial Pioneer Award for his "significant, innovating contribution to pro football."

It wasn't the only time Gehrke's creative juices helped improve the game. Two years before his helmet artistry, Gehrke had his nose broken several times in the 1946 season. In the off-season, and with the help of machinists at Northrup and his grandfather, a shoemaker, Gehrke played the entire 1947 season with what's believed to be the first-known facemask. It was hardly a perfected product—the apparatus interfered slightly with Gehrke's line of vision—and he eventually went back to a standard helmet in 1948.

In 1950, Gehrke was traded to the Chicago Cardinals and then the San Francisco 49ers. With a steady job at Northrup Aircraft, Gehrke retired from football. But he remained heavily involved in the game. Tom Harmon, a former teammate with the Rams, was broadcasting 49er games on Sundays and college games on Saturdays, and he needed some help balancing his workload. Harmon called on his old roommate to see if he could help out. Gehrke drew up charts to aid Harmon during the broadcasts, and Gehrke gave occasional commentary. Writer Peter Vischansky, in a 2000 edition of *The Coffin Corner*, suggested that Gehrke was "maybe the first color man in history."

Gehrke and Harmon worked together for 13 years when Gehrke returned to the pro game on a full-time basis as a scout for the Denver Broncos, which were then part of the American Football League. A fellow Utah alum and ex-NFL great, Mac Speedie, was hired as Broncos coach, and he wanted Gehrke on his staff. Back then, the pay at the pro level paled to what Gehrke made at Northrup Aircraft, so Gehrke initially turned down Speedie's offer. Eventually, Speedie was able to find Gehrke's price, and Gehrke joined the staff.

Out of the humble surroundings typical of an AFL franchise came Gehrke's final lasting contribution to the game. Having quickly earned a promotion to director of player personnel, Gehrke also doubled in what we would know today as a special teams coach, working with the kickers and punters. Using aluminum pipe, Gehrke crafted the first kicking cage. Inevitably in a tight game where a field goal can determine the outcome, the television cameras will focus on the kicker, isolated on the sidelines and warming up using Gehrke's invention.

Gehrke rose all the way to general manager and vice president of the Broncos, helping to shape the franchise's first Super Bowl entry in Super Bowl XII, which the Broncos lost to the Dallas Cowboys 27–10. A few years later, ownership changed and Gehrke resigned, but he landed on his feet as GM of the United States Football League's Denver Gold. When that league folded in 1987, Gehrke's career in pro football had finally run its course.

"I spent the better part of my life in football, and I'll be best remembered for some work I did with a paintbrush, but that's okay," Gehrke said. "I've been called the da Vinci of football helmets, and that's not all bad."

40 John Mooney

If there's anything you need to know about John Mooney's career at the *Salt Lake Tribune*, it's that he was around Utah football so long that he started covering the team when Ike Armstrong was coach and didn't stop writing until after Ron McBride's rookie season as head coach in 1990. It seems unfathomable that any Utah athletics writer will ever be around the program for as long as Mooney was, which makes it all the more fitting that the press box at Rice-Eccles Stadium carries his name.

Today's technology gives fans greater access than they ever had in Mooney's era. In fact, today's world of sports media coverage—and the constant rush to break a story first via non-traditional sports media outlets like Twitter—might have undermined the influence Mooney had in the Utah sports media during his career, which spanned all or part of seven decades. But old-time Utah fans look back fondly on Mooney's writing and keep waiting for another writer like him to arrive on the scene.

Don't count on it. Mooney was one of a kind, one whose combination of wit and love for the U would have him labeled as a "homer" by today's more cynical journalists.

Dick Rosetta—a man Mooney often jokingly referred to as his "illegitimate son" because he made it his mission for Rosetta to succeed in his role as sports editor at the *Tribune* (and he ultimately did in 1990 before retiring in 2002)—recalled his first memories of Mooney. It's quite possible many other scribes had similar encounters in press boxes all over the country.

"He was this pudgy guy, and he was always hunt-and-peck on his typewriter, pushing that carriage back and forth, humming and [with] a cigar rolling back from one side of his mouth to another. Just totally concentrated.

"I stood by that typewriter where he was typing…. It was my first pass through the *Tribune* [office], and he looked up and said, 'What do you want?'"

Like so many Irish-Catholics, Mooney could be both gruff and charming. The latter side often showed up in his "Observation Ward" musings, with which he closed all of his columns. One of Rosetta's favorites: "The doc told me to watch my drinking, so I found a bar with a mirror."

"People thought that he thumbed through a book for stuff like this," Rosetta said. "Nuh-uh. John would sit there tapping his foot with his eyes closed…and then all of a sudden he'd type out an 'Observation Ward.'"

Born and raised in Chicago, Mooney first began his writing exploits at the University of Iowa. He came to Utah in 1939 to write for the old *Salt Lake Telegram*, which was the *Tribune*'s afternoon edition. In 1949, after the *Telegram* was discontinued, Mooney became sports editor of the *Tribune*. He was a prolific writer, often writing a column every day. Even after age started slowing him down, Mooney was good for at least two columns per week. *Deseret News* columnist Lee Benson, upon Mooney's retirement, calculated that Mooney had written more than 13,000 columns, or enough to fill more than 90 300-page books…and that's not counting the game stories, features, and sidebars he wrote on U athletics.

That's not bad for a guy who didn't have access to today's technology or who thought home row was a canoeing event at a nearby lake. He finally compiled a book, titled *Disa and Data*, a compilation of his best work that took its title from his daily columns.

Mooney's influence was largely felt in the Intermountain West, but it extended elsewhere at historic moments. As the president of the Football Writers Association of America (FWAA) in 1969, Mooney was key in getting President Nixon to attend the Texas-Arkansas game to celebrate the 100th anniversary of college football. That the game ended up deciding that year's national champion added to the lore of a rivalry that was already established in the sport. Mooney won national awards from the FWAA and the College Sports Information Directors, and he was inducted into the Utah Sports Hall of Fame in 1978.

"Mooney was the icon out here. He was a kingmaker," Rosetta said. "In the Intermountain West, he won every national award you could win in sports writing. He was truly a legend but a Ute through and through."

41 Brian Johnson

"Roll Tide!" was a familiar call to Utah fans making the trip to New Orleans for the 2009 Sugar Bowl, one that grew louder as kickoff approached and thousands of Alabama fans made the short trek to the Big Easy to make their presence felt.

That might have been an intimidating sight for Utah fans, who consistently travel well to bowl games but had never been outnumbered by nearly a 4-to-1 count. But if you happened to be around Brian Johnson and his family in the days leading up to the game, walking with him along Canal Street, you would have heard him and his crew giving the same chant.

And to Alabama fans, no less.

"We did that all week," Johnson said. "My family and a couple of my cousins and good childhood friends came up, and we called it the Alabama Smash. We would go around to all these Alabama fans, and we would sarcastically say 'Roll Tide!' and try to get them to acknowledge us and give us a high five. It was a pretty funny deal, and we had a good time with it.

"They really didn't [recognize me]," Johnson said. "It was actually my cousin, Aaron Mitchell, who started it. It started at the Poinsettia Bowl the previous year against Navy. We just kind of carried it over to the next year's bowl game, and it took on a life of its own. We'd be walking down the street in New Orleans, and even some of my teammates started doing it. But it went to a whole new level because the whole week all we heard was 'Roll Tide.' It was literally like the ESPN commercial. We had some fun with it, but they were an awesome bunch."

This isn't meant to diminish Brian Johnson's career at Utah, but the Baytown, Texas, native had been through too much at Utah *not* to be unflappable. He took his first snaps as a 17-year-old true freshman. The following year, he had the unenviable task of replacing Alex Smith, the greatest player in Utah history. Unfortunately, Johnson's season ended prematurely with a knee injury that required surgery, which forced Johnson to take a redshirt year. After a season-opening shoulder separation against

Oregon State caused him to miss nearly four games, Johnson was being dealt from the bottom of the deck physically in 2007.

"My knee, at the time when a decision [had] to be made, it was probably about 85 percent," Johnson said. "It was functional enough to play, but it wasn't 100 percent.

"That was the most frustrating season of my career at Utah," Johnson said of the 2007 season. "Before I went down in the [Oregon State game], I felt like I was playing at a level higher than I probably played in 2008.... I was throwing the ball well, my arm felt great, and my legs felt great. [After the injury] I had to find ways to win the game without my normal abilities. I think that helped us find a way to grind out things in 2008.... But it was definitely a frustrating time."

Then came the 2008 season, which firmly established Johnson as a Utah legend.

Johnson came out on fire in the opener against Michigan, throwing for 305 yards and a touchdown in a 25–22 victory. But he also threw an interception in each of the first six games, and Utah had to pull games out with late rallies against Air Force and Oregon State.

The Air Force comeback was largely due to the ground game with Matt Asiata and Darrell Mack. But against Oregon State, Johnson was the key factor in a 31–28 comeback victory, and he took off from there. Starting the following week against Wyoming, Johnson's passing yardage increased in every game the rest of the year, and he threw for 17 touchdowns against just three interceptions in being named Mountain West Conference Offensive Player of the Year.

He saved his best for last, throwing for 336 yards on 27-of-41 passing attempts as Utah drilled Alabama 31–17 in the Sugar Bowl.

Roll Tide? More like Rolled Tide.

"All we heard was that they were the better team," Johnson said after the game. "Nobody thought we could do it—the national pundits, no one. But we're the best team in the country."

Before injuries to his knee and shoulder reduced his carries in Utah's spread-option attack, Brian Johnson was one of Utah's most productive running quarterbacks. Here he breaks off a sizeable gain against Utah State in 2005. (AP Photo/Douglas C. Pizac)

Johnson was barely old enough to drive when Urban Meyer spotted him at Baytown Lee High School, signing him when he was only 16. With no other experienced quarterback behind Alex Smith, Johnson saw extensive mop-up duty as a 17-year-old freshman. It was just his second year of playing quarterback, having played wide receiver behind future Iowa signee Drew Tate as a junior before taking the reins as a senior.

Johnson gave professional football a brief shot, but a shoulder injury suffered in the Sugar Bowl prevented him from ever being at

100 percent for tryouts in front of NFL scouts. He quickly turned to coaching, first as a graduate assistant at Utah before becoming quarterback coach for the 2010 season.

42 The Utah Pass

Whether it is fashion, music, architecture, or cinema, the old axiom of what's old is new again eventually applies.

The same can be said for offensive formations in football. And there's no better example of that at Utah than the Utah Pass, which was designed by "Cactus" Jack Curtice in the 1950s. The Utah Pass was put into mothballs after Curtice's departure for Stanford, only to be brought out of storage and dusted off by Urban Meyer during his two-year stint at Utah.

That's not to say it went entirely unused between Curtice and Meyer. Bear Bryant made it a staple at Alabama during his wishbone days, renaming it the "Whoopee Pass." Because it was a forward pass, it posed almost no risk to the offense. Misdirection by the quarterback made it almost impossible for a defender to be in position to cover the running back, and a bad toss would result in no worse than an incomplete pass.

In an era when the passing game was not nearly as sophisticated or emphasized as it is today, the Utah Pass was an effective, no-frills method for whoever decided to use it.

"There's really no answer for that play," said then defensive coordinator Kyle Whittingham to Meyer during 2003 spring drills.

And Curtice was anything but no-frills. Lee Grosscup credits his former coach with being "15 to 20 years ahead of his time." As innovative as Curtice was, Grosscup believes the concept was taken from another legendary coach some 30 years previously—Stanford's Pop Warner.

"You'd think that I invented the play," Grosscup said.

Grosscup didn't invent it, but he played a significant role in showing off its effectiveness. In 1957, Grosscup arrived at Utah after a year in junior college, preceded by his freshman year at the University of Washington. That season, Utah made its first ever trip east of the Mississippi River to play Army. Although it had been more than a decade since Army had its run of three national titles from 1944–46, it still had coach Earl "Red" Blaik and was a consistent winner.

So pleased was Utah with its performance, and so impressed were the East Coast media with this team from the Rockies, that the Redskins felt as if they had won the game. Grosscup earned All-America honors and finished 10th in the Heisman voting—largely on his game against Army, against whom Grosscup passed for 316 yards. His 1,398 passing yards led the nation, and Grosscup would be a first-round draft pick of the New York Giants in the 1959 NFL Draft.

Utah finished 6–4 in 1957 but managed to win the Mountain States Conference title. Curtice left for Stanford the following year but never enjoyed the success he had at Utah and Texas Western (now Texas–El Paso). Success for Grosscup wouldn't come in his short three-year NFL career; success came in the broadcast booth as an announcer for ABC on its college football broadcasts.

Flash forward to 2003. Grosscup handled color commentary duties for the University of California when the Bears made a trip to Salt Lake City for a nationally televised ESPN broadcast, and you can imagine his surprise to see his old school running a play he helped make famous.

"I think it's brilliant," Grosscup said.

With Meyer's spread-option offense, the Utah Pass received a twist. Under Grosscup, the Utah pass was a two-man operation between the quarterback and running back. Under Meyer's spread-option offense, a flanker was used—usually Paris Warren. It was a true triple-threat formation for Utah because Smith could pitch to the running back, keep it himself, or utilize Warren with a well-timed Utah Pass. And like Grosscup, the play helped propel Smith into Heisman consideration.

"In a way, this has come full cycle," Grosscup said.

43 The 1964 Liberty Bowl

Beyond the fact that this was Utah's first bowl appearance since 1939 and just its second in school history, the 1964 Liberty Bowl against West Virginia was historic for a much bigger reason—it was the first-ever college football game played indoors.

The invitation was a tremendous honor for both Utah and West Virginia. The bowl slate was significantly lesser than it is today, and the Liberty Bowl was one of just eight bowl games played that year. But that honor was a designation that practically came with an asterisk—the first five years of the Liberty Bowl were played outdoors in the Philadelphia cold, and Northeast writers jokingly dubbed it the "Deep Freeze Bowl," along with other less-flattering titles. An exotic locale? Maybe for someone from Greenland.

The previous year's game between North Carolina State and Mississippi State drew less than 10,000 fans at John F. Kennedy Stadium and created a financial bath for game promoter A.F. "Bud" Dudley. Something else needed to be done—most notably finding a suitable climate in a tourist destination that would draw fans.

Atlantic City, New Jersey, once a thriving tourist destination but no place to visit in the dead of winter, made Dudley an attractive offer by allowing the game to be held at the Atlantic City Convention Center, then the home of the Miss America Pageant. Before the city legalized gambling in the 1970s, Atlantic City was a town gone bust. It had been a spot for the Northeast's affluent in the 1920s, but the Great Depression, World War II, and more importantly the availability of air travel to Florida and other destinations had depressed the city's economy.

A group of businessmen offered Dudley a $25,000 guarantee to move the game, which Dudley accepted.

"It was unusual," Dudley told the *Salt Lake Tribune*. "No one had ever done it. It got a lot of publicity."

Three issues remained: seating, playing conditions, and the teams. The first one wasn't viewed as a problem by Dudley, who figured he had 90,000 less problems by playing in the 10,000-seat Convention Center than he did in the 100,000-plus seating of JFK.

The development of artificial turf was in its early stages, so it was not available for this game. A natural grass surface measuring 4 inches deep was built on top of 2 inches of burlap padding underneath, and the whole thing was placed on top of the concrete floor.

To keep the grass from dying, artificial lighting was brought in and kept on 24 hours each day. The cost was more than $16,000. To justify the experimental surface, the Convention Center played host to nearly a dozen high school and small college games leading up to the Liberty Bowl. By the time Utah and West Virginia kicked off, the field conditions were worse than suboptimal. Adding (or subtracting) to the conditions were the end zones, which were only 8 yards deep because the center's floor wasn't long enough to accommodate a standard-sized football field.

The novelty of broadcasting a football game indoors was too powerful for ABC to resist, and the network gave Dudley nearly

$95,000 for the broadcast rights—albeit with strings attached. The Liberty Bowl organizers immediately selected West Virginia and reportedly voted 6–1 to invite Villanova. That made sense given 'Nova's proximity to nearby Philly. But ABC refused to televise a game involving a lower-division opponent and insisted on Utah and All-American Roy Jefferson, which ended the regular season ranked 14th in the final Associated Press poll.

For those of you who don't get the irony involved, let's spell it out. Everyone associated with the Utah program in the 2004 and 2008 seasons felt cheated to varying degrees when discussion over national title contenders came up and Utah was rarely mentioned. Yet here is an instance where the purported East Coast bias didn't rear its ugly head; the East Coast promoters actually took the better team instead of the team in the bigger city that could potentially draw more viewers and fans.

If any team didn't belong, however, it was West Virginia. Utah jumped out to a 25–0 lead behind long touchdown runs by Ron Coleman and Andy Ireland, while Pokey Allen added a rushing touchdown and Jefferson kicked a pair of field goals. Utah tacked on another score when quarterback Dick Groth passed 33 yards to Bill Morley.

The game only drew 6,050 fans, and the lopsided affair likely had viewers changing the channel. But the power of TV was on display, and with that added revenue, Dudley was able to pay both teams $60,000 each for their appearance and still come away with a $10,000 profit.

It would be Utah's last bowl victory for 30 years. Yet in 2003, Utah made a return visit to the Liberty Bowl, which had moved to Memphis immediately after Utah's visit. That game, between Ole Miss and Auburn, drew 38,000 fans and has been a fixture on the bowl calendar ever since.

44 The "Utah Man Fight Song" Lyrics

First verse:

I am a Utah Man, sir, and I live across the green,
Our gang it is the jolliest that you have ever seen.
Our coeds are the fairest and each one's a shining star,
Our yell, you'll hear it ringing through the mountains near and far!

Chorus:

Who am I, sir,
A Utah Man am I!
A Utah Man, sir,
And will be 'til I die.
Ki-yi!
We're up to snuff, we never bluff, we're game for any fuss.
No other gang of college men dare meet us in a muss.
So fill your lungs and sing it out and shout it to the sky,
We'll fight for dear old crimson for a Utah Man am I!

Second verse:

And when we prom the avenue, all lined up in a row,
And arm in arm and step in time as down the street we go.
No matter if a freshman green, or in a senior's gown,
The people all admit we are the warmest gang in town.

(Chorus)

Third verse:

We may not live forever on this jolly good old sphere,
But while we do we'll live a life of merriment and cheer,

And when our college days are o'er and night is drawing nigh,
With parting breath we'll sing that song:
"A Utah Man Am I!"

Legend has it that Harvey Holmes, like most of the contemporaries of his era who coached both the football and basketball teams at Utah, wrote the words after hearing the lyrics to "My Name is Sigma Chi." Those lyrics were written by Charles H. Eldridge in 1885, who penned them to the music of an old folk song titled "Old Solomon Levi."

Dig around enough, and you'll find additional versions of "Old Solomon Levi." It's an authorized march for a regiment of the Canadian armed forces, and it was part of a recording titled "Square Dances" by Carson Robison and his Pleasant Valley Boys released back in 1945.

Today, you'll hear "Old Solomon Levi" most frequently at Utah sporting events, especially at football games, where the Rice-Eccles Stadium faithful sing along with the Pride of Utah marching band after every touchdown.

The song enjoyed a renaissance of sorts when Urban Meyer demanded his players learn the words so they could sing the song before the student section after every game. And the lyrics came under further scrutiny when said student section billed itself as the MUSS. According to Webster's, the word "muss" is defined as disorder, or to make messy or untidy. At Utah, "muss" is an acronym for Mighty Utah Student Section.

Mike Lageschulte, who was Utah's play-by-play radio announcer from 2007–09, punctuated every touchdown call with, "Start playing Utah Man!"

The basics every Utah fan must know reside in the first verse and chorus because the time it takes to sing those parts of the song matches up nicely with the time allotted between an extra point and the kickoff. There is not a better way to celebrate a touchdown or a Utah victory than with a rousing rendition of "Utah Man."

45 Robert Rice

Robert Rice was a lot more than just another rich alumnus and booster who wanted to get involved and help his school's football program. That his name was the only one on the football stadium for nearly 30 years until renovation, expansion, and the 2002 Winter Olympics added the name of the Eccles family alongside his own says enough about Rice's commitment to Utah football.

However, it was Rice's commitment to another athletic endeavor—physical fitness—in which he achieved his greatest notoriety and helped so many people.

As a one-time Mr. Utah body builder, Rice expanded his mark in the health and fitness industry by forming a gym in 1952. That one gym grew into more than 200 nationwide as part of the European Health Spas chain—the first of its kind in the U.S. and a forerunner to other national chains like 24-Hour Fitness and Gold's Gym. European Health Spas counted more than a half-million members in the 1970s when Rice sold the business. But he remained active in the industry, owning and operating other fitness centers nationwide and serving as chairman, president, and chief operating officer of Spa Fitness Centers Inc.

Not everyone in the sports community bought into Rice's methods of physical fitness, most notably coach Jack Curtice, who told his players not to go to Rice's gym. "Your muscles will get big and you won't be able to move," Curtice said.

The moral of that story? Coaches should stick to coaching football.

In 1972, President Nixon appointed Rice to serve on the Council of Physical Fitness, a position Rice held for four years. In that same year, Rice gave $1 million to the U to help refurbish the crumbling stadium, which was built in 1927 and had been named Ute Stadium up to that point. Part of the donation also went toward improving the program's methods of conditioning its players.

"I have always thought that sport underlies what we actually face in life," Rice said shortly after making the donation. "Watching teams and individuals become great at sports is important, I think. The good athlete has the advantage of taking advantage of what gifts he has."

"After [the donation], we no longer sat in the cheap seats," said Jay Rice, Robert's son, at his father's funeral in 2007.

Robert Rice not only contributed financially to help build the Utah program, he contributed genetically, as well. His grandson, Lance Rice, was Utah's starting quarterback in parts of three seasons from 2000–02, leading Utah to an eight-win season and a Las Vegas Bowl victory against USC in 2001.

Rice was 78 when he died of cancer, but before he passed away, University of Utah president Michael Young visited Rice and told him, "You're probably the best friend the University of Utah ever had."

It was a fitting tribute for a great Utah Man.

46 Tailgating in the Guardsman Way Lot

When the topic is Tom Barberi, two things come to mind—his time as a local talk show host, mostly at KALL 700 and currently on the Web at UtahFM.com, and his war cry of "Utah by 5!"

But did you know that Barberi was also largely responsible for creating the tailgating scene at Utah? Obviously the festival that takes place every game day at the Guardsman Way tailgate lot was the development of something much bigger than one person, but it was Barberi in 1971 who helped institute the idea of a paid lot where people could bring their cars, trucks, or motor homes and turn game day into an all-day affair.

"Coming from the Bay Area, I loved the rivalry and tradition of Stanford and Cal," Barberi said. "Neither team was ever a powerhouse, but the Stanford-Cal game was huge. Tailgating under the eucalyptus trees in Palo Alto near Stanford's rickety old 90,000-seat wooden stadium was a great way to spend an entire day.

"The U had a great marching band and drill team but no tailgating. For me football is more than just a game. It's an all-day event. I asked for a meeting with the athletic department officials and told them I wanted to start tailgating at the U games, and [I] asked if they would give us some space in the west lot. They recognized the potential to generate more interest in the football program and gave us a small area."

The first tailgate lot passes cost just $5, and Barberi used his radio show as a vehicle to promote tailgating to fans. Initially, fans were a little confused as to what constituted a proper tailgate, but it didn't take long for them to get into the act and embrace the pregame party that makes college football Saturdays so enjoyable.

Greg Finch, a Salt Lake City financial planner, has been going to Utah games since 1984 and has seen tailgating at the U evolve by leaps and bounds.

"On a day where the weather wasn't perfect, you could pull in and park anywhere you wanted," Finch said. "Twenty years ago, it was a small crowd, and it slowly built over the years—not just with tailgaters but the number of people that come to the tailgates. Most tailgates had no more than five to 10 people in the past. Now you have tailgates where 50 people show up.

"It wasn't an 'in' thing to do, but now it is," Finch continued. "In the old days, it was quiet. People would go and if it rained, there would only be a few motor homes. The best way to explain it [is that] you go in on that first row along the grass [which runs right next to Guardsman Way]—that's a real desirable spot. In the old days, we could get there three or four hours before the game and park there. Now if you're not there the night before, you can't get it."

There are drawbacks to the entire process. First, the cost of a tailgate pass is $225 per year, and the few spots that become available each year are quickly snapped up by the athletic department's largest boosters. And as Finch hinted, the crowds attending the games have gotten bigger, but the Guardsman Way lot remains the same size. Plus, it's located next to the Veterans Administration hospital, so there's no overnight parking until Friday night. The lot is locked down after 6:00 PM, and there's no way to get in until the next morning. Plus the spaces aren't numbered, so it's tough to keep your same spot on a game-to-game basis, much less year to year.

Those things are easily forgotten once the excitement of the game draws near, the food comes off the grill, and the beer—yes, there are plenty of Utah fans who consume alcohol—comes out of the cooler. It's not hard for fellow Ute fans to make friends with one another. Get to know someone with a tailgate pass, or someone who has a standing invite to his friend's tailgate party, and join in on the fun.

47 Luther Elliss

The Four Corners area will never be confused by anyone within college football as fertile recruiting grounds. But in the tiny town of Mancos, Colorado, the University of Utah struck it rich with Luther Elliss, a player whose impact extended far beyond the football field.

Getting Elliss to Utah wasn't a miracle. He was an intriguing curiosity in his home state—enough of a curiosity to earn an invitation to walk on at Colorado, plus he got an offer from Colorado State. No, the miracle came in just discovering him. Credit for that goes to Sam Papalii and a future NFL head coach by the name of Brad Childress, who spent a year as an assistant coach under first-year head coach Ron McBride in 1990.

"They were looking at a kid out of Moab or Monticello or Montrose," Elliss said, "and we had to play them, and they were watching film and that's how they saw me—playing against one of those teams.

"I thoroughly enjoyed playing sports, but I really didn't think I had a chance of playing Division I. Being in a small town, where I grew up in the southwest corner, there weren't too many guys in the whole county, let alone in our district, who were being recruited to play Division I in *any* sport."

And football wasn't even Elliss' preferred sport—he loved basketball. He was on Rick Majerus' radar, and with Deion Sanders at the height of his two-sport fame, Elliss set out to do likewise.

"I did football and track as just a way to [pass time] to basketball," Elliss said.

Things changed quickly at Utah. As a true freshman, Elliss saw himself thrust into the starting lineup as an undersized defensive

Utah First-Team All-Americans
(By year, position, and selector)

1929: Earl "Powerhouse" Pomeroy, fullback, International News Service

1932: Frank Christensen, fullback, Jack Johnson, tackle, Lawrence Perry, I.N.S.

1938: Bernard McGarry, tackle, Central Press Football

1941: Floyd Spendlove, tackle, Collier's Little All-America

1957: Lee Grosscup, quarterback, Football Writers Association of America, Look, Newspaper Enterprise, Williamson

1961: Ed Pine, center, Williamson

1962: Dave Costa, tackle, Williamson

1964: Roy Jefferson, cornerback, The Sporting News

1970–71: Marv Bateman, punter, FWAA, TSN; FWAA, Time

1973: Steve Odom, return specialist, FWAA

1981: Steve Clark, FWAA

1984: Carlton Walker, FWAA

1985: Erroll Tucker, return specialist, FWAA, TSN, Football News

1991: (Consensus) Luther Elliss, defensive tackle, Associated Press, American Football Coaches Association, FWAA, Scripps-Howard, UPI.

2002: (Consensus) Jordan Gross, offensive tackle, FWAA, Walter Camp, AP, CNNSI.com, Sportsline.com

2004: Alex Smith, quarterback, FWAA, SI.com

2004: Chris Kemoeatu, guard, FWAA, SI.com

2006: (Consensus) Eric Weddle, defensive back, AFCA, SI.com, Rivals.com, CBSSportsline.com, TSN, CollegeFootballNews.com

2007: Louie Sakoda, punter, FWAA, CBSSports.com

2008: (Consensus unanimous) Louie Sakoda, kicker, AP, Walter Camp, FWAA, AFCA, TSN

2009: Zane Beadles, offensive tackle, FWAA, College Football News, Phil Steele

2010: Antoine "Shaky" Smithson, return specialist, Walter Camp, Scout/FoxSports.com

tackle. Basketball season rolled around, so it was time to head to the gym, right? Not so fast.

"I had to gain weight and really hit the weight room," Elliss said. "I was embarrassed the way I lifted weights my freshman year, and [I didn't] have the strength that some of my teammates did. Part of my love for basketball was I didn't lift weights in high school. I didn't want to hurt my shot. And Coach McBride told me I would not be playing basketball after my freshman year.

"I enjoyed feeling the pain, [getting] the opportunity to compete against my fellow teammates, setting an example, feeling the encouragement from them, and being a leader in there. I believe leaders should lead more by action than anything else, and I thought, 'If you want to help this team, get in there and lead them in all areas.'"

Elliss moved to defensive end in 1992, beginning a three-year reign of terror against offensive lines and backfields, although he finished his college career where he began it—at defensive tackle. Elliss could rush the passer and contain the edge, as his career marks of 18 sacks (sixth all-time) and 47 tackles for loss (first all-time) indicate, but the position switch prior to his senior year didn't bother him in the least.

"Most of the time on the offensive line—not all the time—but if you have a weaker link, it would be the center. He's usually a smaller, quicker guy. With my size and strength, I could take advantage of a lot of centers in the league."

The final play of Elliss' home career at Utah resembled that remark. BYU and quarterback John Walsh had gotten into the fringes of field-goal range in the final seconds of the 1994 Holy War. On the outside, Bronzell Miller made a BYU tackle look like a turnstile. Up the middle, Elliss and Jeff Kaufusi collapsed the pocket. Miller's sack forced Walsh to fumble, and Elliss recovered to seal Utah's second straight 34–31 victory.

"It was an exciting game, back-and-forth…. Bronzell and I just told each other, 'I'll meet you at the quarterback.'"

"It was an exciting moment in our careers and for the seniors and the impact we had on the program in ending it that way. Utah football was not the same. It was something different and something to be reckoned with."

Elliss would go on to play in the NFL for 10 years, mostly with Detroit, although he made it home for the final year of his career by playing for Denver. In 1999–2000, Elliss was a Pro Bowl selection. Today, he's back at Utah finishing up his degree, working with the team as a graduate assistant, and looking at coaching as his next career move.

48 The Rice Bowl: 1988 Holy War

As noted in the acknowledgments at the beginning of this book, one of my primary inspirations in writing this book came from an online effort by one of the most knowledgeable sources of Utah football history. "The Greatest Utah Football Games Ever," written as a blog by Adam Miller in the summer of 2007, listed and ranked the 35 most significant wins in program history.

Personally, I thought Miller did a great job, and we've talked periodically about the program's history. He asked me to contribute a sidebar to one of his entries, the 1969 game between Utah and Wyoming, which also explained how Utah was robbed of a title it deserved.

My biggest issue was his placement of the Rice Bowl, which Miller placed third on his list—not third in the 1980s but third all-time. Even in Miller's revised rankings after Utah's historical 2008 season, this game ranked fifth—ahead of both the 2004 and 2008 Holy Wars, when there was much more at stake. In this author's opinion, it's the only entry I openly questioned him about.

For the purposes of this book, the Rice Bowl doesn't rate higher than the 2004 game, which was covered in earlier entries, or the 2008 game. Nonetheless, it is impossible to discount what this victory meant to loyal Utah fans who had witnessed tail-kicking after humiliating tail-kicking at the hands of BYU. Never throughout the two-decades-long odyssey through the Dark Ages had Utah football shined like it did on that November 19 day in a 57–28 clubbing of BYU.

The goal posts came down, Coach Jim Fassel did all he could to hold back tears, and diehard members of the Ute fan base, in between wiping their own eyes, could strut proudly for a week…or the entire off-season, if they so chose. The jubilation was justifiable.

Utah entered the game as 11-point underdogs, but BYU was carrying baggage and was ripe for an ambush. After starting the season 7–1, the Cougars inexplicably dropped a 27–15 decision to San Diego State, which had been blown out by three touchdowns the week prior against Utah en route to a 3–8 mark. The loss officially knocked BYU out of the WAC title race.

Quarterback Sean Covey, who had missed time already that season due to injury, went out with another knee injury, so a not-ready-for-prime-time freshman named Ty Detmer was taking meaningful snaps. On Utah's side, sophomore quarterback Scott Mitchell was ramping up his efforts to rewrite the record books— his 631 yards passing earlier that year against Air Force is far and away a Utah record—and the Utes had won three straight after a 2–5 start.

Despite Mitchell's interception on the opening drive of the game, this one was over early. After recovering a BYU fumble on the ensuing drive, running back Eddie Johnson ran three yards and two yards for scores to give Utah a 14–0 lead. The dam broke for good when Covey threw the first of five BYU interceptions right into the arms of defensive lineman Sam Tausinga, who ran 17 yards for scores and a 21–0 lead. Detmer relieved Covey in the second half but threw three interceptions as BYU turned the ball over eight times.

Johnson, or E.J. as he was known in Ute circles, added two more touchdowns as part of a 203-yard day from scrimmage (112 rushing, 91 receiving), and Mitchell threw for a ho-hum 384 yards and three scores, two to tight end Dennis Smith.

"If I never play a football game again," E.J. said after the game, "this will be the best day I've ever had."

No doubt many Ute fans, who had seen only one previous victory against BYU in the past 16 years, felt the same way.

49 Utah Traditions, Part I

These are the traditions every Ute fan who wants to be neck-deep in the history of the program should be able to explain to younger Ute fans or to football fans in general. Anyone who remembers the first college football game he or she attended quickly picks up on the fact that there is so much action that takes place outside the field of play. Here are some of the historical items of note that make Utah football games a special and memorable experience:

The Pride of Utah Marching Band: It's one thing to play a musical instrument. It's another to be part of a marching band and still another to do it and look good in front of thousands of people. Maybe that was former University of Utah President A. Ray Oplin's vision when he hired Ohio State band leader Ron Gregory to lead the first marching band at Utah in 1948.

Gregory brought much of the flair and showmanship of his Buckeye bands, instituting a "Script Utah" formation. With no "I" to dot, the tuba section crossed the "T" in Utah, although that formation has been passed over in favor of a Block U formation. The band was a major part of football and basketball games for more than two decades, but the protest era of the 1960s saw support dwindle for such traditions like a marching band, and the Associated Students for the University of Utah discontinued funding for the band in 1969.

A fundraising effort brought back the band in 1976, and it has been a staple (along with the Crimson Line dancers) at home football, basketball, and women's gymnastics meets. It also travels to several away games, most notably at Utah State and BYU. In 2009, the Marching Utes performed at President Barack Obama's inauguration day parade.

"We think our band is awesome," said Coach Kyle Whittingham. "They're a top-notch band, and I wish they could travel with us every week.

"It's such a boost to our football team to have that band in the stadium—just the atmosphere it creates," he added. "Between the band and the MUSS, I think we have as good a home atmosphere as anywhere in the country."

Bubbles and Crazy Lady: Two women, one tradition. Utah certainly didn't field the first band to play the Blues Brothers theme song at a sporting event, and it certainly won't be the last. But a halftime performance song turned into a musical staple at football games, and sometime in the 1983 season the song caused one fan—known to Ute fans as Bubbles, but on her driver's license as Judy Lagerstrom—to start dancing wildly during the break between the third and fourth quarters. Bubbles did her thing for 17 years.

When Bubbles decided to retire her dance moves, in stepped Terri Jackson, who has fully embraced the nickname Crazy Lady, to continue the tradition. It's one that won't stop anytime soon.

"They'll have to drag her out of there when it's time to go," said Terri's husband, Scott. "She'll be 97 years old and still try to get up there and dance. She'll be a really 'Crazy Lady' at that point."

The Beehive Boot: This award commemorates state supremacy in football and has always been contested between Utah, BYU, and Utah State—although FCS Weber State is also eligible to win the boot, as well. Beginning in 1971, BYU has won the boot most often, with 22 wins in the series, followed by Utah with 11 and Utah State with seven.

Usually, the boot winner has often come down to the Utah-BYU game, but there have been years in which the winner of that game hasn't won the boot. In years in which the teams all go 1–1 against each other, or in years where all three teams haven't played each other, statewide media pick a winner. That happened in 1973, 1997, and 2010, and in all three years, Utah State won the trophy.

50 Classic Finish II: 1995 Air Force

"The sign of a classic college football game, no matter how small the states or how far from the spotlight, is that for both the winners and the losers it remains unforgettable."

—Kelli Anderson, *Sports Illustrated*, 1996 College Football Preview

One of the great attributes developed by Utah teams during the Ron McBride era was resiliency. And never during McBride's 13 years at Utah was such a trait on a greater display than against the Air Force Academy on October 21, 1995.

The ultimate account of this game came from *Sports Illustrated* in its 1996 College Football preseason edition. The article went beyond the miraculous comeback and dove deep into how the game affected—for better and for worse—some of the game's most critical figures. Especially poignant was what was written about Air Force running back Jake Campbell, whose season ended with a torn posterior cruciate ligament as he dove for a third-quarter touchdown that put the Falcons up 21–7.

Upon arriving back in Colorado Springs the next day, Campbell found out his father had died after a long bout with cancer.

Tragic things happen to good people, but Campbell's loss was a double-whammy for the Falcons, who had to endure a record comeback at the hands of the Utes. To this day, no team has scored 15 or more points in the 10 seconds it took Utah to erase AFA's seemingly insurmountable lead and claim victory.

With a change at quarterback from Brandon Jones to Mike Fouts, Utah had won three of five since opening the season with home losses to Oregon and Stanford. One of those wins was a heart-stopping 25–21 victory against Fresno State, which saw Utah score 15 points in the final three minutes to pull out the victory.

But with just more than a minute to go and Utah 64 yards from the end zone, that Fresno State comeback wasn't on the minds of the hundreds of people who filed out of Rice Stadium. Imagine the surprise for some when they reached their cars, tuned into the KALL postgame broadcast, and found out that Utah had won the game!

Two plays covered all the yardage Utah needed on its four-play scoring drive. First, Terrance Keenan turned left, right, then left again to grab a 51-yard bomb to the AFA 17. Two incomplete passes later and Rocky Henry got between a couple of Falcon defenders and hauled in Fouts' pass for a touchdown to cut the deficit to 21–13.

It's important to note that overtime didn't exist in college football in 1995. Today, teams would kick the extra point and not think twice about getting the deficit to seven points. McBride was thinking win first. By initially going for two, McBride still left Utah with an option to tie the game if his first two-point attempt failed.

It didn't. Operating out of the Duck formation, Chris Fu'amatu Ma'afala took a pitch left and followed a convoy of blockers into the end zone to make the score 21–15.

Up next was the predictable onside kick. But instead of getting the ball to hop high in the air where maybe a Utah player could get to it first, or at least create a mad scramble for the ball, kicker Dan Pulsipher sent a line-drive that pegged Air Force's Nakia Addison in the chest. The ball bounced to an open spot on the field, and Utah's Artis Jackson recovered to put the Utes back in business at the Air Force 45.

A false-start penalty pushed the Utes backyards, but that was of little consequence to Fouts, who told sophomore wide receiver Kevin Dyson, "Get on your horse. I'm going to launch it."

Dyson beat a backpedaling Kelvin King, caught the ball in stride at the 5, and strolled into the end zone to tie the game. "I didn't think in a million years he'd go deep," King said. Pulsipher, who was under the presumption that Utah was already ahead, snaked the PAT inside the right upright to give Utah the victory.

Incredibly enough, Utah would tack on another touchdown on an 85-yard interception return by Cal Beck, but offsetting penalties on the return nullified the score. At 22 points in 41 seconds, even the football gods agreed it was overkill.

Utah wouldn't lose the rest of the way that season, finishing 7–4 and earning the school's first conference title since 1964. Air Force rebounded as well, beating Fresno State the following week to earn a share of the WAC title, just its second in school history and its first in a decade.

"That's incredible," McBride said. "We've won two like that this year, and you might not win two of those in a lifetime. It goes to show when there's life and there's breath, you've got a chance."

There's breath, which the Utah team clearly had on that day, and there's breathless, which is the condition Utah fans were left in after the most inexplicable comeback in school history.

51 How O.J. Simpson Almost Became a Ute

Sports are filled with what-ifs. What if Ron Zook hadn't been fired midseason at Florida, allowing the Gators to make their play at Urban Meyer? (He probably would have ended up at Notre Dame, one of the three schools with no buy-out clause in Meyer's contract.) What if Utah finished the job like it should have in 1994 and went undefeated? (In the pre-BCS era, who knows? But likely they would have gone to the Holiday Bowl.) What if Rick Majerus used his bench just a smidge more in the 1998 NCAA basketball championship game against Kentucky? (It's tough to say, but if Alex Jensen is a senior instead of a sophomore off a two-year Mormon mission, Utah wins.) Okay, this is a football book. But that last one is impossible for Utah fans to ignore.

All of those scenarios, however, pale in comparison to the biggest what-if in the entire history of Utah sports.

What if O.J. Simpson had been a Ute?

Now before you say that Simpson wouldn't have received the recognition and notoriety at Utah that he received at USC, you would be partially right. There would have been no Rose Bowl heroics and likely no Heisman Trophy. But barring injury and an offense that would have featured his talents, Simpson still would have drawn heavy demand from the NFL. He still may have been the first pick in the 1969 draft. Look at the pedigrees of the No. 1 picks that followed him:

1970—Terry Bradshaw, QB, Louisiana Tech
1971—Jim Plunkett, QB, Stanford
1972—Walt Patulski, DL, Notre Dame
1973—John Matuszak, DL, University of Tampa
1974—Ed "Too Tall" Jones, DL, Tennessee State

This list includes three no-name programs and a Pac-8 school that was far from USC or UCLA. Sure, Patulski played for the most storied program in the nation, but he's also widely viewed as one of the biggest draft busts of all time. Furthermore, Utah has since produced an overall No. 1 pick in Alex Smith.

Going to Utah likely would have had very little if any adverse effect on Simpson's pro career.

So what happened to keep O.J. Simpson from becoming a Ute? Utah coach Mike Giddings knew of the talented player back in Simpson's high school days at Galileo High in San Francisco, and Giddings kept close tabs on Simpson after Giddings left his defensive coordinator post at USC to take the head coaching job at Utah in 1966. There was a gentlemen's agreement that Giddings wouldn't use his knowledge of USC's recruiting targets while at Utah, but Simpson was a special case because he couldn't get into USC without taking the necessary math credits in junior college. At Utah, he could satisfy the admissions requirements with one year of math credits.

"He wasn't a dumb guy, but [Simpson] needed help getting into USC," Giddings said.

Freshmen were ineligible anyway at the time, but Arizona State was also hot on the Juice's trail. Giddings reached Simpson by phone in the summer of 1966 at the San Francisco airport, where Simpson was about to board a plane to Phoenix for an official visit.

"You promised me that if you didn't go back [to junior college], if you wanted to play three years, then you would come to Utah," Giddings told Simpson over the phone.

Simpson relented and boarded a plane for Salt Lake City. By all accounts, he enjoyed his trip—at least enough to give Giddings a verbal commitment. He wouldn't return to San Francisco City College for his sophomore year, and he was ready to give up his dream of playing at USC.

However, two snags arose. First, since Simpson was on an official visit, he couldn't simply enroll at Utah and join the team. Even current NCAA rules state that a recruit making an official visit must fly back to his city of origin. Outside of official recruiting trips, it is illegal for a school to provide transportation for a recruit. So Simpson had to fly back to San Francisco. Second, all letters of intent must be signed by a parent or legal guardian, and Simpson's mother was in the San Francisco Bay area.

No problem, Giddings thought. He assigned an assistant coach to follow Simpson home, boarding the same flight back to San Francisco. The coach's marching orders were simple—get Simpson's mother to sign the letter of intent, help him pack his bags, load up Simpson's car, and point him east on Interstate 80.

However, when player and coach landed in San Francisco, the coach went to make a brief visit with some family members and let the Juice loose. This proved to be fatal for Utah's hopes of getting Simpson to Salt Lake City. Since it was USC that tipped off Giddings to Simpson's official visit to Arizona State, USC assistant coach Marv Goux was already on his way up the California coast to change Simpson's mind. While Giddings' assistant was away, Goux whisked Simpson back to San Francisco City College and enrolled him for a second year. The rest, they say, is history.

Goux died in 2002, but he and Giddings remained friends. As for Simpson's future? Well, a lot of lives might have been changed had Simpson gone to Utah, according to Giddings.

"When I knew him, I didn't see any of that side," Giddings said of Simpson's trial and acquittal for double murder in 1995, along with his conviction for kidnapping and armed robbery in 2008. "Maybe I didn't know him that well. But we were friends.... An American tragedy is what it is."

Thankfully, it's not a University of Utah tragedy.

52 The Romney Brothers: Utah's First Family of Sports

The contributions of Utah alumni to other athletic programs are significant and have been noted elsewhere in this book. But no family had the impact outside of the U in the first half of the 20th century as did the five Romney brothers, all of whom starred in multiple sports at Utah and whose influence in some instances helped shape Utah athletics even after their departure from the U.

E.L. "Dick" Romney: Dick Romney was a four-sport star at the U, leading Utah to the 1916 AAU title—one of three national championships recognized by the school. Like many of his contemporaries, Romney coached both football and basketball while at Utah State, going 128–91–16 in the former, with a 224–158 ledger in the latter. Utah State's football stadium bears his name today, and after his Aggie days, Dick served as commissioner of the Mountain States Conference from 1949–59. No one was as instrumental in securing a national broadcast partner for the 1953 Holy War—the first televised football game in the state of Utah—than Romney, who served as chairman of an NCAA committee on television rights and broadcasts.

G.O. "Ott" Romney: BYU fans will be the first to tell you that its football history pre–LaVell Edwards is nothing to strut over. But

Ott Romney, the oldest of the five Romney brothers, had little to do with that, compiling one-fourth of BYU's 16 winning seasons from 1922–71, including a school-best 8–1 mark in 1932, a standard that wouldn't be equaled or surpassed for 47 years. He won big in basketball, too, compiling a 144–31 mark at Montana State prior to his time at BYU, with his 1928–29 squad being crowned national champions by the Helms Foundation. In 1912, Ott was an All–Rocky Mountain Conference end for Utah and caught a 45-yard touchdown pass from cousin Lon to lead Utah past the Colorado School of Mines 18–3 for a victory that was instrumental in Utah's first conference title.

Milt "Mitt" Romney: He was known as the "Utah Flash" during his playing days with the University of Chicago, where he helped lead the team to the Big 10 championship as a senior quarterback in 1922. Milt played all three offensive backfield positions for six NFL seasons with the Racine Legion and the Chicago Bears. Nicknamed "Mitt"—yes, he's a distant relative of 2008 presidential candidate and former Massachusetts governor Mitt Romney—he was also the head basketball coach at the University of Texas for one season. At Utah, he was an All–Rocky Mountain Conference halfback as a freshman before moving on to Chicago to play under legendary coach Amos Alonzo Stagg.

W.W. "Woody" Romney: Woody lettered in football in 1917 and was captain of the 1919 U basketball team, one of the better squads Utah had before World War II. He was also a longtime football and basketball coach at several high schools in Idaho and Utah. But it was as a basketball referee where he earned his highest marks—his "other" job after his position as vice president at Continental Bank.

Floyd Romney: Another star performer for the U who transferred to another school, Floyd followed Ott to Montana State after lettering for two seasons at Utah from 1920–21. After his collegiate career, he was a longtime high school coach at West High School in Salt Lake City.

It would be easy to rate the brothers' significance in terms of their documented accomplishments, but longtime *Deseret News* sports columnist Hack Miller best described the brothers' impact on the Utah sports scene:

"The thing for which most of these old-timers should be honored is not what they did for athletics in their prime but what they have done for sports since then."

It's a fitting tribute for Utah's First Family of Sports.

53 How Utah Won the MWC Title with Just Three Points

There have been many phrases and clichés to describe the intensity of the Holy War. "For all the marbles" has rarely been one of them, at least when the marbles being talked about involved a conference championship.

During the rivalry's first 50 years, the Utah-BYU game was rarely played at the end of the season, muting the effect it had on the 19 conference titles Utah collected over that time frame. When LaVell Edwards started his career at BYU by winning 19 of his first 21 games against Utah, BYU had either already clinched the conference crown or just needed to beat up on another hapless Utah squad to clinch it outright.

While Utah had defeated BYU in 1995 and 1999 to earn co-championships, the last time Utah entered the Holy War with its championship hopes firmly in its control was in 1981. Even after Del "Popcorn" Rogers opened the game with an 80-yard touchdown run, host BYU rolled to a 56–28 victory in the last game before Cougar Stadium was expanded to its current state.

More than two decades later, the fortunes had changed for both programs. Utah had Urban Meyer and entered the game 8–2, while BYU was headed to its lowest win total in 33 years under Gary Crowton.

The respective position of the two teams in the standings wasn't the only thing different about this game. The temperature at kickoff was 19 degrees—bitter cold even by Utah standards—and snow and ice covered the field. It was especially tricky for the Utah offense, which relied a lot on motion and misdirection in Meyer's spread offense. The sun made a late appearance and the snow stopped falling, but it wasn't nearly enough to change the playing conditions.

The story of the day, however, was the Utah defense, which had no such problem in pitching a shutout, the first suffered by BYU in 361 games, an NCAA record.

"This was one of the greatest moments I've ever had," said Utah coach Urban Meyer. "I've never been part of a 3–0 game. Period."

Meyer could have ruined that distinction by tacking on a salt-in-the-wound touchdown after Eric Weddle recovered a fumbled BYU punt on the Cougar 22 with 2:57 left in the game. After Brandon Warfield ran 13 yards for the game-clinching first down on third-and-7, Utah took a couple of knees to run out the clock, then celebrated the program's first outright championship since 1957.

With that merciful decision not to score, Bryan Borreson was assured a spot in Ute lore. His 41-yard field goal with 8:43 left in the second quarter accounted for the game's only points.

It wasn't a great day for the Utah offense, but a sterling effort by the defense held BYU to 41 yards passing while picking off two passes. The defense allowed the Cougars to cross midfield only once, a drive that ended with BYU's only scoring chance of the day in Matt Payne's 51-yard field-goal attempt.

"We wanted a shutout," Ute senior cornerback Arnold Parker said. "Winning 3–0 is better than winning 70–3 as far as we are concerned."

"Our mission was to win the game and the conference title," said Ute senior safety Morgan Scalley, who played despite undergoing knee surgery just five days before the game. "Getting the shutout was the icing on the cake."

That icing was spread even thicker when Utah finished its season with a 17–0 shutout against Southern Mississippi in the Liberty Bowl to cap the program's second 10-win season.

54 The North End Zone

Wrigley Field has the Bleacher Bums. The New York Rangers of the NHL have their Blueseaters at Madison Square Garden. Every stadium has its share of loyal, vocal fans that add to the game experience, with some cheering sections having carved out notoriety on a national scale.

The North End Zone at Rice-Eccles Stadium isn't on the same level as the Bleacher Bums or Blueseaters. But it is developing a reputation as a no-holds-barred section of the stadium to cheer on the Utes. All of the views from Rice-Eccles Stadium are fantastic, but spectators in the NEZ have been treated to their share of game-changing plays and fantastic finishes that nearly split eardrums or, in the case of the 2006 Holy War, crushed the spirit of Utah fans.

"The North End Zone are the cheap tickets," NEZ season-ticket holder Heidi Pferdmer said. "It's the regular Joe fan. They're there because they love the sport and they love their Utah football."

"They're not big-time donors, they're not big-money people, but they support their team in other ways that are immediately evident, just by the noise that we generate," said Ray Lindenburg, a U. alumnus. "People want to sit there because they feel like they can be part of the outcome of the game and that's the special part of being in the North End Zone."

The North End Zone, prior to the expansion that turned Rice Stadium into Rice-Eccles Stadium, featured a large asphalt surface behind the playing field and in front of the seats, which was general admission seating. After the renovation, the asphalt surface was removed, the seats were extended to just behind the end zone, and the decibel level reached new heights.

"The way that the MUSS is located in the stadium and where we're located in the stadium, it makes for a great bookend," Lindenburg said. "We do a great job. I won't take anything away from [the MUSS], but I think we're louder. We relish it when teams have to come down—whether they're on offense, backed up at their own end, or we're on defense and we need to make a stop. A lot of the fans want to be there just for that—the adrenaline, the screaming—that's what people look for when they're sitting in that part of the stadium."

"There's an energy in the MUSS," Pferdmer said, "but I believe the loudness is more in the North End Zone."

As with any section that has developed that kind of reputation for loud, intimidating behavior from its fans, security has an extra challenge in making certain things don't get too out of hand. Mostly, according to Lindenburg, their efforts are centered around preventing illegal consumption of alcohol within the stadium. Unlike other sections of the stadium, which, shall we say, are a little more serene, it's perfectly acceptable within the friendly confines of the North End Zone to stand, yell, and scream as loud as you want.

"They don't want to necessarily sit down," Lindenburg said. "They won't stand for the whole game, but they don't want to have someone yell at them for blocking their view."

That end of the stadium was never louder in 2008 when TCU kicker Ross Evans missed a pair of field goals late in the fourth quarter—bouncing one off the left upright—that prevented the Frogs from extending a 10–6 lead and kept the door open for a late Utah rally.

Maybe the football gods were paying Utah back, since it was the opposite upright off which Utah kicker Ryan Kaneshiro bounced a kick to end the 1998 Holy War, a 26–24 BYU win. But no finish at that end of the field could top the ending of the 2006 Holy War. With Utah leading 31–27 and just four seconds left in the game with BYU at the Utah 11, BYU quarterback John Beck spent an eternity in the pocket and bought enough time to throw across the field to Johnny Harline all alone in the end zone for the winning touchdown.

"I'm pretty certain I was closer to Jonny Harline than any Utah defender," Lindenburg said. "Before the play, we had gathered up our towel and blankets—we were getting ready to rush the field. It went from the height of ecstasy to the depths of despair."

55 Utah Sports Bars

If you're not aware of the increasing difficulty in getting tickets to a Utah game, consider yourself warned. Average attendance for Utah games during the last three seasons has been better than 100 percent of Rice-Eccles Stadium's official capacity of 45,017. While Utah tickets represented an incredible bargain for many years, the program's entry into the Pac-12 Conference warranted a justi-fied—and in many spots, a substantial—hike in ticket prices.

So if through a lack of availability or cash you find yourself outside the stadium gates on game day, consider watching the game at one of the following sports bars. Utah's liquor laws are legendary for their quirkiness, but steps have been taken in recent years to make wetting one's whistle more convenient.

For example, the private club status—where one had to be a member and pay an annual fee, or you had to find a club member to sponsor you—has been abolished. However, heavy restrictions remain near campus on the sale of alcohol, meaning there are no established bars within walking distance of campus, although beer is sold at several nearby restaurants. Most of these established sports bars are easily accessible by car or public transportation.

Lumpy's, 3000 S. Highland Drive or 145 W. Pierpont Avenue: The original Lumpy's, located about five miles south of campus, has the longest history of being a U bar. It has long operated a shuttle bus to and from games, and it is decked out with plenty of Utah memorabilia. The menu has the typical sports bar offerings, but what sets Lumpy's apart is its weekend brunch menu—perfect for those early-starting games. Ute fans at the Highland location will be attracted to the Ute omelet, which fea-tures grilled onions, green and red peppers, diced Canadian bacon, ham, and cheddar-jack cheese. The downtown location's brunch menu is significantly more expansive.

The Green Pig Pub, 31 E. 400 South: When the land upon which Port O'Call stood was bought by the federal government to make room for an expanded federal courthouse, the days of this landmark three-floor bar were numbered and it was leveled in 2009. Port's closing scattered several veterans of the bar industry to open their own places, and one of them, Bridget Gordon, opened her own place just a couple of blocks away. The burgers are a visual delight, but the green chili verde nachos represent the menu's eclectic side. With the University TRAX line just outside the front door, the Green Pig is ideally located for pregame and postgame festivities as well as in-game fun.

Legends, 677 S. 200 West: This bar bills itself as a Utah bar, but it is also the meeting spot for Nebraska Cornhusker and Florida Gator expatriates. The menu features more than standard bar fare, with pasta, steak, and Mexican entrees, but the poutine—beer-battered fries slathered with cheese and brown gravy—and a massive appetizer sampler will satisfy any taste.

The Huddle, 2400 E. Fort Union Boulevard (7200 South): If you're away from downtown or your home base is closer to Salt Lake County's major ski resorts in Big and Little Cottonwood Canyons, then The Huddle is probably for you. What's great about The Huddle is the difficulty in telling what's represented more—televisions or flags of major programs. Don't worry—there are plenty of Utah items lining on the walls and hanging from the rafters, as well.

Fiddler's Elbow, 1063 E. 2100 South: Since Fiddler's Elbow shares a kitchen with the adjacent Salt Lake Pizza and Pasta, this is an ideal place to go if your party has different ideas on where to go for something to eat. Like Lumpy's, it features an outstanding brunch menu and doesn't lack for televisions, pool tables, or atmosphere.

56 1994 Freedom Bowl

Call it magical, miraculous, or heaven-sent. Those were the adjectives that were freely tossed around after Utah defeated Arizona 16–13 in the 11th and final Freedom Bowl, a victory that capped

Utah's greatest season up to that point, both in win totals and poll finish.

How many teams win games with 75 yards of total offense? Arizona's defense, ranked No. 2, was clearly worthy of its standing, holding Utah to just six yards rushing. Yet that dominance was trumped by key plays from a pair of true freshmen in Cal Beck and Kevin Dyson. But more on them in a moment.

Utah's first score was set up by a turnover deep in Arizona territory, and Charlie Brown converted it into a six-yard touchdown run. The teams were tied at halftime 7–7.

Arizona kicked a pair of field goals in the fourth quarter, but the last one came with a heavy price. On two occasions, wide-open Arizona receivers dropped passes in the end zone that would have given the Wildcats an insurmountable two-possession lead.

Jason Jones' punt landed at the Arizona 1-yard line, and the Utah defense, which wasn't too shabby itself in surrendering 184 yards, forced a punt. Rather than risk having it blocked for a touchdown, the Wildcats conceded a safety and took a free kick from its own 20.

Beck, a recruiting afterthought from Cottonwood High whose primary goal entering the season was just to be on the 65-man traveling squad, worked his magic for the second game in a row after setting up the game-winning score in the Holy War with a long kickoff return. This return covered 72 yards and set up Utah on the Arizona 5.

"As we were waiting for the kickoff, I turned to Clarence Lawson and said, 'Do you remember when I told you before the BYU return that this was the biggest return of our lives? Well, I lied. This one is the biggest,'" Beck said.

Beck did his part. With just a little more than four minutes left in the game, the offense had to do its job—no small task given the defense it was going up against.

Mike McCoy's first pass was nearly intercepted. The second was batted down, and his third missed Curtis Marsh in the end zone.

In the huddle, Utah called Jumbo Scramble Zone Pass Right, a rollout pass play designed to go to tight end Rick Tucker. Two problems quickly emerged—Tucker was covered, and Arizona lineman Chuck Osborne broke through the Utah line and got his hands on McCoy. McCoy was about to hit the deck like so many Mike Tyson knockout victims before him, but he managed to fling the ball toward the end zone.

Racing along the back of the end zone was Dyson, a freshman from nearby Clearfield High. He reached out with one hand and snagged the ball for a miraculous touchdown. Arizona wasn't able to do anything with the ball on the ensuing drive, and Utah got one of its five first downs on a 10-yard pass play to Tucker to run out the clock.

For McBride, who served as an assistant under Arizona coach Dick Tomey for three seasons before coming to Utah, it was a dream fulfilled.

"This is as big as it comes," McBride said, clutching one of the game balls firmly in his right arm. "I've been through a lot of highs and lows in this profession. This is history—it's never been done at Utah."

57 Good-bye to the Mountain West Conference

The 2010 season proved to be a mixed bag for Utah. An 8–0 start and rise to fifth in the national polls was tossed in the gutter after a 47–7 thrashing at Rice-Eccles Stadium at the hands of TCU. That was followed by a sleepwalking effort against Notre Dame on national TV that had various pundits tossing out the words "fraud" and "overrated" in reference to the Utes.

Those were fair comments. Utah had built up its glossy record largely by stomping patsies and squeaking out wins against the two semi-decent opponents it had played. It was destroyed by a legitimate top-three team and steamrolled on the road by a name program, albeit one that had also lost to Navy and Tulsa.

With two games left against up-and-coming San Diego State and the Holy War grudge match against Brigham Young, losing out was a real possibility if the Utes continued to trudge along and feel nothing but pity for a lost opportunity.

What followed were two of the greatest gut-check games in program history and a with-honors departure from the Mountain West Conference, even if the team's goal of finishing at the top of its class with a conference championship went unfulfilled.

Against resurgent San Diego State and its high-powered passing offense, Utah gave up 528 yards passing to Ryan Lindley and trailed twice by 17 points in the first half. But Jordan Wynn threw for 362 yards of his own, including a 47-yard Hail Mary to Kendrick Moeai to end the first half to get Utah within 3.

Lindley escaped a fierce Utah rush to start the third quarter, and Vincent Brown leaped between two Utah defenders to haul in a pass and race 90 yards for a touchdown early in the third quarter to give the Aztecs a 10-point lead.

Utah's defense kept SDSU out of the end zone the rest of the way en route to forcing three Lindley interceptions, the last by Brian Blechen in the end zone with 1:22 left. Matt Asiata and Eddie Wide scored on a pair of one-yard runs, while Greg Bird blocked a punt that set up Utah on the doorstep for Wide's winning score with 10:21 to play. Utah had escaped.

"A lot of things smiled on us," said quarterback Jordan Wynn, whose passing yardage marked a single-game best. "Those two weeks were pretty bad, and we needed a win desperately."

Against BYU, Utah's situation appeared dire as it was shut out through three quarters. Wynn was benched to start the second half,

Utah Trivia

Q: Name the only former Utah head coach to coach a future Utah head coach?

A: Mike Giddings, head coach for the Hawaiians of the World Football League in the 1970s, had Jim Fassel as his quarterback for parts of two seasons in 1974–75. Fassel also threw the last pass in the league's two-year history, which folded three days after the WFL's final game on October 19, 1975.

Q: What was Mike McCoy's connection to Super Bowl XXXIII?

A: During his collegiate career, McCoy handed the ball off to the starting running backs for both teams in that game—Jamal Anderson of Atlanta and Terrell Davis of Denver. Davis and McCoy were part of George Allen's first recruiting class at Long Beach State, and both saw time as redshirt freshmen in the 1991 season. After Long Beach State dropped football, Davis went to Georgia, and like Anderson, was a late-round draft pick, going in the sixth round of the 1995 draft.

Q: If 34–31 is Utah's lucky number on the scoreboard, then what is it for uniform numbers?

A: One could make a case for several numbers, but four stand above the rest: 11 (Alex Smith, Paul Kruger, Lee Grosscup, Pokey Allen, and Carl Harry), 32 (Jamal Anderson, Eddie Johnson, and Eric Weddle), 43 (Anthony Davis, Kautai Olevao, Jack Steptoe, and Norm Thompson), and 68 (Norm Chow, Zane Beadles, and Chris Kemoeatu).

Q: Name the only Super Bowl–winning coach to lead a team into Salt Lake City to play Utah?

A: Before he won Super Bowl XXXIV with the St. Louis Rams (in addition to losing Super Bowl XV with the Philadelphia Eagles), Dick Vermeil was the head coach at UCLA for two seasons. In his first year as Bruins head coach, Vermeil and UCLA prevailed over Utah 27–14, one of Utah's better showings in a 1–10 season, given that a better Utah team lost 66–19 the year before in Pasadena.

Terrance Cain threw two interceptions in as many possessions, and BYU was getting a mistake-free game from freshman quarterback Jake Heaps in building a 13–0 lead.

Wynn completed a 12-yard pass to Jereme Brooks on third-and-10 to put Utah in range for a Joe Phillips' 40-yard field goal. Then Heaps aided the Utah comeback with his first big mistake of the day by botching a handoff that was recovered by Junior Tui'one at the BYU 37.

Wynn struck quickly, connecting with Devonte Christopher for a juggling 37-yard touchdown on the next play from scrimmage to get Utah within 3. But BYU came right back as Heaps directed a 15-play, 56-yard drive that chewed up more than six minutes off the clock to give the Cougars a 16–10 lead.

Then came easily the craziest drive of Utah's season in which it both punted the ball away and threw an interception yet managed to keep possession and get the go-ahead score.

First, Phillips shanked a 27-yard punt, which hit a BYU player. Bird alertly pounced on the loose ball at the BYU 46. Two plays later, Wynn rolled out and threw to fullback Shawn Asiata, but the ball went through his hands and right into those of BYU's Brandon Bradley for his first career interception. But as Bradley was being tackled, the ball was ripped free by Moeai who recovered it at the BYU 38.

BYU appeared to have a good argument that Bradley's knee was down before the ball came out, but after a lengthy video review, the officials let the play stand as it was called on the field. Wynn threw to Dallin Rogers for a 29-yard gain to the BYU 3, and Matt Asiata punched it in on the next play to give Utah a 17–16 lead with 4:24 left.

Heaps completed all four of his passes in an 11-play, 54-yard drive that had the 6–5 Cougars on the verge of pulling off a huge upset of the 9–2 Utes. Strangely, BYU played for the field goal at the end of the drive, not allowing Heaps to throw a single pass as Utah used all three of its timeouts. Still, the 42-yard field goal for Mitch Payne, while not a gimme, was more than makeable.

Thanks to Brandon Burton, no one will know if Payne's kick would have been good. Burton flew in from the left side of the line, past BYU's Mike Muehlmann, and dove to block Payne's kick. After a decade-plus of close games that had gone BYU's way, it was Utah's turn to provide the heartbreak finish for its rivals.

"I was just standing on the sidelines rubbing my lucky dimes together," Coach Kyle Whittingham said. "But then it was elation, and I breathed a sigh of relief."

Fans on both sides are used to carrying such bitter or glorious memories of the Holy War into the off-season, but with Utah's departure to the Pac-12 Conference and that league's insistence that the Holy War not take up the final date of the regular season, it could be some time before this game provides the final word on the success or failure of each team's regular season.

58 Classic Finish III: 2008 Oregon State

"When we were down eight, I saw a few people leaving and thought, 'They're about to miss a show.' I thought there was no way we were going to lose this game."

—Brian Johnson on his thoughts
with Utah trailing Oregon State 28–20 late
in the fourth quarter of their 2008 game

Self-confidence is an intangible that's not easily quantified in a quarterback. Maybe it can be determined by fourth-quarter comebacks or in road games against teams with winning records. However you want to measure it, those who have seen him play can safely say Brian Johnson had an unshakable belief in his team and his ability to lead it to victory.

It's one thing to say that there was no way Utah was going to lose to Oregon State, as Johnson did after Utah's 31–28 victory against the Beavers. But no sane person would have predicted a Utah victory *in regulation*…not after being shut out for the first 28 minutes of the second half. Not after Oregon State stretched a one-possession game to the max on Brady Kamp's two-yard touchdown reception with 2:18 seconds left to go in the game. And certainly not against an Oregon State team that had slapped silly No. 1 Southern California in its last game.

Maybe, just maybe, the anemic Utah offense would wake up, string together a drive, and put itself in position to tie the game late, burn most of the clock, and send the game into overtime.

The Utes did well with the first part of the comeback, going 60 yards in four plays—all Johnson completions—to get within two points on Braden Godfrey's 25-yard touchdown catch.

The touchdown was the easy part. The two-point conversion proved a little stickier. Johnson threw incomplete to David Reed in the end zone, but a pass interference call gave Utah a second chance. This time, Johnson rolled right and beat an OSU defender to the pylon to tie the game.

There was still 1:29 left in the game, but that turned out to be Oregon State's problem, not Utah's. Horrible clock management by OSU coupled with a 31-yard punt put the Utes back in business from their own 45-yard line with 1:06 left. Two completions put the ball to the Oregon State 40 before Johnson connected with Brent Casteel on a 16-yard pass, placing the Utes in field-goal range for All-America kicker Louie Sakoda.

Two plays later, Sakoda drilled his kick from 37 yards. Utah, which had entered the game ranked 15th in the country, had escaped.

David Reed's long kickoff return helped set up Utah's first touchdown against Oregon State. (AP Photo/Douglas C. Pizac)

The last time Sakoda was in such a situation, his game-ending field goal gave Utah a 17–14 victory at Air Force in the penultimate game of the 2006 season. He wasn't looking back on that kick for inspiration as he trotted onto the field in 2008.

"When I got out there, the only thing going through my head was concentrating on making the kick," Sakoda said. "This was the biggest kick of my career, without a doubt."

So went Utah's quest for its own brand of perfection. Turnovers and periods of stagnation on offense ultimately gave way to a couple of clutch drives and eventually a Utah victory. Six games into the 2008 season, Utah had its share of moments where defeat was a real possibility. It would face another such moment against TCU.

But it was out of these moments where the character of the 2008 Utah team was built. It might not bedazzle you with style points, but when the job had to be done, the Utes were certain to finish it.

59 Polynesian Power

The Polynesian influence on the University of Utah football program can be attributed to two primary factors—the influence of the Church of Jesus Christ of Latter-day Saints in Polynesian communities and countries, and Ron McBride.

The former extends all the way back to 1843, when Mormon missionaries landed in Tahiti and proselyted there and in surrounding islands. The first Mormon Polynesian community in Utah was Iosepa. When translated from Hawaiian, Iosepa means Joseph, in honor of Mormon Church founder Joseph Smith. The town was founded in 1889 in Tooele County, adjacent to Salt Lake County. Although many of those settlers returned to Hawaii at the start of the 20th century when a Mormon temple was built in Hawaii, there remains a strong Polynesian presence in Utah today.

McBride's history doesn't go back nearly as far, but like the Iosepa settlers, he is a pioneer of sorts in recruiting the Polynesian community, or at least as far as Utah football is concerned. While previous Utah coaches made efforts to recruit in Hawaii and other South Pacific island countries, McBride's experience—which went all the way back to his days as a coach at Gavilan Junior College in the 1960s—helped open doors that were partly shut during previous Utah football regimes.

"I've loved having Polynesian players on my team for years," McBride said. So tight was McBride's bond with the Polynesian community that he was a strong candidate for the Hawaii job after the 1998 season.

As Utah head coach, McBride's first recruiting coup in Hawaii came with offensive lineman Roy Ma'afala, a four-year letterman from 1991–94. Ma'afala was a product of St. Louis High in Honolulu. The Crusaders are the dominant prep program in the state and have produced several NFL players and dozens of collegiate players. One of those future NFL stars was Roy's brother, Chris Fuamatu-Ma'afala, a 6-foot, 280-pound running back, who as a true freshman was a vital component of Utah's 1995 Western Athletic Conference title team. His size and speed made it almost impossible for a single defender to bring him down in the open field.

The list of Polynesian contributors to Utah football is lengthy, but here are profiles of the most notable and accomplished:

Ma'ake and Chris Kemoeatu: Ma'ake was an All–Mountain West Conference defensive tackle at Utah before making it in the NFL with Baltimore, Carolina, and Washington. Chris followed three years later and earned All–MWC first team honors as a senior offensive lineman before being drafted by the Pittsburgh Steelers in the 2005 draft. With a high-powered offense that scored points at a dizzying pace, Chris Kemoeatu's role on the 2004 Utah team was often overlooked. But after Appalachian State upset Michigan in its 2007 season opener, at least one coach recognized how vital Chris was to Utah's offense.

"When [Meyer] was at Utah, we got our hands on every bit of Utah tape we could," said Appalachian State head coach Jerry Moore. "It wasn't so much Alex Smith. We were just infatuated with how physical their right guard played."

Another younger brother, Tevita, lettered in 2003–04.

Doug, Jason, Jeff, and Henry Kaufusi: The first two Kaufusi brothers listed were four-year letterman on opposite sides of the ball—Doug played on the offensive line from 1998–2001, while younger brother Jason, currently an assistant coach at Weber State under Ron McBride, played in Utah from 2000–03. Both men twice earned first-team All–MWC honors. Two older brothers, Steve and Rich, played at BYU, with Steve serving as Utah's defensive line coach before taking the same position at his alma mater. An adopted sibling, Pasa Tukuafu, also played for Utah.

Kautai Olevao: Olevao is best remembered for a crushing hit he put on BYU's Ronney Jenkins in the 1998 Holy War, but his career was much more significant than one play. Along with Luther Elliss, Olevao is the only Utah defensive player to ever be named first-team all-conference three times—once in the WAC and twice in the MWC. Like the Kemoeatus, Olevao is a product of Kahuku High on the island of Oahu's north shore.

60 Holy War Hijinks

If you can't beat 'em, embarrass them. And for most of the Holy War, the best way to do that for fans of both Utah and BYU is to engage in pranks on select institutions, buildings, and even the home of one of the rivalry's radio broadcasters. What is desecration for one side is justifiable comeuppance for the other.

Today, with the intensity surrounding the game spilling over to the fans and occasionally causing serious injury to one another and other unfortunate incidents, plus with school presidents pleading for more fan civility, it might not be the worst thing for fans to channel that physical rage into more pranks like those of yesteryear, pranks where the only damage done is to one's pride and not his nose or jaw.

But as University of Utah Police Department Sgt. Lynn Rohland said, "Once you get into hurting an individual or causing property damage or destruction, then it's no longer a prank—it's criminal. There's a big difference between the two."

You can decide under which categories the following incidents fall. Just remember that BYU started it all, and Utah has been merely defending its honor ever since.

In 1939, BYU students painted the Block U blue and wrote "Scalp Utah" on campus sidewalks. Utah students responded by dousing the steps to the Maeser Building, a sundial, and the campus' main flagpole with red paint.

With only one win against Utah—and during World War II no less—BYU pulled off its biggest "victory" in the rivalry by placing a giant lit "Y" above Block U in 1956. Utah did an end run around the Intercollegiate Knights—a BYU spirit club that expected retaliation and guarded the "Y" in Provo—and burned a "U" in a lawn smack dab in the middle of BYU's campus. Utah ran up the score in the Holy War Hijinks three months later by stealing BYU's victory bell and taking it back to Salt Lake City.

More red paint flowed in 1967 when several U students slapped on a few coats of red paint to BYU's bronzed cougar at the entrance to the campus grounds. This was the first incident in which there were documented consequences, as several students were caught and paid a $100 fine.

After the 1981 season, BYU backers painted the score of that year's football game (56–28) on the Park Building and the Huntsman Center. They were also caught and ordered to pay a $1,400 fine to clean up their unsightly mess.

In 2004, the most serious incident from a law enforcement perspective took place. The "Utah Eight" were a group of baseball players who painted the "Y" red. The players—which included a former Utah quarterback named Ryan Breska, a Purdue transfer on the wrong end of a quarterback battle in the 2002 season that included Brett Elliott and Alex Smith—took pictures of themselves and their handiwork. But when Breska went to a local department store to pick up the developed photos, police were waiting to arrest him. Apparently, the photo lab technician was a BYU fan, saw the photos, and tipped off police.

Pay a fine and the matter is settled, right? Not in Provo, where the baseball players were charged with second-degree felony mischief, which carries a maximum sentence of 15 years in prison and a $15,000 fine.

For an act of vandalism that BYU grounds crews had cleaned up by noon on the day it was discovered? "[It] seems a little much," Breska said. Utah fans agreed. Naturally, the Provo sentiment was to hang 'em in the town square at high noon. Fortunately, cooler legal and judicial heads prevailed, and the players pled to a Class B misdemeanor and agreed to pay nearly $6,300 in restitution.

Somewhere Paul James might be wondering where the law was all those years ago when his house was first covered in toilet paper, which was followed up by Utah fans leaving wrecked cars and junkyard-bound tires covered in red paint and often decorated with language not suitable for a family publication.

James was a former broadcaster for Utah football, but he went south after the 1967 season and was BYU's radio voice for the next 30-plus years. Utah fans have been making James pay for his decision ever since—or at least until he retired after the 2000 season.

"It was the unique feature of the Utah-BYU game because I know I'm going to get trashed," James said.

61 The Dyson Brothers

If the Romney brothers are Utah's first family of sports for the first half of the 20th century, it's hard to imagine a better set of brothers at Utah in the second half of the century than the Dysons—wide receiver Kevin and defensive backs Andre and Patrick.

It's impossible to talk about the Dysons without first mentioning Kevin, who was on the receiving end of the biggest touchdown in school history when he caught Mike McCoy's five-yard pass to win the Freedom Bowl against Arizona in 1994. And with apologies to the 1972 squad for its comeback against Arizona, Kevin's 50-yard touchdown reception against Air Force the following season capped the most miraculous comeback in school history.

Utah would never reach the heights that it did in Kevin's first two seasons, but no one could fault his effort or production. Against nationally ranked Kansas early in the 1996 season, Dyson had 172 yards receiving plus a score in a wild 45–42 Utah victory. The following season, Dyson spoiled New Mexico's bid for a rare 10-win season by returning a punt 75 yards for another score in a 15–10 Ute victory. And in his final Holy War, Dyson had nine catches for 143 yards as the Utes prevailed 20–14.

Kevin Dyson ranks first all-time at Utah in receptions, second in yards, and tied for fifth in touchdowns. Not bad for a guy who had five different quarterbacks during four seasons.

The 2000 season was a frustrating, underachieving year for Utah as it finished 4–7, but it wasn't the fault of the defense, especially Andre Dyson, who created more magic with the ball in his hands than any Utah defender before or since. That year Dyson was responsible for five turnovers—four interceptions and a fumble. He scored touchdowns on four of those plays. Older brother Patrick also got in on the act with an interception and a kickoff return for a touchdown.

With 36 of Utah's 234 points that season, Andre and Patrick were responsible for 15 percent of Utah's points in 2000.

The 1999 season was much better for everyone involved. Andre had two interceptions in a 20–17 Holy War victory, including the clincher with 1:09 left. He also knocked down a pass late against Fresno State to seal a 17–16 Las Vegas Bowl victory and a 9–3 season for Utah that saw the team claim a share of the Mountain West Conference title. And Patrick earned MWC special teams player of the week honors for returning a kickoff for a score against San Jose State.

Kevin and Andre were early-round draft picks in the NFL, both by Tennessee. Kevin went in the first round in the 1998 draft, while Andre went in the second round of the 2001 draft. Both would reach the pinnacle of every player's career by playing in the Super Bowl—Kevin first with Tennessee, then with Carolina, while Andre started for Seattle in its Super Bowl loss to Pittsburgh. Sadly, neither one emerged with a ring. Kevin was tackled a yard short of the end zone in the 1999 Super Bowl against the St. Louis Rams with the Titans down seven points. Earlier that postseason, Dyson carved out a piece of history that was much more positive, running back a lateral off a kickoff return 75 yards to give the Titans an improbable victory in what later became known as the Music City Miracle.

62 Where to Go When the Game Is Over

You've had your pregame tailgate party. You've (hopefully) watched the Utes crush another foe on its schedule. You're not ready to go home or back to the hotel because the game-day experience shouldn't be limited to your activities at or around Rice-Eccles Stadium. So here are some offerings of what to do and where to go after the stadium crowd has emptied and the tailgaters have packed up.

Many of the following places are located along or close to 400 South, which is a major east-west artery leading to the University of Utah. Others require a little more of a drive, but Salt Lake City is easily navigable by car and public transportation is plentiful, so none of these places qualify as off-the-beaten-path establishments.

Red Iguana, 736 W. North Temple: There are two additional locations—one just around the corner from the original at 866 W. South Temple called the Red Iguana 2, and a bistro at 28 S. State Street called Taste of Red Iguana. But the original location, which opened in 1985, is accessible en route to Salt Lake International Airport, and it bills itself as the Home of Killer Mexican Food. Few who have eaten there could disagree. The wait can be lengthy—a good rule of thumb is to expect at least 30 minutes at any time, or longer during traditional dining times, but the wait is more than worth it.

The Red Iguana features everything one would expect on a Mexican food menu, but the mole—a generic term for the sauces used in various dishes—can only be described as outstanding. As a food critic for *City Weekly* once wrote, "Simply put, you could travel far and wide and never find a more satisfying dish than Red Iguana's red pipian mole.'"

Litza's Pizza and Hires Big H Burgers, 716 East 400 S. and 425 S. 700 E.: The two eateries go hand-in-hand at two other locations in Midvale and West Valley City. Hires, established by Don Hale in 1959, came first. Litza's followed in 1965. Of the burgers, one *Deseret News* foodie opined, "The Hale Family makes burgers like we should raise kids. From start to finish, they leave nothing to chance or to the kindness of strangers." Hale worked into his 90s before he died in January 2011 at the age of 93.

Trolley Square, 600 S. 700 East: Before it became one of Salt Lake City's premier shopping and dining destinations, Trolley Square was exactly as its name suggests—the launching point for Salt Lake City's 144 trolley cars, a role it served until 1945 when trolley lines were discontinued. Little was done with the lot until 1972 when the existing trolley barns were converted into a two-story shopping center.

The center's water tower is covered with neon lighting that at one time served as a weather indicator of sorts, but today it consists of continuing lights that alternate between red and blue and can be seen for several miles across Salt Lake City. Inside, brick and wooden floors, winding hallways, and wrought-iron balconies add to the center's charm and décor. Trolley Square features many national high-end retailers, but it is also home to some great eating establishments, most notably the Desert Edge Brewery at The Pub, Rodizio Grill, and Poundcake's Eats, located inside the Wise Guys Comedy Club.

The New Yorker, 60 W. Market Street: The first of the Gastronomy restaurants, The New Yorker opened in 1978 in the old New York Hotel and is one of Salt Lake City's best fine dining establishments. Gastronomy partners John Williams and Tom Guinney had a vision of bringing the ocean's delights to the desert and arranged for fresh seafood to be flown in daily, and their vision was legitimized by Salt Lakers who continue to flock to the chain's seven additional restaurants and three fish markets. One of them, the Market Street Broiler and University Fresh Fish market, is located just a block away from the University of Utah at 260 S. 1300 East.

63 Utah's Twin No. 1 Draft Picks

Utah fans owe a debt of gratitude to St. Louis Rams quarterback Sam Bradford. If Bradford, an Oklahoma redshirt sophomore, had declared for the NFL Draft after the 2008 season like many believed he would, Utah's distinction of being the only school to field No. 1 overall picks in the NFL and NBA drafts would have been in jeopardy since Sooners hoopster Blake Griffin went No. 1 overall to the Los Angeles Clippers a couple months after the NFL Draft. Instead, Bradford played another season, and although he suffered a pair of injuries that ultimately cost him the 2009 season, he still managed to be the first player taken overall, albeit one year after Griffin.

So again Sam, thank you for staying in school and allowing the University of Utah sole distinction of a tremendous honor.

Two things swung open the door for Alex Smith to be selected first overall by the San Francisco 49ers in the 2005 NFL Draft. It certainly helped that Heisman Trophy–winner Matt Leinart decided against forgoing his senior year at USC. That said, Leinart would have been in a tough position to show the scouts much physically, as evidenced by his decision to have elbow surgery following the 2004 season. It's very possible Smith would have been the No. 1 overall pick even with Leinart in the draft, but Leinart's absence made Smith the front-runner to be no worse than the first quarterback chosen, and almost certainly the top pick, given San Francisco's struggles at the position in the 2004 seaosn.

If Leinart's absence from the draft didn't solidify Smith as the top pick, his pro day workout at the University of Utah certainly did, which drew representatives from every NFL team. One scout called it a "paramount" workout.

"Those guys, the quarterbacks, get nervous sometimes in that situation, and then they are all over the place with the ball. He didn't look that way at all," the scout added, saying that Smith looked "natural."

It marked the end of a rapid climb out of obscurity for Smith, who was just a little more than two years removed from a burned redshirt year after an aborted appearance against San Diego State in which he didn't complete a pass and had an interception returned for a touchdown.

Andrew Bogut's career at Utah didn't get off to such a rocky start. If anything, perhaps too much was expected from Bogut in his freshman year—he was coming off an MVP performance in the FIBA Junior World Championships in which he averaged 26 points and 17 rebounds as the Boomers won the gold medal. Still, he was Mountain West Conference freshman of the year after averaging 12.5 points and 9.9 rebounds.

Like Smith, Bogut exploded onto the national scene in his second year of full-time action at Utah, averaging 20.4 points and 12.2 rebounds per game. The 7–0 Australian swept the sport's major honors, winning the Naismith and Wooden awards, as well as being the leading vote-getter on the Associated Press All-America team. Bogut was chosen first overall by the Milwaukee Bucks and has gotten better and better with each year in the NBA, having earned third-team All-NBA honors after the 2009–10 season.

64 Utah's First Dynasty: 1928–33

Prior to the arrival of Urban Meyer and the 2003–04 seasons, it had been 50 years since Utah successfully defended its conference crown. In the first half-century of Utah football, such defenses were often successful. But no era of Utah football reached the heights of the 1928–33 teams, which won six consecutive Rocky Mountain Athletic Conference titles. Here are some key moments, players, and games from that era of dominance that all Utah fans should be aware of.

Players

Frank Christensen, 1929–32. Utah's only three-time All-American, "Crashing Chris" was a third-team selection as a sophomore and junior before earning first-team honors from United Press and the World Telegram as a senior fullback. Christensen wasn't Ike Armstrong's first choice to replace Earl "Powerhouse" Pomeroy at fullback entering the 1930 season—Preston Summerhays started against Nevada in the season opener but went down with an injury that would sideline him for several weeks—but the Granite High product made a seamless transition, rushing for 100 yards or more the next seven games while leading the team in rushing in all eight games.

Marwin "Marvin" Jonas, 1927–30. Utah's offense was a machine in Jonas' senior year, and Jonas' blocking from his center position was a big reason why Christensen had as much success as he did running the ball. Jonas was Utah's first two-time All-American, earning third-team honors from Consolidated Press as a junior as well as second-team honors the following year. Although his pro career consisted of just two games with the Brooklyn Dodgers in 1931, Jonas became Utah's first player ever in the NFL.

Jack Johnson, 1929–32. The first Utah product with staying power in the NFL, Johnson played for seven seasons with the Detroit Lions. Johnson and Christensen were also members of Detroit's first NFL championship team in 1935. Johnson, a tackle, actually scored two touchdowns in his pro career—one on defense, and another on a 48-yard pass play in his final season of 1940.

Other players of note include George Watkins, end, second-team All-American; Alton Carmon, tackle, third-team All-American; and Earl "Powerhouse" Pomeroy, fullback, who had several All-American honors as a senior, including a first-team selection by International News Service.

Games

1930: Utah 34, Colorado 0. On the road and against a team that finished 6–1–1, Utah showed that the gap between first and second was indeed that wide with a blowout of the Frontiersmen (as they were known before they adopted the Buffaloes as their name). Utah's offense—with Christensen on punishing runs and Watkins on deep routes from quarterback Ray Forsberg—was well-established. Colorado took away the deep pass and limited Utah to just 40 yards on 3-of-14 passing attempts, but Christensen made up the difference offensively with a 201-yard, three-touchdown effort.

1931: Washington 7, Utah 6. The Redskins had won a school-record 16 straight games and hadn't lost in 24 games going all the way back to a 16–7 loss to Creighton in 1927. That streak should have been extended for at least one more week before a University of Washington record opening-game crowd of 24,000. Out of the single-wing, Christensen threw for a touchdown in the third quarter that got Utah within a point, but quarterback Fred "Tabasco" Tedesco's extra point was blocked and the Huskies escaped en route to a 5–3–1 season.

Honors

Until the 1964 Liberty Bowl team, the 1930 Utah edition was probably the greatest unit ever assembled in program history. Not only did it outscore the opposition 340–20 with five shutouts in going 8–0, it featured three players who earned All-American honors of some kind—a standard that wouldn't be equaled until the 1994 team. The 1930 Utes also occupied eight of the league's 11 all-conference slots.

Although the 1929 team also went undefeated at 7–0 and was almost as stingy on defense in giving up just 23 points, its offensive output was 121 points less than the 1930 squad.

While it is difficult to judge teams of this era against the rest of the country given the rarity of inter-sectional games, much less bowls, this particular Utah team would have been at best a tough out for some of the best teams of the time. One website operator who has compiled power rankings for every year since the first college game was played in 1869 has Utah at No. 17 in his final 1930 rankings.

A stronger schedule in 1931, one which featured two narrow road losses against quality teams (Washington and Oregon State) had Utah finishing 19th in these same power polls—probably the strongest evidence *against* Utah being a team that could take on and defeat the Notre Dame, Alabama, and Southern California teams of the day. In fact, Utah opened the 1932 season against USC and was soundly defeated 35–0, but they went 6–1–1 that year.

65 How a Ute Took Center Stage in the Heidi Game

If it isn't the greatest moment in Charlie Smith's football career, it is easily the most memorable. But for that moment to attain such a status, nobody could see it.

Or that's the story anyway about the events of November 17, 1968, when the Oakland Raiders, for whom Smith played running back, and the New York Jets kicked off in a key AFL battle that would later live on in football lore as the Heidi Game.

The Heidi Game was a seminal moment in the history of television and sports. With less than a minute to go and the Jets leading

32–29 on Jim Turner's field goal with 1:05 left, the ensuing drive by the Raiders for the go-ahead score was cut short when NBC, precisely at 7:00 PM Eastern Time, began its broadcast of the children's movie *Heidi*.

Thousands of enraged viewers lit up NBC's switchboard with calls, anger that likely intensified when NBC ran a message across the bottom of the screen during a key moment in the movie that the Raiders had come back to win. NBC issued a public apology upon the film's conclusion, and the method networks use to handle late-running games was forever changed.

In a 2010 issue of *TV Guide*, the Heidi Game was listed as the No. 5 Biggest Blunder. And a 1997 poll conducted through select NFL media members to celebrate the NFL's 10,000th regular-season game, the Heidi Game was chosen as the most memorable game in pro football history.

Never mind that it wasn't an NFL game—the two leagues wouldn't officially merge until the 1970 season, although the leagues had already announced their plans to merge by the time the Heidi Game was played. The reaction to the game's finish not being broadcast was enough evidence for anyone who still scoffed at the AFL's significance that the league had arrived, offering a compelling, competitive product on the field.

It's also not true that no one saw the finish on television. Those in the Pacific and Mountain time zones saw it, as those regions of the country had not yet reached prime-time programming hours as the game concluded. But given the population density of the U.S. at the time, it's not the grossest of exaggerations to say almost no one saw the final minute. And the technology in use at the time made it impossible for the network to switch back to football.

That fateful minute was largely dominated by Smith, a rookie running back drafted in the fourth round of the AFL-NFL Draft. Smith would play eight years in the AFL and NFL—seven with the Raiders and his final season with the San Diego Chargers in 1975.

He had a productive NFL career, rushing for 3,351 yards and 24 touchdowns on 858 carries while catching 141 passes for 1,596 yards and 10 more touchdowns. He was never a star, but he was always a solid pro.

As a senior at Utah in 1967, Smith led the Utes in rushing with 588 yards and four touchdowns on 154 carries. His 27.2 kickoff return average was a single-season school record that stood until Steve Odom broke it in 1973, and Smith's 100-yard kickoff return for a score against Arizona State is tied with six others for the longest such play in school history.

After Turner's field goal, Smith returned the ensuing kickoff to the Raider 23. On the first play from scrimmage, Raider quarterback Daryle Lamonica hit Smith with a 20-yard screen pass. A 15-yard facemask penalty against the Jets moved the ball to the Jet 42.

NBC went to a commercial break, but after the commercials, viewers were brought to a little girl dancing in the Swiss Alps and not the gridiron. Back at the Oakland Coliseum, Lamonica hit Smith on a route in the middle of the field, and Smith took it the rest of the way for a 43-yard score and a 36–32 Raider lead. Single-handedly, Smith accounted for every yard gained in the drive.

There were still 42 seconds left, however, which was plenty of time for Joe Namath and his Jets to tie the game or even win it outright. But Earl Christy fumbled the squib kick, and Oakland's Preston Ridlehuber scooped up the fumble and fell over the end line for a score—the Raiders' second touchdown in nine seconds.

It was a memorable last drive for Smith, who was already in the middle of several key moments in the game, most of which went against his team. He lost a fumble at the Jet 1-yard line and had a 65-yard touchdown pass nullified by a holding penalty. He did score on a three-yard run in the third quarter to give the Raiders a 22–19 lead, however.

"I thought I had lost the game with my fumble," Smith said. "[The finish] sure gave me a lift. But it turned out to be my best day in football."

The Jets, however, would get revenge when the two teams met for the AFL title game later that season. The Raiders, AFL champions in 1967, couldn't defend their title, losing the game (27–23) and the right to represent the league in Super Bowl III. In the big game, the Jets pulled off one of the biggest upsets in NFL history, beating the Baltimore Colts 16–7.

66 The 1989 Holy War

Ugh.

That's about all anyone associated with the Utah program could say after the 1989 Holy War, which was perhaps the lowest point in the Holy War history for the Ute side. At the very least it has to rank among the worst moments in the rivalry's history. About the only consolation Utah fans have is when the occasional BYU fan reminisces on the good ol' days, and how nice it would be for a repeat of this game, is that such a prospect will likely never happen again in their lifetimes.

How bad was it? Even before kickoff, Ute hopes of a repeat of the previous year's game, the 57–28 Rice Bowl victory, were diminished significantly with the absence of starting quarterback Scott Mitchell, who was injured during practice leading up to the game.

But Mitchell didn't play defense, and it was on that side of the ball where Utah fielded unquestionably its worst defensive unit ever, giving up by a runaway margin various school records for yards and points. BYU was easily the best offense Utah had gone up against. If ball-control CSU could score 50 on the Utes at Rice Stadium, there was no telling how many trips to the buffet line BYU would make on the Ute defense.

The Cougars didn't just feast on the Utes—they gorged themselves in racing to a 28–0 lead in the first quarter and a 49–0 lead late in the first half. The then-record crowd of 66,110 at Cougar Stadium loved every minute of it. (And don't ever let BYU fans kid you into believing beating Utah isn't a big deal.)

The final statistics? Wes Craven couldn't write something this ghoulish. BYU did all it could to keep the score down, but it still averaged 10.7 yards per play, and quarterback Ty Detmer led eight touchdown drives in as many possessions. It's scary to think how many points BYU would have scored had it not substituted liberally on defense, allowing Utah quarterback Mike Richmond to throw for 393 yards and four touchdowns—most in the second half. You see, BYU ran only 70 plays—hardly an exorbitant amount—but all that did was translate into a *point per play* for the Cougars.

"Mitchell would have made a difference," said BYU assistant coach Dick Felt. "But he wouldn't have changed our offense. Our offense was a machine."

Utah had endured several blowout losses at the hands of BYU over the years, but this one was tough to top. Never before had a team scored that many points against Utah, and the 49-point margin of victory was just one point shy of the all-time mark, a 56–6 BYU victory in 1980.

After five years of Fassel, which featured exciting and explosive offenses but some of the nation's worst defenses, Utah decided it couldn't beat BYU at its own game. Three days after the Utes finished their season with a 42–38 home loss to Air Force, Fassel was fired, a move he felt was at odds with what he had been taught about the mission of collegiate athletics.

"I think in college athletics there's a hypocrisy that reeks," said Fassel, who by all accounts got players to go to class and graduate, shortly after he was fired. "I think within college athletics there's a wear-it-on-your-shirtsleeve attitude of, 'What are we really here for? What is our main primary goal?' and that's to educate people. I think a lot of times that's lip service."

Fassel admitted to having bitter feelings about college athletics, and those feelings might explain his career choices since Utah. He has never taken another college job and has worked almost exclusively in the pro ranks, highlighted by a stint as New York Giants head coach and a trip to Super Bowl XXXV. At the start of the 2011 year, he was the head coach of the Las Vegas Locos of the United Football League, and he won that league's championship in his first two years as head coach there.

67 Utah Traditions, Part II

Whether you're a longtime season ticket holder or someone who makes shotgun visits to Utah, there are events all year long that every Utah fan can take part of to get closer to the program and its players. Some events are held during the season, while others fall in the off-season. Most importantly, however, is that all of them are free.

Go to a Utah spring game: This has evolved into a huge off-season event at Utah from the days when the spring game was held on an outdoor practice field next to the Dee Glen Smith football center. Now it's played in Rice-Eccles Stadium, and while Utah's crowd won't remind anyone of Alabama or Nebraska, it draws a solid five figures and grows in attendance every year. It's a great time to pick your under-the-radar player who will shine next year or judge for yourself how the team's two-deep is shaping up.

But there's more to the event than just the game. Fans are encouraged to tailgate, and there's even a tailgating competition, although that requires some pregame registration. All of the players are made available for autographs after the game, and there is also an alumni touch football game, so it's a prime time to catch up with some of your favorite former players.

Get the team fired up on a Ute Walk: It sounds strange that players would stay in a hotel for home games, but coaches like to build a routine that has everyone on the same page for game day. For Utah players, their routine at Rice-Eccles Stadium begins when the team is dropped off along 500 South and begins its walk toward the stadium. Fans line up along the sidewalk, the Pride of Utah marching band is playing, and cheerleaders throw T-shirts into the crowd. If you're too busy getting in some last-minute tailgating to welcome the team as it comes onto the field, you can at least make the short trek from your Guardsman Way tailgate to get the team fired up as it walks to the game.

Attend Fan Fest: When the athletic department was forced to make some budgetary cuts leading up to the 2009–10 school year, one of the ways the department thought it could achieve its fiscal objectives was to cut funding for Fan Fest, probably the most fan-friendly event put on by the athletic department and holder of a summertime spot on the calendar since 2000.

That turned out to be a rare mistake for athletic director Chris Hill.

"We were wrong," Hill said. "We should have found money elsewhere to do that because [Fan Fest is] a good family thing for people to do."

Fan Fest takes place at Rice-Eccles Stadium prior to the beginning of the school year, usually in late August. What's great about Fan Fest is that it's not restricted to the football program. Many of the athletes that make up the rosters of Utah's 17 sports are in attendance, and they are exceptional about signing autographs and posing for photos.

The event draws several thousand fans, so don't go expecting to get an up-close-and-personal visit with every one of your favorite athletes. Naturally, the football players get most of the attention since the event is held just days before the start of the regular season, but that means it's an opportune time to get to know and visit with athletes of some of Utah's lesser-publicized teams. You can also play some games, eat some food, maybe win a prize or two, and just soak up the sunshine. Fan Fest promises to be a great time for any fan of Utah athletics.

68 Rivalry Rewind: Arizona State

Maybe this entry should be titled "Rivalry Renewed" in light of Utah's arrival into the Pac-12 conference for the 2011 season. As the teams gear up for their first game as conference rivals since 1977, this series will mark a good opportunity for Salt Lake City and Phoenix sportswriters and broadcasters to take a trip down Memory Lane.

It won't be the first such trip for Utah and conference rivals of days gone by. Colorado also returns to the Utah schedule on an annual basis for the first time since 1962 but for the first time as a conference rival since the 1946 season. While Utah and Colorado have played more games against each other, Utah-ASU is a tad more contemporary and, most importantly, features more meaningful games.

In its 16 years in the WAC, Arizona State was clearly the dominant program. It recorded only one losing season and won seven conference titles from 1969–77. ASU went 5–1 in bowl games, including victories in four of the first five Fiesta Bowls, beating high-caliber programs such as Pittsburgh and Nebraska along the way. The high point was the 1975 season, in which the Sun Devils went 12–0 and finished second in both major polls to one-loss Oklahoma.

During that time, Utah would prove to be the thorn in Arizona State's side. The Utes recorded three victories against the Sun Devils in that era, more than any other WAC team. From 1969–73, ASU lost a total of three conference games. Two of those were against Utah. And one of them, in 1973, cost ASU an undefeated season.

"We were leading 30–3, and I got hit hard and left the game for two-and-a-half quarters," said quarterback Don "Brownie" Van Galder. "I wore the doctor out and told him 'I'm good to go.'" Van Galder told the *Salt Lake Tribune* after the game that he was experiencing double vision—a sure sign he had suffered a concussion.

After a goal-line stand in which fans and coaches were certain Arizona State got a fifth down, a mistaken assumption based on a scoreboard operator and statistician who fell asleep at the controls, Van Galder reentered the game for an injured Lou Onofrio and drove Utah for the game-clinching score in a 36–31 victory.

"Those guys would hit you," Van Galder said. "I hurt so bad after playing them. They even hit you late a little bit sometimes. They wouldn't mind. They definitely hit you."

But the story of that game was Utah's defense, which probably got a little help from the snow and cold, which were conditions that Arizona State wasn't accustomed to playing in. ASU fumbled nine times, losing six, while quarterback Danny White threw four interceptions. The only reason the game didn't remain lopsided was that Utah fumbled eight times, losing four, in addition to an interception.

"They may be devils in the sun, but they are angels in the snow," *Sports Illustrated* wrote in its weekly college football recap.

Even in victory, beating Utah was never easy for the Sun Devils. ASU's 59–48 win in 1972 featured the most points ever given up by the defense in its entire WAC history.

"That was a craaaa-aazy game," Van Galder said. "We were down [52–26], and we were getting hammered. We came out in the second half and started chipping away. Eventually, it was 52–48, and we had the ball and we were driving to beat them. I called a play to the tight end—we hadn't called it all game and it was just a little pop pass, trying to dink it to him, and it went right through his hands and right to their guy."

In 1969, Utah gave up 15 quick points to the Sun Devils, then scored 24 unanswered in a thrilling 24–23 victory. Fred Graves, who would later become Utah's offensive coordinator under Ron McBride in 1995, threw an option pass 15 yards to Billy Hunter for one score, and starting quarterback Ray Groth ran seven yards for the go-ahead score in the fourth quarter.

Even stranger than Utah's upset of ASU in 1973 was Utah's 31–28 victory in Tempe in 1976. Utah had won just four of its previous 30 games under Tom Lovat, but the Sun Devils were in the midst of their first losing season in Frank Kush's 19 years at Arizona State. Just as surprising was Pat Degnan's 79-yard touchdown pass to Mike Cordy for the game-winning points, since it was Degnan who threw a school-record eight interceptions against Arizona State the year before.

69 Steve Odom

You can almost tell the age of any Utah fan by asking this question: Who is the greatest kick returner to play at Utah?

Your twentysomething set will argue for Antoine "Shaky" Smithson. Those in their 30s whose first memories of Utah football came late in Ron McBride's tenure as Utah coach will likely argue for Steve Smith. Parents of today's Utah students will make their case for Erroll Tucker.

Make your case for Steve Odom, however, and it's clear you've seen a lot of football at Utah. You would also have a compelling argument for a player whose name is still plastered all over the Utah record book.

"Eventually all of those records will come down, but I'll always have to say the things I did on the field were not done alone," Odom said. "I'm seeing faces and hearing names as I speak who were on the field making those things happen with me.

"A good example, my senior year I remember returning a punt and it wouldn't have happened if Steve Marshall hadn't been on the field," Odom said. "Seldom do you hear communication when you're returning a punt or kick, but I remember when we played Arizona.... All of a sudden I'm hearing Steve's voice, 'Up the middle, Odom! Up the middle!' He was reading what was happening in front of me as it was going down. I caught the ball, and I did exactly what he said—I ran up the middle and gained some yardage. Those are stories you don't forget because it really does reinforce that you don't do that kind of thing alone."

Alone is where Odom stood at the end of his Utah career in virtually every receiving, punt, and kickoff return mark at Utah. Today several of those marks have been surpassed, most by his aforementioned successors, but Odom still holds single-season and career marks in kickoff return yardage and punt return average, and his six kick returns for touchdowns have never been matched.

But just as meaningful for Odom are the memories and friendships he forged while at Utah, among them Marshall, who was

Odom's roommate during their first two years at Utah, and a local family with whom he remains in touch.

"The boosters had a program where they asked a family in the community at Utah who wouldn't mind taking on one of the kids that's there and let them be part of their family," Odom said. "During holidays and downtime between semesters, they would have a family that would be like a family to them and help with the transition between high school and college. That was very important for me. If it wasn't for Bruce and Judy Bell, I would have been out there all alone. And they were just a wonderful, wonderful family...they still are my family. I remember them cheering for me from the stands and talking to me like [they were] my mother and father.

"The University of Utah is a lot like Green Bay—family-oriented. It was just a wonderful organization with great support."

Odom played six NFL seasons, mostly with the Green Bay Packers, but he was hatching plans for his career after football. He went back to school and earned postgraduate degrees in psychology from Biola University and worked in that field for several years before getting into law enforcement with the Berkeley, California, police department.

"I integrated all of my experience in the things that I liked into a nice little package and that's how and what I did—law enforcement, psychology—and everything was good."

Now retired, Odom spends a lot of time traveling the world, having gone to Hong Kong, Singapore, Australia, South Africa, Morocco, and several European countries.

"[Retirement] goes by fast, let me tell you," Odom laughed. But probably not as fast as Odom was in returning punts, though.

70 Classic Finish IV: 1990 Minnesota

This game was destined to be an afterthought of the sports-minded public in the state of Utah—especially after BYU defeated top-ranked and defending national champion Miami to help kick off Ty Detmer's Heisman-winning campaign that same night. But for what the Utes didn't gain in press clippings and national prestige by beating Minnesota 35–29, they gained in intangibles for a rebuilding program in just its second game under new head coach Ron McBride.

Yet this game still managed to produce one moment that would easily have made any Top 10 plays for the day's events of September 8, 1990. And it's one that still lives on in the minds of Ute fans and the players who were part of a game that started out with all appearances of a Utah blowout. The game seemed destined to end with a Utah collapse, only to see the Utes pull off a miraculous finish for a 2–0 start for just the fourth time in 30 years. In 2007, Scout.com put together a list of the 100 Greatest Endings in College Football History from 1970 to the present, and this game squeaked onto the list at No. 99.

"What draws people to [remembering this game] was that you have these emotions," LaVon Edwards said. "You're thinking these guys are about to win this game, then they're about to lose this game, and now they're going to win this game."

Utah gave Minnesota a standing eight count by storming out to a 19–0 lead after one quarter. Although the Gophers got off the canvas and showed enough signs of life to keep them in the game, Utah held a two-touchdown margin at 29–14 as the fourth quarter began.

"We had great control of the game," said Edwards, who is currently a regional sales manager for Qwest in Salt Lake City as well as a youth baseball coach. "We were thinking we should be able to finish these guys out, but you always expect a team to make a run on its home field."

That run came, but not without some generous gifts by the Utes:

- Quarterback Mike Richmond—second string for the season opener the week before against Utah State—threw for 317 yards and a touchdown on 24-of-31 passing attempts. After his second interception, which led to the Gophers' tying score early in the fourth quarter, he was replaced by Jason Woods, who sustained a bruised knee in the opener and was far from 100 percent.

- Utah's last offensive possession ended when Woods fumbled without being touched at the Gopher's 7-yard line. Earlier in the series, Woods had a perfectly thrown bomb drop through the hands of Khevin Pratt.

- Minnesota's tying touchdown was set up by a late-hit penalty after a Dave Chaytors sack that would have put the Gophers in fourth-and-20. Instead, Minnesota had a first down at the Utah 29.

And those were just the second-half mistakes. When Minnesota kicker Brent Berglund came in for a 29-yard field goal with just eight seconds left, it appeared certain Utah would have plenty of moments they would look back on with regret.

Special teams coach Sean McNabb called for Middle Block, a play in which the Utes crash down on the middle of Minnesota's offensive line, with players behind rushing forward and jumping to block the kick. Nose tackle Greg Reynolds, whom Edwards said was the strongest person on the team, burst through, got his hand up, and blocked the kick, which bounced once and directly to Edwards to the left of the defensive line.

Minnesota never had a chance of catching Edwards, who was almost at full speed before any Gopher player realized he had the ball.

"I had a nice convoy of guys blocking for me," Edwards said. "The cool thing [was] ESPN showed the split-screen image of Mac running down the sidelines and me running."

Edwards joked that McBride "killed my NFL hopes—that old man is running stride for stride with me, and he's not running a 4.4 40."

The consolation prize, however, is a good one—playing a key role in a victory that jump-started a moribund program while installing a winning attitude that would go a long way into making Utah football respectable again.

71 Scott Mitchell

Scott Mitchell, a hotshot quarterback at nearby Springville High School, grew up the truest of true Cougar Blue fans. There was no better school for Mitchell to showcase his talents than BYU, and he seemed destined to follow in the footsteps of Gifford Nielsen, Marc Wilson, Jim McMahon, Steve Young, and Robbie Bosco. Your favorite pair of jeans couldn't make for a better fit than the one between Mitchell and BYU.

Nobody inside of Utah County, and precious few outside of it, thought Mitchell would end up anywhere else. But a funny thing happened en route to Mitchell's ascension to the BYU Quarterback Factory throne. Not only did he sign with Utah, he made it his duty to remove as many of his schoolboy idols from the NCAA record books as he possibly could.

Credit Utah head coach Jim Fassel, who had tutored John Elway at Stanford before heading east to Salt Lake City, and offensive coordinator Jack Reilly for not believing what everyone else had assumed. The two went after Mitchell like paparazzi after a movie starlet, and their efforts weren't lost on Mitchell or members of his family, all of whom shared Mitchell's passion for BYU football.

Mitchell enjoyed his time at a Utah camp more than his time at a BYU camp in the summer before his senior year, adding to the difficulty of his decision. And then there was the specter of all the highly touted quarterbacks he would have to compete against at BYU. Upperclassmen Steve Lindsley and Bob Jensen, who mostly filled the gap between Bosco and Ty Detmer, didn't quite live up to the standard set by their predecessors, but both men were nonetheless capable quarterbacks. Farther down the depth chart was Sean Covey, who played at Provo High and was just as highly sought as Mitchell.

In short, there were no guarantees at BYU, but there was plenty of opportunity to be had—and quickly—at Utah. So Mitchell became a Ute, and the Utah sports information department found out quickly what its counterparts at BYU had been accustomed to for so many years...namely that no record was safe and to have plenty of correction fluid on hand.

Mitchell's bonanza year came in 1988 when he was a sophomore. It was Utah, not BYU, that led the nation in passing offense that year as Mitchell set 24 school and 10 NCAA records. When he completed that year with a 57–28 blowout in the Rice Bowl, Mitchell had thrown more times (533 attempts) and for more yards per game (392.9) than any quarterback in NCAA history at that time.

The quarterbacks' names that were erased as a result of those marks included Bosco and McMahon.

"My dream was always to play like those guys," Mitchell said after his Utah team put up more points than any previous Ute squad did against BYU.

Mitchell's 631 passing yards against Air Force that season are still a single-game record at Utah by 120 yards. The second-highest record is also held by Mitchell. No Utah quarterback other than Mitchell has thrown for 500 yards in a game, and Mitchell led the nation in three different categories in his sophomore season, including total offense, total yards passing, and yards passing per game.

While Mitchell's name is all over the Utah record books to date, he is nowhere to be found in the most important statistic—victories. As prolific as Utah's offense was under Mitchell and during the Fassel era, its defense was equally as generous. Five of the six highest totals for yards surrendered happened in Fassel's five years, with the stop unit in Mitchell's junior year giving up a school-record 6,411 yards, or 534.5 yards per game. Utah went just 15–20 during Mitchell's three seasons.

The defense ultimately proved Fassel's undoing as the 1989 season featured two of the most embarrassing losses in school history—a 50–10 thrashing at home by Colorado State on homecoming, which was followed two weeks later by a 70–31 loss to BYU in which the Cougars led 49–0 at halftime. Injury forced Mitchell to miss the latter, and he had his worst game as a Ute in the former. In between, Mitchell made his last start as a Ute, a 41–39 victory against a two-win Lobo team.

With Ron McBride coming on board and with uncertainty over how he would fit in with the new staff, Mitchell declared for the NFL Draft and was taken in the fourth round by Miami. Mitchell backed up Dan Marino, played well after Marino's season-ending Achilles' tendon injury in the 1993 season, and parlayed that into a lucrative deal with the Detroit Lions. His best NFL season was in 1995 when he threw for 32 touchdowns and 4,338 yards. In his 11-year career, Mitchell threw for 95 touchdowns for four different teams—Miami, Detroit, Baltimore, and Cincinnati.

72 Bruce Woodbury

There aren't many relationships with the Utah football program that have lasted longer than the one Bruce Woodbury has enjoyed for almost all of his 64 years.

Woodbury, or Woody as he was affectionately known during his time at the U, figures he has been going to games since he was four years old, tagging along with his father who was a professor at the U's medical school.

Woody went to the U and was sports editor of the school newspaper, the *Daily Utah Chronicle*, during his senior year. Upon graduating in 1972, he became the assistant sports information director under Ron Fessenden, shedding the assistant tag six years later. In 2000, he became the athletic department's director of community relations, handing over the SID reins to Liz Abel.

"It was time to retire, and I'm not wishing to go back," said Woody, who along with his wife, Nancy, began serving a Mormon mission in San Diego in January 2010. "But it would be fun to be in the Pac-12 and experience all that. When I get back, I'll still help in the press box…. But yeah, to make a huge move like that, it would be fun to do that."

It's a far cry from Woody's first years on the job, which coincided with Utah's worst performances and the rise of a national power 40 miles to the south in Provo.

"The first few years I'm there, we won five games in three years," Woodbury said. "It was real hard. BYU was getting better, the Aggies were pretty good, and we struggled. We were getting our brains beat out. That was a tough time."

The action was much better away from the field, especially when it came to the old Skywriters Tour, a week-long tour of traveling beat writers, columnists, and sports information directors to each of the cities in the Western Athletic Conference. Young sports fans might have a hard time wrapping their minds around this, but there was a time when the daily newspaper wasn't just the most comprehensive source for sports—it was the only source. The Skywriters Tour gave newspapers an opportunity to devote a solid week to college football leading up to the start of the season, giving their writers the opportunity to get creative with their expense reports.

"I can't tell you who the writer was," Woodbury said of a Skywriters stop in Salt Lake City. "They really had a tough night the night before. One of the guys came up and told me, 'I just can't write my Utah preview. Could you write my Utah preview and send it to my newspaper?'

"He couldn't write his story, so I wrote it, put his byline on it, and telecopied his story to the newspaper."

Woody was just as adept at handling imbibing boosters as he was writers. According to John Mooney in *Disa and Data*, "The Tempe Quarterback Club is notoriously rowdy, and visiting press agents fear facing these guys, some of whom start drinking at noon and are prime hecklers by the time the evening speakers arrive.

"So Woodbury is just getting warmed up in his prepared talk when someone shouts, 'Is that a toupee you're wearing?'

"Without missing a word, Woodbury flipped off his hair piece and threw it at the heckler. It brought down the house and was such a hit Bruce thought about working it into his pregame sales pitches."

Another time, Woodbury told of an incident in Hawaii. Aloha Stadium is located right in the middle of a jumbled mass of freeways, and he had just a few minutes to make his flight back to the mainland. He knew of a way through one stadium gate that would get him to the terminal in about 10 minutes, but this time it was guarded by a giant of a man, one who told Woodbury he needed to take another route and wouldn't budge despite Woody's pleas to let him through.

"I saw a space between the curb and the barricade," Woodbury said. "I hit the gas, and the guy jumped on my hood spread eagle. I knew if I stopped now, I'd never make the plane.

"So I just kept going, got on the plane, and went back to Salt Lake. I was very concerned at the rental car counter, but nothing happened. That was in 1979, so I think I'm okay now because the statute of limitations has run out. But SIDs do stupid things."

Technology changed the duties of a sports information director, for better and worse. Woody recalled the days where he could spend a day touring the city's newspapers, television stations, and wire services. He could eat lunch with Mooney and other scribes at Lamb's Café. Today's sports media need merely a laptop computer or other wireless device, and he or she can get all the basics and then some.

"I couldn't do it anymore," Woodbury said. "It's a lot harder than it used to be."

The job responsibilities have changed, but the relationships built during his time at the U have remained, especially at rival schools. Dave Schulthess at BYU was one. "I learned a ton of stuff from him, and he's our chief rival," Woodbury said. "Always great. Love that man. He was awesome."

Somewhere across the Intermountain West, there's likely an SID or two saying the same thing about Woody.

73 Rivalry Rewind: Colorado

One of three long-ago conference rivals that Utah will battle again as it joins the Pac-12 Conference for the 2011 season is the Colorado Buffaloes. (Arizona State and Arizona are the others.) Known as the Frontiersmen for many of their years in the Rocky Mountain Conference, Colorado will take up the final spot on the schedule that had long been reserved for Brigham Young.

While it will take some time for this rivalry to reach the levels of the Holy War—and it probably won't ever become that bitter—fans on both sides will likely enjoy having another close geographic rival.

If history is to indeed repeat itself, this game will regularly be for the Pac-12 South crown and the right to play in the conference's new title game. After all, it was Utah and Colorado that routinely traded off spots at the top when both shared the same conference some 60 years ago. From the teams' first meeting in 1903 to the time Colorado left for the Big Eight conference after the 1947 season, the two teams had combined for 27 conference titles—14 by Colorado and 13 by Utah.

As conference mates, this rivalry was a dead heat at 21–21–2. When Colorado joined the Big Seven, it started gaining traction and pulling ahead of Utah, going 9–3–1. Of course, there have been some great historical games involving the two teams, both as conference and non-conference rivals.

1936: Colorado 31, Utah 7; 1937: Colorado 17, Utah 7. This game is memorable for the extraordinary efforts of one player, Byron "Whizzer" White. Before he became known as a U.S. Supreme Court justice and confidant of President John F.

Kennedy, White used two games against Utah to establish his legend as an American sports hero. In the first game, despite Colorado gaining just three first downs, White threw for one score and ran for another. However, he ran back three kicks for touchdowns (two punts, one kickoff) in a 31–7 victory. The following year, with Utah leading 7–3 heading into the final quarter, White ran back a punt 95 yards for one score and tacked on a 57-yard touchdown run in a 17–7 Colorado victory. This game alone nearly won White the Heisman Trophy, but he finished second to Clint Frank of Yale.

1961: Utah 21, Colorado 12. Colorado was undefeated and had already accepted an Orange Bowl berth when it hosted 5–3 Utah. The Buffs got on the board first, but Utah dominated thereafter in beating the Associated Press' No. 8 team and Big Eight champions. Marv Fleming, who would later play in five Super Bowls with Green Bay and Miami, had catches to set up Utah's first two touchdowns, and Doug Wasko had a pair of short touchdown runs. This would remain Utah's biggest victory over a ranked foe until 1973.

1922: Utah 3, Colorado 0. So you thought the 2003 Holy War was the only outright conference title decided by such a low score? Well, you'd still be right—this knock-down, drag-out happened in Utah's third game of the year, not its last. Neil Smith's 30-yard drop-kick field goal provided the game's only points, and his reward was being pulled from the game. That's how things often went in the era of limited substitution, and it would be the last time Utah played a 3–0 game for 81 years. The moral of the story is that 3–0 Utah victories mean a conference title is around the corner.

1943: Colorado 22, Utah 19. The youthful manpower needed to fight World War II depleted many a roster during this timeframe. Utah, under Coach Ike Armstrong, was no exception. In

1942, Utah lost for the first time ever to BYU. And in 1943, Utah recorded its only winless season. This game was as close to victory as Utah would get in going 0–7 while being outscored 297–38 and being shut out five times.

74 Louie Sakoda

The first major duty for any new college football head coach is to deliver a signing class. Since most coaches are hired in December or January, and National Signing Day is on the first Wednesday of February, time is of the essence. Verbal commitments need to have their pledges reaffirmed, and prospective pledges need to be sold on the mission and direction of the new staff. It can be a very chaotic time, especially for a first-year head coach.

Coach Kyle Whittingham's first class rates a smashing success. Not only did it feature NFL Draft picks in offensive lineman Zane Beadles and defensive backs Sean Smith and Brice McCain, it contained several notable contributors in quarterback Brett Ratliff, running back Darrell Mack, and defensive linemen Soli Lefiti and Kenape Eliapo.

But go back and look at the official press release announcing the Class of 2005 signees, however, and the one player who had the biggest impact and is arguably one of the most decorated players in school history isn't even listed.

Just exactly how did Louie Sakoda end up at Utah?

Special teams coach Jay Hill, who is responsible for recruiting the state of Utah but also has Las Vegas as his territory, attended a kicking camp held by one-time All-American kicker Chris Sailor in

Louie Sakoda went from being a recruiting afterthought to the most dependable and dominant kicking specialist in the history of Utah football. (AP Photo/ Lenny Ignelzi)

January 2005. By Sakoda's account, he had a great showing, and Hill told Louie that the two sides needed to keep in touch.

Sakoda's only true scholarship offer was from FCS Idaho State, but he didn't even make an official visit there. Utah wouldn't bring Sakoda on an official visit, but Sakoda was intrigued to the point where he paid his own way on an unofficial visit.

"I was bombarded by the coaches at Idaho State. For Utah, I wasn't as bombarded," Sakoda said. "I wasn't being offered a scholarship, but there was a promise: 'We need a guy, and you seem to be it.... We can't give you a scholarship now [because] we don't have enough for this year. But if you come and show enough during training camp, we will sign you as soon as we legally can.'"

As things turned out, a scholarship was available on Sakoda's first day at the 2005 training camp, and Utah offered it immediately.

"We had to go at it in a roundabout way, and I had to trust them and they had to trust me, but it ended up working out and that was [my recruiting] process," Sakoda said.

Sakoda handled the punting and kickoff duties as a true freshman in 2005, but in 2006 he established himself as a true weapon as Utah finished first nationally in net punting. This was easily Sakoda's best year statistically as a punter, yet he inexplicably wasn't a finalist for the Ray Guy Award, which is given to the nation's best punter. Sakoda added more to his plate by handling the placekicking duties, although Ben Vroman—who walked on at Utah a week after Sakoda arrived and eventually earned a scholarship of his own—took over the kickoff duties.

"I don't think it was the lack of due diligence [on the voters' part], but it was highly political, just like a lot of these awards are," Sakoda said. "To go through that season and to have those stats... and not even make it into the top three was more frustrating.

"At the same time, at the end of the day, if your performance can statistically show that you help your team win, that's really what you're there to do."

There is no question Sakoda did just that while at Utah. In 2006, his field goal on the final play of the game beat Air Force 17–14 and guaranteed Utah a bowl invitation. In the bowl game against Tulsa, he kicked four field goals and had three punts that averaged 47.3 yards. Against TCU, Sakoda placed a staggering seven of nine punts inside the 20-yard line, single-handedly keeping the nationally ranked Frogs and their offense on their heels all game long as Utah registered a 20–6 win.

Sakoda remained a solid punter after the 2006 season, but he became an even bigger weapon in the kicking game. In 2007, he made 87 percent of his field goals, and in 2008 he raised his success rate to 91.7 percent by making 22-of-24 field goals and 56-of-57 extra points. His 122 points are a single-season school record, and he was voted Utah's first unanimous All-American, as well as being both a Guy and Lou Groza Award finalist. And it's probably redundant to add that he was also a three-time Mountain West Conference Special Teams Player of the Year.

75 Wayne Howard

The end of a coach's tenure at any school is often not a pretty sight. But at least the split has an explanation or answer and is rarely unexpected. Ambitious coaches take jobs at schools they feel are more suited to their career paths, like Urban Meyer and Cactus Jack Curtice did by going to Florida and Stanford, respectively. Others are fired for failure to meet expectations, such as Chuck Stobart, Tom Lovat, and Ron McBride, to name a few.

And then there's the saga of Wayne Howard, who wasn't fired for lack of performance. All Howard did in his final year in Salt Lake City was lead the Utes to an 8–2–1 record, and only a late-season 7–7 tie against New Mexico kept Utah from the unthinkable for that era—namely entering the Holy War with a piece of the WAC crown in its hands.

So that must have been good enough for Howard to be enticed by a bigger opportunity at a more prominent school, right? Again, that was not the case. When Howard walked off the Cougar Stadium turf after a 56–28 defeat in the 1981 Holy War, it ended up being the final game he coached in at any level.

A little more than a year later and some 2,000 miles to the east, Philadelphia Eagles head coach Dick Vermeil (who actually coached against Utah in two games when he was UCLA's head coach in the 1970s) unexpectedly stepped down just two years after leading the Eagles to the Super Bowl. Vermeil cited burnout, an interesting term for the times to describe the burdens of coaching pro football. In psychological terms, "burnout" is defined as long-term exhaustion coupled with diminished interest.

Were the demands of coaching football really that great? Vermeil's departure from the game for 15 years—he would return to coach the St. Louis Rams in 1997 and lead that franchise to its first Super Bowl title after the 1999 season—certainly gave people interested in the game a reason to think about and chronicle those demands. Vermeil wasn't the last coach to succumb to the demands of coaching, but he probably wasn't the first, either.

To this day, Howard maintains he wasn't pushed out at Utah. Never mind that he couldn't have been technically fired since he never worked under a contract during his entire five-year stint with the Utes.

"I said I would stay for five years, and [athletic director] Arnie Ferrin said he'd keep me for five years," Howard said from his home in Myrtle Beach, South Carolina. "When my five years were up…I thought I left the program a lot better than it was when I came. There was nothing sinister or anything like that—I got along very well with the administration. Ferrin and [Vice-President for University Relations] R.J. Snow, they were the best I could hope to work for."

The strongest physical evidence Howard gives in explaining his decision to simply walk away from the game came during the 1980 season at Wyoming. Howard passed out during that game, and he suffered headaches as a result of that fainting spell for some six to eight months after the fact. Howard faced some brutal attacks on his character after his first season when he blistered BYU for putting its starting quarterback back in the game after the outcome had long been decided in an attempt to set an NCAA record.

"The hatred between BYU and Utah is nothing compared to what it will be," Howard said afterward. "It will be a crusade to beat BYU from now on."

"The things I said, I didn't do [it] on purpose to get people upset, but a crusade? I guess that's a bit of a religious word, so I can see why people might feel that way," Howard said.

Salt Lake Tribune sports writer John Mooney came to Howard's defense, and although he didn't absolve Howard for his remarks, he said this about Howard's critics: "If I didn't know the Righteous Brothers were a singing duo, I'd swear it was a BYU group taking upon itself to censure Coach Wayne Howard for his remarks last week."

Howard had a bit of a last laugh the following year as Utah came back from a 22–0 deficit to beat BYU 23–22. And with his final season, his short-term future at Utah was secure. So why walk away?

"Without a doubt, I was too emotional to just maintain my coaching duties day by day," Howard said. "I got excited at times, to say the least. I don't know if it was burnout. It could be."

Shortly after announcing his intention to leave Utah, Howard interviewed for the California vacancy, one that was ultimately filled by Joe Kapp, a Bears alum.

But even if he had been offered the job, Howard said, "I don't know if I would have taken it." Today, he has no regrets about how his career ended.

"There are some things you miss—the camaraderie you have with your coaches, the relationships you have with your players, the challenge of winning and losing," Howard said. "You think about those things, but not with regret. You don't get a chance to do many other things in life. I was looking to try something new."

Howard went into real estate—his specialty was building apartment complexes—and taught at Long Beach City College before retiring 19 years ago and moving to South Carolina with his wife, June. He still follows the Utes and maintains no ill will toward his former program.

"I like to watch Utah games on TV when we can get them," Howard said, "but I follow Ron McBride a lot closer at Weber State. And I root for Utah very strongly against BYU."

76 The Andersons

It's only fitting in a program filled with so many major contributions from brothers that arguably two of Utah's greatest running backs share not only the same last name but physique, punishing running style, and NFL bloodlines.

But for the umpteenth-million time, Jamal and Mike Anderson are *not* related. Still, even after you learn more about their contributions at the pro and college levels, as well as their vagabond-like journeys to stardom in Salt Lake City and eventually in the NFL, shouldn't it be possible that they are at least distant cousins of some kind?

Jamal Anderson didn't grow up privileged, but he grew up around fame. His father, James—a one-time member of the police department in Newark, New Jersey—was a bodyguard for Muhammad Ali from 1973 until the fighter's career neared an end in 1980. After moving to Southern California, James established his own security firm and claimed Sugar Ray Leonard, Richard Pryor, Mike Tyson, and Donna Summer among his list of clients.

Notoriety eventually came for Jamal, but it was never easy. As a junior college transfer from Moorpark Community College, he had to fight for carries in a crowded Utah backfield that featured Keith Williams and Pierre Jones—two backs with extensive experience at Utah. But in 1993, the backfield was all Jamal's, and he responded with a 958-yard season. His breakout game came against San Diego State and Marshall Faulk, with a career-high 23 carries for 156 yards and three touchdowns.

"Man, good job. Good job," Faulk told Anderson after the game.

Although Jamal outplayed the Heisman finalist in that game, NFL scouts weren't as enamored. When he was told he could expect to be a middle-round pick on draft day, Anderson's mood darkened as he dropped deeper in the draft. Finally, in the seventh round, the Atlanta Falcons called his name. It couldn't have been a worse fit—the Falcons already had Craig "Ironhead" Hayward in the backfield, and the run-and-shoot offense employed by coach June Jones rarely used any two-back sets.

But Jamal managed to make the team, and he became a starter in his third season, rushing for 1,055 yards—the first of four 1,000-yard seasons. After Jones was fired and replaced by Dan Reeves, Anderson's workload grew even more. His 1998 season was one of the best in NFL history—an NFL-record 410 carries, plus 1,846 yards and 14 rushing touchdowns. Even better, the Falcons made the Super Bowl but lost to John Elway and Denver.

A season-ending knee injury early in the 1999 season started Jamal's decline in productivity, although he would rush for 1,024 yards in 2000, and another injury in 2001 finished his career. Today, Anderson's engaging personality is on display as a commentator in the sports media world.

At least Jamal had a background in athletics. Mike Anderson didn't even play sports during his high school days in Fairfield,

South Carolina. Instead he played in the school band. It wasn't until he enlisted in the Marines that he joined organized competitive sports for the first time, playing for the 11th Marine Regiment team at Camp Pendleton outside San Diego. A coach from Mt. San Jacinto College spotted Anderson and convinced him to enroll at and play for the school.

Success came quickly for Mike at every level thereafter. He rushed for more than 3,000 yards at Mt. San Jacinto, and he burst on the scene at Utah with 1,173 yards in 1998. Injuries forced him to miss two games the following year, but he still managed to finish with 977 yards in the regular season. He then exploded for a school-record 254 yards in the Las Vegas Bowl as Utah defeated Fresno State.

Even without that game (official statistics did not recognize bowl game performances until 2002), Anderson remains the only Utah running back to average more than 100 yards per game for his career at 102.4.

Mike's biggest drawback as he entered the NFL Draft was his age. With his service in the Marines and four years of college football, Anderson was just two weeks shy of his 27th birthday when he took the field for the Denver Broncos, who selected him in the sixth round. Injuries thrust him into the lineup in Week 2, and Anderson responded with a 31-carry, 131-yard, two-touchdown performance in a victory against Atlanta.

In Week 13 against New Orleans, Anderson set a single-game rushing record for rookies (since broken) with 251 yards and four touchdowns on 37 carries. For the season, Anderson gained 1,487 yards and 15 touchdowns on 297 carries—all career highs. *USA Today* named him NFL Rookie of the Year, while the league voted him NFL Offensive Rookie of the Year.

Like Jamal, injuries took their toll on Mike too soon for him to have a truly great NFL career, although he did rush for 1,014 yards with Baltimore in the 2005 season at the age of 32.

77 Crazy Eights: How Utah Lost the 1994 WAC Title

As the 1994 season stretched into November, everyone knew Utah was on the verge of a special season. Ranked in *Sports Illustrated's* Top 25, the Utes rapidly climbed in the polls to No. 8 in the Associated Press poll. Wins over Oregon (which stormed through the Pac-10 en route to its first Rose Bowl since 1958) and unbeaten Colorado State gave the Utes validity on the national scene.

But at 8–0, there was some business to take care of in road trips to New Mexico—a team that defeated Utah in Salt Lake City the year before—and Air Force, always a nemesis for Utah teams, which claimed just one victory in program history in Colorado Springs.

In the span of eight quarters, the Utes first lost any claim of being included in talk of national title contenders, then lost almost all hope of winning a conference title. The only consolation prize for Utah players was watching the opposing team's fans rip down the goal posts—a sign of some kind that defeating Utah was worthy of such a raucous celebration.

"The hopes of the undefeated season, the Holiday Bowl, it was all gone," said free safety Harold Lusk. "There are certain games in life that you never forget, and those are two of the three—New Mexico, Air Force, and a Central Coast Section semifinal game when I was in high school at Monterey High."

Against New Mexico, Utah raced out to a 21–3 halftime lead. Charlie Brown scored a pair of touchdowns, and freshman wideout Kevin Dyson scored on a 56-yard touchdown pass from Mike McCoy.

And that was it for the Utah offense. It ran just eight plays in the third quarter, and the fourth quarter ended with a punt, a fumble by Rob Hamilton, and a missed 29-yard field goal by Dan Pulsipher with 4:04 left in the game—a huge break for the Lobos as they could now win with just a field goal.

The defense failed to deliver a knockout blow, although it did have its chances. Lusk tried advancing a fumble instead of falling on it, and the Lobos turned that miscue into a field goal. Cornerback Kareem Leary had a pick-six called back because of a pass interference penalty on strong safety Mark Rexford.

All of those missed opportunities could have been secondary had Utah stopped New Mexico on fourth-and-3 from its own 26. But a missed tackle by Keith Hamilton on Gavin Pearlman resulted in a 56-yard gain to the Utah 17.

Utah's boat was taking on way too much water now, and Nathan Vail's 32-yard field goal with as many seconds left won it.

"We didn't make the plays, plain and simple," McCoy said after the game. "It was nothing they did. We have no excuses. Championship football teams find a way to win these games."

"That New Mexico game, I remember Coach McBride saying we didn't practice like we should in practice. He said we lost focus," Lusk said. "It was devastating, but not as devastating as the Air Force game. We went down there for business. Walkthroughs were good, and it just seemed like we let it slip away."

Again, Utah jumped out to a big lead, scoring on its first three possessions for a 17–0 lead. But then Beau Morgan, making just his second start of what turned out to be an illustrious career for the Academy, got the option rolling. And Utah couldn't stop it.

"He started to become 'ungettable,'" Lusk said. "We had worked on option, and all of a sudden everything we were doing wasn't working. We missed tackles. Coach McBride never singled out the offense or defense, but we knew the defense had not performed the way it should have."

Air Force cut the lead to a touchdown by halftime, then owned the third quarter with a pair of scoring drives to take its first lead.

Utah tied the game right before quarter's end on a Brown catch-and-run out of the backfield, but Air Force regained the lead with a field goal.

With 1:20 left in the game, Air Force appeared to put the game away with a touchdown by Jake Malloy to go up by nine. But Utah blocked the extra point and Leary ran it back for two points to keep Utah within a touchdown of tying the game. Unfortunately Utah could get no further than its own 49, and McCoy was intercepted on fourth down to end the game.

For the second straight week, Utah felt jobbed by the officials. New Mexico was aided by a two-point conversion pass that should have been ruled with the receiver out of bounds, and Air Force was the beneficiary of at least two good spots as well as an apparent fumble that was ruled an incomplete pass.

"It seems like it's been ragged against us since the Colorado State game," wide receiver Deron Claiborne said. "They're not for us, that's for sure."

Utah would get off the couch the following week against BYU with its second straight 34–31 victory, but later in the day, Colorado State would stage a comeback of its own, coming back from 21 points down to defeat Fresno State 44–42 to earn its first WAC crown since joining the league in 1968.

78 Chuck Stobart

Urban Meyer wasn't the first head coach hired by Utah directly from the Mid-American Conference. After Wayne Howard's sudden resignation after the 1981 season, Utah athletic director Arnie Ferrin moved quickly to replace him, hiring University of

Toledo coach Chuck Stobart on December 13, 1981—just more than three weeks after the Utes concluded their season with yet another Holy War thrashing at the hands of BYU.

Thus began the Tough Luck Chuck Era at Utah. Stobart had experienced decent success at Toledo—his final team went 9–3, won the MAC, and defeated San Jose State in the California Bowl 27–25. That wasn't the last close game Stobart won as a head coach; it just seemed that way for Utah fans, who too often saw their team on the wrong end of a close game.

Many younger Ute fans would argue that Ron McBride is Utah's patron saint for close losses. Taken in context, Stobart made McBride look like Knute Rockne. Stobart's three-year mark at Utah was 16–17–1. In his final year, Utah went 6–5–1 after a pair of 5–6 seasons. Improvement, right? Not in the eyes of Ferrin, who didn't fire Stobart but told him he'd be better off looking for work elsewhere because Utah was going to shop around for a new head coach. If both sides failed in their efforts, it was quite possible Utah would welcome back Stobart for a fourth year.

Instead, Utah hired Jim Fassel, and Stobart began a four-year odyssey as an offensive coordinator at three different schools before becoming a head coach for the third and final time at Memphis. Stobart helped the Tigers score one of the program's biggest wins with a 24–10 upset of No. 16 Southern California to start the 1991 season, but he was fired after a six-year record of 29–36–1 despite winning records his last three years.

"Maybe my best game [as a head coach]," Stobart said of the Southern California game some 20 years after the fact.

There are no such victories at Utah—only a never-ending streak of close losses and agonizing finishes.

In 1982, Stobart's first season, Utah went 5–6 with all four of its Western Athletic Conference games decided by less than five points—three of them on the road. Two of those losses were at Hawaii and Wyoming, arguably among the toughest road trips the

WAC could offer. With non-conference games at Arizona State and Texas, it was one of the most ambitious schedules the Utes had ever played. And even Utah looked respectable in those games, losing by 13 and 9 points to a pair of teams that combined to go 19–5 that season.

Optimism took a hit in 1983. The Utes remained stagnant, going 5–6 with two conference losses by two and three points. Again, both were on the road, specifically to Colorado State and Air Force. The CSU loss was particularly galling, since the Rams entered the game 0–4 and had scored just 33 points in four games—two less than they scored against Utah in victory. Games for the Beehive Boot were dreary—a four-point loss to Utah State followed a week later by a 55–7 alley whipping at the hands of BYU. It was surpassed only by a 56–6 beat down in 1980 as the worst Holy War loss in school history.

The 1984 season was outright cruel to Utah. While BYU was embarking on its greatest year in school history with a national championship, Utah remained stuck in neutral. Sure, the Utes posted a 6–5–1 mark, but those five losses were by a combined total of 28 points…29 points if you throw in the tie to San Diego State.

And those losses weren't to patsies. Tennessee went 7–4–1 and defeated Utah by six. Washington State went 6–5 and beat Utah by two. Wyoming and Hawaii again proved to be road stumbling blocks, as Utah lost by seven and three points, respectively. The Wyoming game was a crusher; Utah was in chip-shot field-goal range only to have quarterback Mark Stephens fumble the ball and watch Wyoming race 80-plus yards for a touchdown in the closing seconds of the game.

Even BYU struggled to put Utah away, winning 24–14 in Salt Lake City. And Utah's consolation prize? Watching BYU go to No. 1 in the polls after that game.

Stobart's record in games decided by seven points or less was 2–11–1. In games decided by more than a touchdown, the Utes were 14–6, and those six losses were to teams with a combined record of 56–15–1. Those can be justified and understood.

Repeatedly losing close games can't. It's what gets coaches fired.

Brad Rock of the *Deseret News* summed up the entire Stobart tenure as well as anyone after Utah's 20–17 loss in Honolulu, the Utes' 11th consecutive road loss.

"Since Stobart took over almost three years ago, it has been the same story of woe, just different towns as the stage. A non-stop procession of almost in the close ones; of freak plays, bonehead plays, interceptions, or penalties, fumbles and decisions that went sour; of normal human mistakes that under the glare of close games take on far more significance than they should."

That's a more elaborate way of saying Stobart was snakebitten.

79 Visit the Charlie Monfort Family Hall of Champions

The first thing Utah fans need to know about the Charlie Monfort Hall of Champions is that it is not open to the public since it's largely used to show off to recruits the legacy left behind by select Utah players and teams. So if you get an invitation, don't turn it down. You'll be in and out in about 30 minutes, but you'll experience a lifetime of Utah football memories.

At the same time, anyone can go up to the front wall made out of glass and peer inside—you'll see it to your left as you approach the front doors of the Dee Glen Smith Athletic Center, which is Ground Zero for the Utah football program. It is right across the street from the Guardsman Way tailgate lot and just a short walk from Rice-Eccles Stadium.

Charlie Monfort

Even though most people outside of Utah who recognize Charlie Monfort know him as the owner of the Colorado Rockies, Monfort wasn't always a baseball guy. "I really wasn't a baseball fan, I was more of a football fan," Monfort said. "I grew up in the beef business, that's our background—our grandparents and parents—so that's where I thought I would be."

The beef business was a family-owned operation—Monfort of Colorado—a meat packing and distribution firm that was sold to ConAgra Foods in 1987. Four years later, Charlie and his brother, Dick, were part of a group that brought Major League Baseball to Denver, with Charlie becoming chairman and CEO of the club in 2003. In 2005, the brothers became the team's primary owners.

The walls feature a field-level, 270-degree view of Rice-Eccles Stadium during the Utes' game against Colorado State in 2008. Because of the glass that makes up the front of the building, the view of the North End Zone isn't included and keeps it from being a full 360-degree view. But if you stand in the middle of the room, it's almost as if your vantage point is from the 50-yard line, right on the middle of the field.

The best parts of the Hall are the video highlights of the players whose jerseys hang prominently on the south wall of the building. The jersey numbers and names of 26 longtime greats are there for everyone to see. Three more players—Marvin Jonas, Earl "Powerhouse" Pomeroy, and Wes Watkins—have no numbers affixed to their jerseys.

Near the base of the wall is a computer that allows visitors to select highlights for any of the players whose jerseys are on the wall. It's unfortunate, but understandable, that video highlights don't exist for players like Roy Jefferson and Lee Grosscup, but there are plenty of great videos from the pre-YouTube generation of players like Mike McCoy and Bryan Rowley. The best video, however, is of Erroll Tucker and his numerous punt and kick returns for touch-downs, two of which came in epic snow games against UTEP and BYU in Tucker's illustrious senior year of 1985.

Finish watching the videos and look at the various artifacts that celebrate Utah's history—from the trophy for the 1928 Rocky Mountain Conference championship to the Fiesta and Sugar Bowl trophies for Utah's two BCS bowl triumphs. There is a section that features the previous season's star players and displays honoring former Ute greats who starred in the NFL.

It is the closest thing Utah football has for a shrine. If given the opportunity to take a look inside, don't pass it up.

80 Steve Smith

Ron McBride wants Utah fans to know they were right. He should have gotten Stevonne "Steve" Smith more involved with the offense during his two years at Utah.

"We were fairly conservative offensively. The offense was built around the tailback and play action. After McCoy left, we weren't as strong at the quarterback position. But we had great tailbacks and good play-action game. We weren't a wide-open offense. We tried to isolate Steve and get the ball to him, but looking back, we probably should have gotten him the ball more."

Getting the ball to Smith almost always meant something good happened. Of his 78 career receptions, 12 went for touchdowns. His career 20.6 yards per catch edges Steve Odom for the best mark in program history.

He was also a dynamic punt returner, holding school records for punt-return yardage in a game and season. Only LaVon

Edwards had more punt-return yardage in his Utah career than Smith, and his four career punt-return touchdowns are matched only by Odom. Smith is also the only Ute to return two punts for touchdowns in a single game, a feat set against New Mexico in the 1999 season.

Prior to playing at Utah, Smith played at Santa Monica City College, where the wide receiver opposite him was none other than Chad Johnson, now known as Chad Ochocinco. One can only imagine the touchdown celebrations that duo produced, but Smith was encouraged by head coach Robert Taylor to play it low-key after scoring. "They put the cuffs on us," Smith said.

At 5'9" Smith didn't have the ideal size sought after for receivers in the NFL. But he clocked a 4.4 40-yard dash time at the NFL Combine and registered a vertical leap of 38.5 inches. Carolina liked what it saw in Smith and took him in the third round of the 2001 NFL Draft.

Used primarily on special teams as a rookie, Smith immediately made an impact with his new team. He became the first rookie chosen to the Pro Bowl as a special teams player in nearly a decade, returning three kicks (two kickoffs, one punt) for touchdowns. Gradually, his role in the offense grew from 10 receptions as a rookie to 54 and eventually 88 in 2003 when the Panthers made the Super Bowl. Smith caught a touchdown pass in that game, a 32–29 loss to New England.

Smith's 2004 season was cut short with a knee injury he sustained in the season opener, but he roared back in 2005 with one of the greatest single-season efforts ever by a wideout, leading the NFL in catches, yards, and touchdowns. He is just one of three players since the NFL's merger with the AFL in 1970 to attain that feat, joining Jerry Rice and Sterling Sharpe.

Three more 1,000-yard seasons followed before Smith came up short in 2009, playing only 15 games and gaining 982 yards. The 2010 season was his least productive since his rookie year;

he caught just 46 passes for 554 yards and two touchdowns as Carolina started four different quarterbacks and skidded to an NFL-worst 2–14 mark.

In 2008, Smith and his wife, Angie, endeared themselves even more to the football program with a $250,000 gift toward an endowed scholarship carrying his name at his alma mater. The first scholarship player to benefit from this gift was David Reed, now with the Baltimore Ravens and, like Smith, an exceptional kick returner in his rookie season.

81 Mac Speedie

The placement of this entry behind Steve Smith is not coincidental. While Smith represents Utah's best hope at gaining a second inductee into the Pro Football Hall of Fame, Speedie held that distinction until Smith started making his mark in the NFL. And both players are the only former Utah players to catch a touchdown pass in an NFL Championship Game.

Speedie was a Hall of Fame finalist in the early 1970s, and as recently as 1983, he was a senior nominee. That he made it that far given his early health obstacles was a miracle. As a young boy, Speedie wore braces on his legs due to a bone deficiency disease. His left leg was slightly shorter than his right, but this didn't deter Speedie, who had "such a backlog of athletic ambition that I wanted to play football, basketball, and track all at one time."

Speedie excelled on the gridiron and at track, tying a national record in the 120-meter hurdles while at South High School in Salt Lake City. He starred in both sports while at Utah and was taken in the 15th round of the 1942 NFL Draft by the Detroit Lions. But World War II called, and like so many athletes of his era, Speedie's debut as a pro player was delayed.

During the war, Speedie played with his base team in Fort Warren, Texas. Another military team, the Great Lakes Navy squad, was coached by none other than legendary NFL coach Paul Brown. Brown convinced Speedie to sign with the Cleveland Browns of the old All-America Football Conference, which was a charter member of the new league.

That started Speedie's run as one of the top receivers in all of football. As a rookie, Speedie showed what he was made of by scoring seven touchdowns on just 24 receptions. Over the next three years, with another Hall of Fame quarterback in Otto Graham throwing to him, Speedie led the AAFC in receptions. And in two of those years, Speedie was the league leader in receiving yards.

The AAFC was no match for the Browns, who went 52–4–3 in the league's short history and at one point won 18 straight games while going unbeaten in 29 straight. The NFL was forced to accept the league as a peer, and the two leagues made peace after the 1949 season when Cleveland, San Francisco, and Baltimore were admitted into the NFL.

The Browns—and Speedie—quickly made their mark in their new league, winning the NFL championship in 1950 and making it to the league's title game the next five years. Speedie led the NFL in receptions in 1952, his last year in the NFL.

But it wasn't his last year in professional football, and Speedie's decision to jump to the Canadian Football League is what he believed cost him a spot in the Pro Football Hall of Fame. The personalities of Paul Brown and Speedie clashed consistently, and Speedie viewed going to Canada as a way to extend his career and release himself from Brown's taskmaster ways.

"I was overlooked, and a lot of it was Paul Brown," Speedie told the *Los Angeles Times* in 1991. "He told me when I jumped leagues that he was going to get even with me. There was a time when it bothered me, but that was years and years ago. It really isn't important anymore."

Speedie was the first of the "Nine Old Men," the Browns' stars of both the AAFC and NFL, to break from the team. Of the other nine, Graham, Marion Motley, Lou Groza, Bill Willis, and Dante Lavelli have been enshrined in Canton. At least one of his former teammates believes Speedie should be part of that group, as well.

"I've written letters for years saying that Mac should be in the Hall of Fame," Lavelli said. "I can't understand it."

"Speedie should be in the Hall of Fame," said former Utah coach Mike Giddings, who worked with Speedie when both men were part of the Denver Broncos organization in the 1970s. "When you referred to the Browns' receivers back then, it was Speedie and Lavelli, not Lavelli and Speedie. Brown never forgave Speedie for going to Canada, but anyone who saw that era will tell you Speedie was one of the great receivers to play in the NFL…and one of the best guys."

Speedie hasn't been forgotten in Utah, where he is a member of the Utah Sports Hall of Fame and the Crimson Club Hall of Fame. Whether Canton comes calling or not, it will be too late for Speedie to enjoy the accomplishment since he died at the age of 73 in 1993.

82 Erroll Tucker

For those who blaze trails, it's always nice when those who follow them take time to pay tribute to those who preceded them. To get an idea of the impact Erroll Tucker had as a kick-return specialist and defensive back at Utah during his senior year in 1985, read what Steve Smith had to say about the Crimson Club Hall of Famer:

"Twenty-four-point-three yards per (punt) return," said Smith, reciting Tucker's numbers. "Three punt returns [for touchdowns] in the same season, three interceptions, two kickoff returns. That man was doin' work. You can't even compare me with him. When you write an essay, you want to write about Erroll Tucker. Somewhere at the conclusion you can include my name."

Tucker could have gone just about anywhere coming out of Long Beach City College after the 1983 season. Ohio State was the biggest program to have a piece of Tucker's ear, but Utah put Tucker's mother a lot closer to see her son play. So Tucker headed off to Salt Lake City where he didn't take long to establish himself as one of the premier kick returners in the country, finishing 8th and 14th nationally in punt and kickoff returns, respectively. In Utah's first game against a Division I-A opponent, Tucker returned one kickoff 72 yards to set up one score while returning a punt 69 yards for a score in a 42–40 loss to Washington State.

The following year, Tucker became the first player to lead the nation in kickoff and punt-return average in the same year—a distinction he still holds today. One Tucker first that has since been matched is being the first player to record multiple touchdown returns off punts, kickoffs, and interceptions in the same season.

Tucker was more than a specialist—he was also an All–Western Athletic Conference defensive back who intercepted six passes in his senior year.

Tucker appeared destined for a lengthy NFL career when he was drafted in the fifth round by the Pittsburgh Steelers in the 1986 NFL Draft. Quickly, Tucker showed off his stuff, returning a kickoff 98 yards for a score against Washington in just his second preseason game. But in the preseason finale against the Giants, those assumptions were grounded.

"Before I knew it, I was down," Tucker said of the moment when one of his own players was blocked into him on a punt return. "I saw Giants Stadium spinning in circles when the pain set in. I broke the fibular [calf] bone right above the ankle."

This turned out to be more than a bad break to Tucker's frame—it was an injury that brought him back to a level playing field in terms of opposing coverage units. Although the bone healed thanks to a steel rod, the sensation in Tucker's foot never felt right. Another surgery loosened the tendons to his ankle, but the surgeries and ensuing rehabilitation cost Tucker the 1986–87 seasons.

As is typical of life in the NFL, the Steelers couldn't afford to keep waiting on Tucker's health to return, so they waived him. Meanwhile, the exercise room became Tucker's playing field, and he threw himself into his rehabilitation efforts. As the 1988 NFL season drew close, Tucker tried out for several teams, even though by his own admission he was only at 85 percent. "If you're at 85 percent, we'll take you," Buffalo responded.

He played with the Bills in 1988–89 but was waived midway through his final season before hooking up with New England for the remainder of the 1989 season. That was the end of his NFL career, but Tucker soldiered on in the World League with Orlando, leading that circuit in punt returns before winning a Grey Cup with Calgary in the Canadian Football League.

Today, Tucker is a physical therapist in Los Alamitos, California, and helps others heal like so many other doctors did with him in his NFL career.

"Going through what I went through was God's gift. With my surgery and my injury, I really have something to give back to others," Tucker said. "That's what prompted me to go into rehab."

83 Dynasty Architect II: Pokey Allen

The rivalry that exists between the Utah and Boise State programs is a recent one. Although Boise State has won the last four meetings of consequence since the Broncos joined the Division I-A/FBS ranks in the 1990s, it's a rivalry largely manufactured by the fans.

Both sides view their team as the preeminent non-BCS program of the 2000s, and as a result, plenty of spite exists toward the other program. With the backing of ESPN and its television contract with the WAC, Utah fans believe Boise State has been undeservingly bestowed the title of "BCS Buster," and a faction of Boise State fans remain puzzled over Utah's invitation to the Pac-10 while the Broncos remain without an invitation to a power conference.

The two teams had three games remaining in a four-game series that began in the 2006 season, games that ultimately were canceled after Utah's invitation to join what is now the Pac-12 Conference, leading to more claims from Boise fans that Utah was ducking the Broncos.

It's too bad Ernest "Pokey" Allen isn't around today to comment about the status both programs have achieved. As a quarterback and defensive back during his collegiate playing days, Allen was selected MVP of the 1964 Liberty Bowl, which Utah won by defeating West Virginia. Allen rushed for one score and intercepted a pass in that game. Not bad for a kid from Missoula, Montana, who almost went to Utah State because he wasn't sure there would be any playing time for him in Salt Lake City. After his playing days at Utah, Allen played in the Canadian Football League for three years.

He remained in Canada for nine years thereafter, all with Simon Fraser University in British Columbia. He returned to the States for an assistant's job at Montana with a one-year stop at Eastern Washington. His first taste of major college football since his playing days came next at Cal, where he was a defensive back coach and established ties with offensive guru Al Borges, who would later assist him at Boise State before directing successful offenses at several top programs.

Allen's first head coaching job came at Portland State where he went 63–26–2 with five appearances in the Division II playoffs. In his last season, his future bosses got a good look at him when he led his Vikings to a 52–26 victory against Boise State, which hired Allen's entire staff away from PSU.

He won quickly with his new school, and the Broncos reached the national title game under his watch in his second year in 1994, losing to Youngstown State and future Ohio State coach Jim Tressel.

For most coaches, such a season would generally signal the start to new opportunities at bigger schools, often a life-changing event. Two days after that loss, a true life-changing event occurred when Allen was diagnosed with rhabdomyosarcoma, a rare and potentially fatal form of muscle cancer. It cast a cloud on all of that season's accomplishments, including Boise State's decision in October to accept an invitation to the Big West Conference and transition to the Division I-A level.

Allen fought through the 1995 season but took a leave of absence after the season. In Boise's first season, when it struggled to a 1–9 start in its first season of I-A competition, Allen returned for two games—a 33–32 victory against New Mexico State, and a 64–19 loss to Idaho. Three weeks later, Allen was dead at the age of 53.

Allen got Boise in the door of major college football, and it has been all smooth sledding ever since for Boise State, which has hired accomplished coaches—Houston Nutt, Dirk Koetter, and Dan Hawkins—and watched them leave for more money and opportunity at other schools. Under Chris Peterson, the Broncos consistently are near the top of the polls and have bullied their way into the conversation when it comes to national title contenders.

And it all started with a very sick man making a brave return to the sidelines, helping salvage a positive memory from a very difficult first season in Division I-A football.

84 Who Are These Guys? Old-School Utah Coaches

Ike Armstrong turned Utah into a regional power during his Utah tenure as head coach from 1925–49. But prior to Armstrong's arrival from Drake University, Utah had already had some very accomplished coaches. One of them was a star at one of college football's first traditional powers, while another used his success at Utah to gain a job with USC. Take that, Urban Meyer!

Harvey Holmes, 1900–03: Career Utah record 16–9–1. Holmes' lasting contribution to the Utah football program was his authoring the words and selecting the music for the Utah Man fight song. On the field, he wasn't half bad, first as a tackle for the University of Wisconsin, then as the first official head coach at Utah before stints at USC (where he also coached the men's track team) and Idaho State. Overall, his coaching record was 62–24–4. He died in Salt Lake City on May 11, 1948—the same day he was to receive a lifetime pass to U athletic events in a ceremony preceding Utah's baseball game against BYU.

Joe Maddock, 1904–09: Career Utah record 36–9–1. Arguably the holder of the greatest playing career among Utah head

Remember These Guys?

Pat Degnan and Dan Hagemann: There was very little to cheer about from 1974–76, when Utah went 5–28 and was one of the worst teams in the nation. In that last year, however, Degnan and Hagemann tossed three of the longest touchdown passes in school history, topped by Hagemann's school-record 98-yarder to Jack Steptoe against New Mexico. The following week, Degnan came on in relief and his 79-yard strike to Mike Cordy rallied Utah past Arizona State for the Utes' first win in Tempe in a decade. Degnan also had a 72-yard scoring pass to Steve Peake against Rice. There have been 37 touchdown passes of 70 or more yards in Utah history, yet three of them came in a year in which Utah went 3–8.

Tony Lindsay: Since freshmen became eligible for the 1973 season, Lindsay is the sole owner of a feat that only one other Utah player on offense has come close to matching. As the team's leading rusher from 1977–80, Lindsay is the only player to lead his team in the same major offensive statistic four times. Countless rushers, passers, and receivers have led the team in their respective category in two seasons, but receiver Bryan Rowley (1990–91, 1993) is the only other Utes player to attain this feat three times since freshmen became eligible. On defense, Mike Bailey (1976–78), Bill Gompf (1979–81), and Mark Blosch (1982–84) each led the U. in tackles in three seasons.

Joe Clausi: How could Utah's worst defensive team in history produce such a dominant record-holder? Clausi's 28 tackles for loss in the 1989 season are seven more than the second-best mark set by Jimmy Bellamy in 1991. Utah's defense gave up a school-record 6,411 yards that year, but without Clausi's 120 yards in losses—the No. 2 single-season mark—it would have been even worse. And if Clausi isn't a household name in your memories of Utah football, consider he's not even the most recognized Utah athlete in his own home—that honor goes to his wife, Utah gymnast and 1988 Olympian, Missy Marlowe.

Eric Jacobson: Maybe Jacobson fits the old football adage that says when your leading tackler is a defensive back that it's not a good indicator of overall defensive strength. Still, Jacobson holds the top two single-season marks for unassisted tackles, set in 1987–88, as well as the career mark of 207. But Jacobson also excelled at the big play, with single-season and career marks for recovered fumbles. His three interceptions against Hawaii in 1987 is one short of Frank Nelson's single-game record of four set in 1946.

Carl Monroe: No running back was leaned on as much as Monroe in the 1982 season, when he set records for carries in a game (45 against Texas-El Paso) and in a season (309). Monroe was just as dependable as he was durable, setting single-season marks for yards (1,507) and 100-yard games (9). But with all of those yards and carries, Monroe doesn't show up anywhere among the school leaders in touchdowns. Ironically enough, he was the first Utah player to score a touchdown in the Super Bowl by being on the receiving end of a 33-yard pass from Joe Montana in San Francisco's victory against Miami in Super Bowl XIX.

Marv Bateman: If Louie Sakoda possessed the most accurate kicking leg in Utah history, then Bateman provided the program with its strongest. The six-year NFL pro, mostly with Buffalo, holds the top two single-season marks for punting average, with a staggering 48.07 average in his senior year of 1971. His career mark of 46.89 yards per punt is more than three yards higher than the second-best career mark held by another ex-NFL'er, Rick Partridge. Bateman also made 21-of-41 field goals during his three years at Utah.

Norm Thompson: Just as Larry Wilson's NFL career was winding down, St. Louis dipped back into the Utah pool for its next great defensive back. Thompson's 12 interceptions at Utah rank sixth all-time, but every player ahead of him played at least three seasons, while Thompson just played two. His seven picks in 1970 is just one behind the school record of eight by C.J. Lowery, and in his nine-year NFL career with the Cardinals and Baltimore, Thompson made 33 thefts.

coaches, Maddock was a multiple-position player for the University of Michigan from 1902–03. Even though he was primarily a lineman playing right tackle on both sides of the ball, Maddock was often used in short-yardage situations by Fielding "Hurry Up" Yost and his point-a-minute teams in those years.

Maddock scored 15 touchdowns in the 1902 season when Michigan outscored the opposition 644–12. Despite what appear to be impressive touchdown totals, Maddock was only his team's fourth-leading scorer that year, but he was the star in two of his team's closest victories that year. He scored three times in a 23–0 victory against Notre Dame and had the game's only points in a 6–0 victory against Wisconsin. Michigan had played in the first Rose Bowl the year before, but it had so thoroughly whipped Stanford that the Tournament of Roses committee decided on chariot and ostrich races for the next 15 years before hosting another football bowl game. Thus there was no postseason game for Maddock and his teammates.

Upon graduation, Maddock set out for Salt Lake City and quickly won over the locals. According to a Texas newspaper in 1905, "He has the Mormons all football crazy. He has written here to say that his team now holds the championship of Utah, Montana, Wyoming, and the greater part of Colorado. When he won the hard-fought battle with Colorado College a week ago, the Salt Lake City papers said, 'Maddock is now a way of saying success.' The great Michigan tackle has taken boys who never saw a football before and made them the star players of the Rocky Mountain States."

Maddock left coaching for the private sector after the 1909 season, but he returned to coach Oregon for one year, going 4–3–2 in 1924, after which he returned to Idaho to run his business interests.

Fred Bennion, 1910–13: Career Utah record 16–8–3. The most significant move during Bennion's stint as head coach was

Utah joining its first conference, the Rocky Mountain Athletic Conference. It was in 1912 that Utah won its first conference title, a title claimed largely by the relevant media of the day. Other sources award that year's crown to Colorado School of Mines, although Utah convincingly won that year's matchup 18–3.

Nelson Norgren, 1914–17: Career Utah record 13–11. The one football and basketball coach at Utah who fared better in hoops than with the pigskin, leading Utah to the 1916 National AAU title—a recognized national championship—was Nelson Norgren.

Norgren's tenure as football coach was so uninspiring that the U made several overtures to Joe Maddock, begging him to come back and recapture the interest and fanaticism he had earlier created around the football program. Almost in a sarcastic tone, the *Deseret News* wrote, "Inasmuch as a successful athletic career for a school means increased popularity and prestige, and since there are such things as box offices and turnstiles at Cummings field, the question of how to revive the 'good old days' is puzzling to the members of the board."

Even some 100 years ago, coaches were under the gun to fill stands and keep fans happy. That's not much different than the pressures today's coaches face. Norgren resigned following the 1917 season after posting a 2–4 mark.

Thomas Fitzpatrick, 1919–24: Career Utah record 23–17–3. Due to World War I, Utah didn't field a team in 1918. Fitzpatrick's 5–2 season in his rookie year made for a good start, and in 1922 he led the U to its second conference championship with a 7–1 mark—a nice rebound for a coach whose administration again made overtures for Maddock to return as an assistant coach as well as athletic director. He reportedly resigned after that season over a salary dispute, but U students took up the cause to bring him back for an increase in pay. Fitzpatrick later was a high school coach in Oakland, California, and the head of officials for the Pacific Coast Conference.

85 The Duck

From the time the University of Utah discontinued the tradition of the Crimson Warrior—which was no more than a student dressed in Native American clothing who rode into the stadium on a horse and planted a flaming spear into a hay bale—to the introduction of Swoop in 1996, Utah athletic teams were without a live mascot of any kind.

In between, however, there was the Duck. The Duck wasn't a mascot, however; it was a wild and crazy offensive formation that Jim Fassel incorporated into the Utah offense in 1987. But it wasn't done in an attempt to show off his coaching acumen.

"You use the Duck in the Big 8, they'll think it's communistic football," said Fassel, who nonetheless used the formation in a couple of plays against Nebraska in a 1989 game.

Rather, the Duck came out of sheer necessity. A shortage of experienced offensive linemen had not only taken away a majority of Utah's talent at the position but had also created a shortage of depth.

The Duck got its name from the family of Disney cartoon characters because the formation was that daffy. Additional twists to the formation were appropriately labeled Daisy and Dewey.

In its base formation, the Daffy Duck set consisted of the center lining up in his normal spot over the ball. The remaining linemen were set wide on one side of the field with a running back behind them. On the other side of the line were the remaining eligible receivers, usually a combination of wide receivers and a tight end.

"What it does is spread the field out and take the line out of the game," Fassel said. "We had a lot of injuries on our offensive line…. It's almost like a seven-on-seven game out there."

While Fassel had the guts to incorporate a scheme he knew would draw attention, not to mention some skeptics, it was offensive coordinator Jack Reilly who came up with the scheme, having used it as a high school coach in California. The Utes had used it sparingly in Fassel's first two years before unleashing it against Wisconsin in 1987 in a 31–28 upset in Madison.

"When we went from the Duck back to our regular offense, the fans booed," Fassel said.

The formation proved effective enough—it certainly was entertaining enough—that Utah continued using the Duck in ensuing years. In Fassel's later years, however, its use was questioned as the Utes continued to struggle on defense. The thinking at the time was shouldn't the coaching staff be just a little more worried about defense rather than working on variations of a situational offense?

With Fassel's firing in 1989, Ute fans thought they had seen the last of the Duck. Offensive coordinator Rick Rasnick, feeling an itch to come up with a creative method to get a touchdown in short-yardage situations, drew up a formation that he showed to Ron McBride, who immediately recognized it as the Duck—with a few twists—from his days as an assistant under Fassel. Renamed "Anaheim" for the city in which Utah was playing in the 1993 Freedom Bowl against USC, Utah used it successfully on a two-point conversion in a 28–21 loss to the Trojans.

In Utah's breakthrough 1994 season—and at the most critical of times—it was used twice. Utah had scored a touchdown to go up 22–17 on Charlie Brown's 44-yard touchdown run, and out came Anaheim for the two-point conversion.

McCoy found running back Rob Hamilton for the two-point conversion, and after Ken Buss blocked a punt to again put the Utes on the CSU doorstep, Anaheim made an encore appearance. Up in the broadcast booth, Dick Vermeil said, "Yeah, I think I've seen something like this back in the old Pop Warner days—they called it 'Formation Zero.'" This time it was tight end Rick Tucker, with three blockers taking on one Ram, who scored easily to give Utah a two-touchdown lead.

The following year in Utah's miraculous comeback against Air Force, offensive coordinator Fred Graves—Rasnick had taken the head coaching job at Eastern Michigan—called for Donald Duck left. Chris Fuamatu-Ma'afala took a pitch from quarterback Mike Fouts and ran in a two-point conversion to get Utah within six points at 21–15.

86 Rivalry Rewind: Wyoming

It's only fitting that Utah has played the Wyoming Cowboys more often than any other out-of-state team. The two campuses are separated by exactly 400 miles, and while that sounds like an ends-of-the-earth drive for fans of many SEC or ACC schools, the six-hour road trip along Interstate 80 was for years one of Utah's shortest trips.

Wyoming is full of extremes. At nearly 7,200 feet above sea level, its elevation is the highest in the Mountain West Conference. And Laramie, with fewer than 30,000 residents, is by far the smallest city housing a MWC member.

It also has, according to longtime sports information director Bruce Woodbury, "as fine a people as you'll find anywhere."

"When you go there you expect to see Bronko Nagurski walking down the street," Woodbury said. "The people are tough, and they love their football. They are cowboys. It's a cowboy town."

Utah leads the series 51–31–1, dominating the first 23 meetings from 1904–48 while going 22–0–1. Wyoming had an excellent run of its own in the 1950s and '60s, winning 12 of 14 from 1955–68. The late '60s were especially glorious for the Pokes as they won three consecutive Western Athletic Conference championships and split a pair of bowl games—beating Florida State in the Sun Bowl and falling to LSU in the Sugar Bowl.

When Utah and Wyoming played on November 8, 1969, at Ute Stadium, the stakes had never been higher for this game. Both teams were 6–1 and were ranked in the UPI coaches poll—Wyoming at No. 16, Utah at No. 18. Utah was unranked in the AP poll, and Wyoming had fallen out of that poll after losing to Arizona State the previous week—its first conference loss in more than three years.

Wyoming backers likely didn't see it coming, but their program was just beginning a decline that would see it go without a conference title for nearly 20 years. It would turn out to be a spectacular fall for a team that entered the 1969 season with high expectations. As it turned out, the social upheaval that this country experienced in the fight for civil rights made its way to the Wyoming campus, even though blacks made up a miniscule percentage of both the student body and the statewide population.

But blacks made up a sizable portion of Wyoming's football team. And when 14 black players went to coach Lloyd Eaton with a request to wear black armbands for its October 18 game against Brigham Young to protest Mormon policy banning blacks from holding the priesthood, they were booted from the team. Thus began the program's most chaotic and turbulent period, with boosters and the athletic department in full support of Eaton's actions, while the student and faculty senates fought for the players' reinstatement.

Wyoming easily defeated BYU but struggled to put away San Jose State the following week, a team that finished 2–8. If the alarm on Wyoming's season wasn't sounding then, it was after a 30–14 loss at Arizona State.

Still, Wyoming held its hopes of a four-peat in its own hands if it could defeat Utah, which had already defeated the Sun Devils. Those hopes were more than alive at halftime as Wyoming trailed by just a touchdown at 17–10.

In the second half, Utah crushed the Pokes and set the stage for a new WAC champion. Fullback Dave Smith scored his second touchdown of the game on a four-yard run—he caught a 50-yard scoring pass in the second quarter—and Norm Thompson ran an interception back 97 yards to salt away the game in the fourth quarter. The 34 points were the most surrendered by Wyoming in a conference game since it gave up 42 points to Utah in 1965— Utah's last win against the Pokes to that point.

Wyoming's downward spiral continued to pick up speed as it lost its final two games of 1969 to finish 6–4, and it went 1–9 the following year. Eaton was fired and Wyoming was branded as an institution that was indifferent, and perhaps hostile, toward providing a climate where black players could feel comfortable.

Over the next 17 years, Wyoming went through seven coaches and won more than 7 games just once (under Fred Akers in 1976). Akers promptly bolted to Texas. It wasn't until 1987 when Paul Roach was able to lead the Cowboys to their last great run, winning back-to-back WAC titles and breaking BYU's stranglehold on the conference.

While the 1969 contest featured the best combined record between the two teams, there have been other memorable match-ups in the rivalry's 106-year history. Among them:

2007: Utah 50, Wyoming 0. If not for the wonders of modern technology, this game probably wouldn't rate anywhere close to memorable. Tipped off to some remarks, including guaranteeing a victory, made by Cowboy head coach Joe Glenn at a mid-week luncheon, and already upset about last year's 31–15 loss at Laramie, Kyle Whittingham was determined to hold Glenn accountable. "You can't just say things and have it go by the wayside," Whittingham said.

Up 43–0 in the third quarter, Utah attempted an onside kick, and Glenn was captured by television cameras extending his middle finger toward the Utah sidelines. The clip went viral, Glenn was fined by the MWC, and Whittingham eliminated his team from any claim on the sportsmanship trophy.

1984: Wyoming 21, Utah 14. The entire Chuck Stobart Era could be summed up by this loss. With just more than two minutes to play and Utah closing in on its first victory in Laramie since 1972, quarterback Mark Stevens pitched to Pete Bendetti, who ran in for the score. The catch? Bendetti was a Wyoming linebacker, and his 90-yard return gave the Pokes the winning points.

The 1996 Bowl Selection Process: In the first year of the 16-team WAC, Wyoming surprised everyone by starting 9–0 and rising to No. 16 in the polls. The Cowboys would finish 10–1 before losing in overtime to BYU in the first WAC title game. Utah finished its regular season 8–3, losing two of three after an 8–1 start. But when bowl bids were announced, Wyoming was left in the cold while Utah was invited to the Copper Bowl to face Wisconsin. No doubt Poke fans had a good laugh when the Badgers and freshman sensation Ron Dayne ran roughshod over the Utes 38–10.

87 The BYU Players U. Love to Hate

What would a rivalry be if there wasn't someone to stand up and wear a black hat? Whether it's their actions on the field, in front of a microphone, or to a newspaper reporter, there is a select group of BYU players who will always bear the brunt of the wrath from the Ute fan base. There are some readers who will insist upon a missing name or a hundred, so for brevity's sake, I apologize if I've missed anyone.

1. Max Hall. Poor Max. So traumatized by unfounded allegations of abuse against his family at Rice-Eccles Stadium in the 2008 game, Hall blasted the entire university after throwing a 25-yard touchdown pass to Andrew George to give BYU a 26–23 overtime victory in the 2009 game.

"I don't like Utah. In fact, I hate them. I hate everything about them. I hate their program, I hate their fans, I hate everything," Hall said.

Most quarterbacks who perform to the rock-bottom levels Hall did in three games against Utah (84.6 passer rating vs. Utah as opposed to 137.7 for his career) are usually a lot more gracious in victory. Not Hall, who added insult to injury by cheap-shotting Utah linebacker Stevenson Sylvester in the back as Hall ran to celebrate his winning touchdown pass.

2. Austin Collie. Rivalries wouldn't exist without stereotypes. Utah fans are drunk, belligerent, and godless; BYU fans are sore losers, sanctimonious, and holier-than-thou. But after BYU's miracle finish in the 2007 game, when Max Hall completed a 49-yard bomb to Collie on fourth-and-18 en route to the winning score with less than a minute to go, Collie did his part to infuriate many Mormon U fans with this remark:

"I wouldn't say it was lucky. We executed the play well…. Obviously, if you do what's right on and off the field, I think the Lord steps in and plays a part in it. Magic happens."

Meanwhile, Utah fans had a pair of perfect scapegoats in Brice McCain and Robert Johnson, who couldn't have possibly been living right off the field, if you're to believe Collie was speaking the truth.

After the predictable furor ensued, Collie had the audacity to play the race card in defending his comments.

"I just think it's absolutely ridiculous that people take something like that and blow it up. I really think it's because I'm a Mormon white kid from Brigham Young University. Anybody else says that from any other team and it's just 'how spiritual that guy is.'"

Whatever you say, Collie.

3. Lenny Gregory. Better known to Utah fans as Lenny Gomes—he changed his name to that of his biological father after his playing days were over—Gregory flipped his lid after Chris Yergensen's missile from 55 yards defeated BYU 34–31 in the 1993 Holy War in Provo.

"Typical Utah bullshit," Gregory said. "All those [Utes] think that's all there is to life. But when I'm making $50,000, $60,000 a year, they'll be pumping my gas. They're low-class losers."

This story has a happy ending, or at least an ending that provides a lesson that fans on both sides should appreciate. Gregory, who is a high school football and golf coach in Georgia, still bleeds blue but admits his words were far from pearls of wisdom.

"Unfortunately, I do see the quote on the Internet every year when people will talk about it. That was one of the stupidest things I ever said. I regret it. It's just one of those things I don't think the coaches appreciated."

All is forgiven, Lenny. And thank you for your contributions to the rivalry.

4. Curtis Brown. You could understand if BYU fans felt bitter toward Utah's historic BCS-busting run in 2004. After all, BYU had long viewed itself as the premier program not in a BCS conference. It had also won the national championship in 1984 as well as producing 1990 Heisman Trophy–winner Ty Detmer.

Not only did it view busting the BCS as inevitable, it saw it as an inalienable right. And to make matters worse, BYU finished off its second consecutive losing season in 2004 and fired head coach Gary Crowton after finishing 5–6.

So after getting steamrolled 52–21 in the 2004 Holy War, one would have assumed BYU players—most of whom had little or no association to BYU when it was a winning program—would choose to remain silent on the accomplishments of their rival. Not Brown.

"USC is a team that will shut you out in the second half," Brown said of the Trojans, who beat BYU 42–10 in September. "That was something Utah wasn't able to do. We hurt ourselves. They didn't stop us."

It might be the first time a player whose team lost by 32 points called his own offense unstoppable. But the only thing unstoppable about BYU was the speed with which Brown's gums flapped.

 Mike McCoy

Mike McCoy was far from being the real McCoy when he started his playing career at Utah.

"When you fumble the first snap and the other team scores shortly after that, that wasn't a good start," McCoy said about his first career start, a 20–13 homecoming loss to lowly UTEP. It was the Miners' only win that year. McCoy had relieved an injured Frank Dolce the week before at New Mexico, and the Utes lost that game as well at 24–7.

Things got better the following week in a 20–13 victory at Air Force, Utah's first win ever at Colorado Springs. While there would be a few more low points for McCoy, by the time he graduated in 1994 he was riding as high as any quarterback in Utah history. Only Scott Mitchell outclassed McCoy statistically, and Mitchell never led a team to a top 10 ranking and 10-win season as McCoy did.

That's not bad for someone who almost certainly never would have come to Utah were it not for Long Beach State's decision to drop football after the 1991 season. McCoy wasn't viewed as being good enough to even warrant a scholarship offer from the 49ers coming out of high school. But he walked on and impressed George Allen enough to the point where McCoy earned a scholarship.

McCoy redshirted in Allen's only season with the 49ers before Allen died suddenly after the 1990 season, then McCoy started five games in Long Beach State's 2–9 season in 1991. Like many schools in the California state system at the time, Long Beach State was drowning in red ink and therefore discontinued its football program.

Then the fun began for McCoy, who by virtue of his five collegiate starts was getting the recruiting attention he never received as a high school player.

"We dropped [the program] in late December, school was letting out, Christmas break was coming up, and the recruiting deadline was coming up for a dead period to where [coaches] couldn't be on the road," McCoy said. "It was like a scavenger hunt for all the coaches to find some guys who had played at the Division I level instead of being junior college guys or high school kids."

Just as important, McCoy could play the following year without the one-year transfer penalty. That turned out to be a key factor in McCoy's ultimate choice of college.

"I took three recruiting trips—Oklahoma State, Wyoming, and Utah," McCoy said. "I thought after talking to everybody and the process of elimination of what type of system I wanted to run in...and I wanted to stay out West.

"I knew it would be a good situation with Frank Dolce only being there for another year.... It would be a good opportunity for me to go in for a year and have two years left," McCoy said. "I knew the quarterback situation, and there was really nobody else there [after Dolce] at that point."

Oklahoma State was running the option at the time, so McCoy quickly crossed the Cowboys off his list. It was much tougher for McCoy to put off Joe Tiller and Wyoming, which emphasized a passing attack that was to McCoy's liking.

Choosing Utah turned out to be a great decision for McCoy, even with an uneven start in McCoy's junior year. Utah then rattled off wins in five of its last six games to earn a bowl berth for the second consecutive year—a program first. Three times in that streak, McCoy threw for more than 400 yards, and in all but one game he threw for at least 377 yards. Only Mitchell had as many 400-yard games in a single season, and Utah needed every last yard to cover for a secondary that was decimated by injuries.

"In that conference back then, any week you could win or lose. The way the competition was and the way the league was set up back then, more often than not the team with the ball last, that's what it came down to," McCoy said.

McCoy's senior year was capped by another victory against BYU—only Alex Smith can boast of a record equal to McCoy's 2–0 mark against BYU—and the school's first bowl victory in 30 years, a 16–13 win against Arizona in the Freedom Bowl.

"To beat the team down south, the team nobody likes in Utah that goes to Utah.... All you heard about was John Walsh and how they were going to beat us, but to beat them back-to-back was a great accomplishment for us and the university," McCoy said.

McCoy's success in the pro game has come as an assistant coach, first with the Carolina Panthers as quarterback coach and now with the Denver Broncos as offensive coordinator. Interestingly enough, Broncos head coach John Fox, who was also with McCoy in Carolina, was an assistant coach at Long Beach State in 1981 before moving up to Utah to be part of Chuck Stobart's first staff in 1982.

89 The Kenneth P. Burbidge Family Academic Center

Kenneth Parry Burbidge was one of the most loyal and generous supporters of the University of Utah, and he was a Utah Man through and through. His efforts as leadership gift chairman in helping to remodel and expand Rice Stadium into Rice-Eccles Stadium were significant, and although he died in 1998 at the age of 68, he was able to enjoy the Utes' first season in the new facility.

But it's with another facility on the U campus where Burbidge's legacy serves as a constant reminder of his dedication to the U—namely the Kenneth P. Burbidge Family Academic Center, which was built in 2001 and is located between the John M. Huntsman Center and the Ute Natatorium. It's just one of many efforts by the university to emphasize the "student" part of student-athlete as it is available for use by every scholarship athlete at the U and not just for those on the football team.

And it took the help of a former Utah coach to push Burbidge into donating to such a project.

"Burbidge calls me just before he passed away. He wants to have lunch and talk about a few things," Ron McBride said. "He told me, 'They want me to build this academic center and put our name on it. What do you think? If you want me to give the money to the football program, I will and you can build something you want over there. What's going to be best?'

"I said the academic center is going to be best, that's what you need to do," McBride said. "That afternoon, he went up and told Chris [Hill] that's what he wanted to do."

A successful lung transplant in 1995 added three years to Burbidge's life and did little to slow down his passion and energy for the University of Utah. He was serving on the Board of Trustees at the time of his death, and he received the Distinguished Alumnus Award in 1994.

Burbidge, along with his wife, Sally, donated $2 million toward the $2.33 million project. At 11,000 square feet, it contains two levels with 40 computer labs, 10 tutor rooms, and three group study rooms. It also houses the athletic department's academic services, compliance and nutrition departments, as well as the life skills program. With the increased attention given to graduation rates by the NCAA, this facility serves a vital role in keeping Utah athletics nationally relevant.

90 1994 Holy War

Although it has been commonplace in recent years for the Holy War to feature two evenly matched, highly respected teams, it wasn't anywhere close to that for the rivalry's first 69 years. During the rivalry's first 50 years, it was Utah that almost always provided the stronger squad. For nearly two decades thereafter, it was BYU that entered the game either with a ranked squad, a conference championship team, or both.

That all changed in the rivalry's 70th edition—a game that featured ranked squads on both sides of the field for the first time ever. And it featured a finish that had one side staring at the scoreboard in disbelief, while the other side celebrated and tore down the goal posts—something it had been forced to watch the opposition do after a pair of heartbreaking losses.

It was Utah 34, BYU 31: The Sequel.

Despite the historic matchup, neither an outright championship nor the WAC's berth in the Holiday Bowl was at stake for this game—sort of. One-loss Colorado State would have to lose to Fresno State later that day to open the door for the winner of the Holy War to claim either a co-championship (in Utah's case), an outright championship (in BYU's case), and the Holiday Bowl berth (still in play for both teams).

When the Rams rallied to beat the Bulldogs, it took all of those equations out of play, putting Utah in the Freedom Bowl against Arizona with BYU in the Copper Bowl against Oklahoma.

Utah entered the game as the more desperate team, having lost two straight games—not to mention its lofty status in the rankings and its long shot status at a claim for a national championship. BYU, on the other hand, had won seven of eight since an early season loss to CSU, although five of those wins were by a touchdown or less. Its one setback in that stretch was a blowout loss at home to Arizona State, which went 3–8 that year.

The warts showed early for BYU, who fell behind 10–0. But the Cougars, who claimed a road victory at Notre Dame as part of their midseason surge, fought back with 17 points in just less than five minutes to take the lead. Dan Pulsipher's field goal cut the BYU lead to four points, and Mike McCoy's 15-yard touchdown pass to Deron Claiborne just before halftime regained the lead for Utah.

The second half, most notably the fourth quarter, featured more of the same. BYU would score, but Utah would come back. The lead changed hands four times in the final quarter, but when BYU scored with 2:15 left in the game, the possibility of Ute fans and players having to endure another blown fourth-quarter lead was as chilling as the Salt Lake City air.

Freshman Cal Beck quickly turned momentum back toward Utah, returning the ensuing kickoff to the BYU 32. Two running plays netted 12 yards before McCoy went back to pass, went through his reads, and checked down to running back Charlie Brown in the flat. Brown survived a tackle attempt by a BYU player inside the 5-yard line and went in for the touchdown with 56 seconds left.

Time remained for BYU, and the Cougars drove to the fringes of field-goal range. But from the Utah 34, Bronzell Miller pressured BYU quarterback John Walsh and forced a fumble. Luther Elliss fell on it with 10 seconds to play, and Utah fans could finally breathe easily.

"This was a real gut check," Coach Ron McBride said. "A week ago we were at the bottom of the barrel. But this team found a way to dig down and win."

91 Carlisle Indian School Comes to Utah

Air travel and interstate highway construction in the 1950s made travel into Utah faster and easier than it was earlier in the century, when most long-distance visitors to Utah came by train. And that difficulty in getting into—and out of—the state of Utah in the first half of the 20th century explains the early schedules of the University of Utah football program.

Outside of occasional trips to Los Angeles for games against Southern California and other smaller schools, Utah played all of its games in the Mountain Time Zone in the program's first 27 years. Neighboring Colorado provided Utah with its easternmost competition.

There was one notable exception, however—the Carlisle Indian School in Carlisle, Pennsylvania. You might recognize Carlisle as the institution that gave us Jim Thorpe. Although Thorpe didn't arrive at Carlisle until 1907, it was coached by another legendary figure in Glenn Scobey Warner, better known as Pop Warner.

Today, his name is all over the game, most notably at the youth programs and cheerleading levels that bear his name.

Warner was in his first stint at Carlisle from 1899–1903 after his first go-round at his alma mater, Cornell. After two years at Cornell, he arrived at Carlisle and turned an average program, but one with plenty of intrigue, into the biggest act in the game.

"Almost from the beginning, they were a great drawing card," said Tom Benjey, a Carlisle historian and author of several books about the Indian school. "They were exotic. You had Wounded Knee in 1890, and three years later [Indians] were playing football against the best teams in the country. Indians were looked on as being backward, drunkards...all sorts of things. So it was kind of a shock to many white people that Indians were smart enough to play football.... But they were great athletes, and they loved to play the game."

Carlisle was not built upon size and strength. Many of its players were impoverished Native Americans who came from the most desperate of backgrounds but who used speed and deception—and their coach's ingenuity—to beat their opponents. Just a month before coming to Utah, Carlisle shocked national power Harvard, leading 11–0 after using the Hidden Ball Trick—a kickoff return was fielded, the remaining players surrounded the return man, and the ball was stuffed into the jersey of a second player. No one on the Crimson knew who had the ball until it was too late to prevent a touchdown.

Tales of Warner's gadgetry—which he justified by saying that there were no rules against it, while also admitting that it wasn't probably the most sporting display—were told in newspapers from coast to coast. Although Harvard rallied for a 12–11 victory, the effort reinforced the belief that Carlisle was the most entertaining, must-see outfit of its time.

Which brings us back to Utah. In 1899, Carlisle made its first trip west, beating Cal 2–0 before unleashing the heavens on

Phoenix Indian School in a 104–0 victory. In 1903, Warner put in motion plans for another western barnstorming tour and arranged games against the Reliance Athletic Association—a collection of former collegiate players in California—and against the Sherman Indian School, which still exists today in Riverside, California. With those games scheduled for Christmas and New Year's Day, and with Carlisle's last game scheduled against Northwestern on November 26, Warner sought a third western team to provide some competition.

Situated almost halfway between Chicago and San Francisco, Salt Lake was perfectly situated for a break in travel and another game.

"I can't recall [Warner] saying why he [traveled west]," Benjey said, "but he recalled the advantages of why he did it."

First, the travel served as a great educational purpose for Carlisle's gridironers. Many of the players had never been to a big city before or seen a building taller than three stories. When the team traveled, they stayed in nice hotels, ate well, and always traveled first-class. They were able to do that because of their drawing power, and they earned the school a lot of money for their appearances.

Carlisle earned whatever fee it was paid for its game against Utah, keeping down the score while shooting off enough fireworks to entertain the fans and give them a different perspective on how football could be played. With coaches Warner and Utah's Harvey Holmes acting as officials, Utah gained just three yards of total offense in the game. Carlisle used its wing-shift play—a forbearer to the single-wing and today's Wildcat formations—to gain yards seemingly at will. Only a superior edge in the kicking game, as well as a snowy field, kept the score from being much worse than the 22–0 margin.

According to the *Salt Lake Herald*, "Salt Lake has witnessed the Carlisle Indians play football, and to say that Salt Lake is happy is putting it mildly. The famous redmen came to this city touted as wonders on the gridiron, and after their exhibition yesterday there are very few who will not say they made good. Football is a popular sport in this city, and many fans worship at its shrine, but it is doubtful if any of those who walked through the snow to see yesterday's contest will not say that it was the most interesting game from every point of view ever played in this state."

It would be another 33 years before any team—Texas A&M in 1936—came close to traveling the distance to Salt Lake City that Carlisle did to play Utah.

92 Utah Traditions, Part III

One part of the great fabric that makes up college football is the set of unique traditions that exist at different schools. And like every tradition, there's usually a good story behind its origins. Read on to get a better grasp on some of the in-game traditions at Utah.

The Third-Down Jump: Any time the defense faces a third-down situation that could result in the offense punting on the next play is always a time to get rowdy. In the MUSS, the students take home-field advantage to another level by jumping up and down; the goal is to create such a distraction for the offensive team that it moves before the ball is snapped, resulting in a five-yard false start penalty. And the MUSS keeps score, hanging a small sign with the number five on it as a tally for all the false starts registered by the opposition during the season.

Throw Up a U.: Like a certain school in Coral Gables, Florida, the University of Utah prominently features the letter "U" in its name multiple times. While Miami likes to call itself "The U," Utah fans know where the real U is located—and until Miami can put a U on a mountain and have it seen for miles across a major metropolitan city, Utah fans will forever claim that they give the letter more recognition than any Hurricane ever could. Therefore it's important to know what the hand signal looks like. Fold your middle, ring, and pinky fingers while extending your index fingers and thumbs. Now put the thumbs together. Congratulations, you've just thrown up a U.

Ute Thunder Cannon: After the playing of "Utah Man," the firing of this cannon—built in 1904 and used in training for World War I—is the most celebrated sound on game day at Rice-Eccles Stadium since it is fired after every Utah score. Owned by the school's U.S. Army ROTC program and the military science department, the cannon has been heard for miles around campus after every score since the 1968 season. It also serves as a call for the Utah cheerleaders to get into action and do a pushup for each point that's on the scoreboard, although that tradition didn't start until several years after the cannon started firing.

In 2002, the cannon underwent extensive repairs to the firing mechanism and the wooden wheels upon which it is perched. Originally, the cannon fired three-pound lead balls with gunpowder, but changes to the firing mechanism allowed it to fire 10-gauge shotgun blanks.

93 Jordan Gross

As Utah's 2002 season went from promising to pitiful, from being a preseason favorite to win the conference to the 5–6 finish that ultimately cost Ron McBride his job as head coach, Jordan Gross' future in the game was skyrocketing in the opposite direction.

Gross had always been a good player for Utah, and he started the last 26 games leading up to his senior campaign. He earned a pair of honorable mention All–Mountain West Conference honors and was widely praised for his versatility, a trait that helped him start games at three different positions on the offensive line as a junior.

As a senior, Gross blew up in the minds of NFL scouts and talent evaluators. Before he ever earned first-team all-conference honors, he was being projected as a high draft pick in the 2003 draft. So how did Gross move up the pundits' draft boards so quickly?

In addition to the requisite physical strength all NFL linemen have, Gross possessed uncommon speed for the position, and his 5.04 40-yard dash backed up what scouts saw on film. He was an exceptional athlete in high school in Fruitland, Idaho, where he played basketball and participated in track and field. In fact, it was a basketball game that McBride attended that gave his future Utah coach enough evidence to offer Gross a scholarship.

"They saw me running and moving. That kind of solidified the scholarship. We lost [the game], and it was kind of a bad game. Evidently, they saw my feet and liked what they saw."

Finally, Gross' ability to fight oncoming defensive linemen went all the way back to when he was six years old and began practicing tae kwon do, a discipline in which he eventually earned a black belt. It didn't hurt that he didn't give up a sack in his final two years at Utah.

"I don't actually think about doing it while I'm playing, but years leading up to this point, when I was growing and hitting my growth spurt, I was doing a lot of kicking and hand-fighting," Gross said. "Those types of things really helped my hand-eye coordination develop faster than they would have."

It all started bearing fruit in Gross' senior year when he was named first-team All–MWC and a finalist for the Outland Trophy.

That spring, as expected, Gross was taken in the first round by the Carolina Panthers with the eighth selection overall, the highest ever by a Utah player at the time.

Gross became a fixture in the Panthers' offense, starting every game and not missing a single offensive snap as a rookie in a season that saw the Panthers reach the Super Bowl. Gross started the first 84 games of his career before a concussion ended his streak in 2008, a year in which he was an All-Pro selection by the Associated Press. In 2009, Gross suffered the first serious injury of his career when he broke his leg and missed the final seven games of the season, but he bounced right back in 2010 by starting all 16 games and earned Pro Bowl honors for the second time in his career.

Gross has maintained close ties with his alma mater, donating $500,000 to the Utah football program in 2009 to endow a scholarship that is given to a player of Gross' upbringing and background, one who comes from a small town. The goal is "to recognize that players from small communities can achieve at the highest level."

94 Morgan Scalley

Morgan Scalley was a Utah fan since he was old enough to remember. Not that it was ever his choice, what with such close family ties to another former Utah player, his father Bud.

"He was my little league coach growing up," Morgan Scalley said. "I always had the red and white, and I grew to love football because of my father and wanted to follow in his footsteps and be the next Scalley running back at Utah."

Morgan, who currently coaches Utah's safeties, was a star running back at Highland High in Salt Lake City, and he got the

Morgan Scalley's dreams of following in his father's footsteps as the next great Utah running back were upended by a coach's need to have him on defense, but he made the most of the switch and earned co-Defensive Player of the Year honors in 2004. (AP Photo/Laramie Daily Boomerang, Michael Smith)

first part of his collegiate ambitions right by earning a scholarship to Utah.

"I never really made plans for what I'd do if I wasn't offered by Utah," Scalley said. "But as soon as the offer came, I jumped all over it. I didn't think about it or say I wanted to weigh my options. For [offensive line coach] Don Eck, who recruited me, and Coach McBride, I was probably one of the easiest recruits they ever recruited."

Fate, however, had other plans, and Morgan's earliest days at Utah couldn't have gotten off to a less auspicious beginning.

There was his first punt return when the public address announcer identified him as "Morgan Stanley." Scalley, who had never fielded a punt during a game in his life, was begging for the ball to bounce to him or stay away from him altogether out of fear of dropping the kick. His second punt return effort saw Scalley gain about 30 yards, but a penalty wiped it out.

Although Scalley got a fair shake at running back leading up to the 2002 season, the arrival of Brandon Warfield from junior college and the return of Marty Johnson from injury clearly put the writing on the wall for Scalley. If he wanted to see the field at Utah, it wouldn't be conjuring up memories of his old man on offense but on defense. It's a turn of events that Scalley and his current boss—head coach Kyle Whittingham, who was then defensive coordinator—joke about from time to time.

"I went into his office when they wanted to make the switch and I said, 'Coach Whittingham, it's always been my dream to play running back and follow in my dad's footsteps and be the next Scalley running back at Utah,' and he said, 'Morgan, it's always been my dream to play center field for the Angels, but it didn't happen.' That was a nice come-back-to-earth meeting with Coach Whit before I made the switch."

As for his sudden role as a punt returner, which came in his freshman year after serving an LDS Church mission to Munich,

Germany, Scalley never saw it coming, even though he had been catching punts in spring drills and two-a-days leading up to the 2000 season. As for being publicly misidentified on the punt team, Scalley kept his sense of humor about it because he was too busy realizing his dream of playing football at Utah. "I wish I made the money that guy did," Scalley joked.

"We were season ticket holders," Scalley said. "I went to all the games growing up. I remember how the stadium changed, how the environment changed, all the names in Utah football history. I would go visit my dad's office, and my mom had put together his newspaper clippings on the wall."

One clipping was from one of the most famous games in Utah history, a 6–0 victory against Utah State in the 1960 season when the Aggies were ranked 16th in the AP Poll. Bud Scalley scored the game's only points late in the game to give Utah its first-ever win against a ranked opponent.

"I always remember looking at that and saying, 'I'm going to do that one day,'" Scalley said. "'I'm going to play for Utah.' It turned out different than I imagined, but I couldn't be prouder. Utah football was all I knew."

Scalley was not only a leader on the 2004 Fiesta Bowl team at Utah, he was also a big-time playmaker, earning co-defensive Player of the Year honors in the MWC as a senior and All-American second-team honors from the Associated Press and *Sports Illustrated*. He earned tryouts with Buffalo and Philadelphia in the NFL, but when those opportunities didn't pan out, Scalley returned to Utah as a graduate assistant, then he became a full-time coach. And for someone who loves Utah football as much as Scalley does, his additional duties as recruiting coordinator shouldn't come as a surprise to anyone.

95 Dee Glen Smith Center

If Rice-Eccles Stadium is the main stage where the Utah football team performs in the form of gridiron clashes while conducting dress rehearsals in the form of practices and scrimmages, then the Dee Glen Smith Center houses all of the program's activity behind the curtain.

With Utah's entry into the Pac-12 Conference, one of the first areas targeted for expansion to serve the greater demands put on the Utah athletic program is the Smith Center. A $20 million expansion project set to begin in 2011 will add nearly 60,000 square feet to the facility and address the athletic program's needs in several areas. Primary among those needs is the university's sports medicine program, which also calls the Smith Center home, as well as a permanent training table.

The addition will also include more space for equipment storage, team meeting rooms, a players' lounge, and the coaches' offices.

The Smith Center was converted into the epicenter for the football program in 1990, but prior to that it housed the motor pool for the Utah National Guard in a facility that was built in 1960. Hence, Guardsman Way is the street address for the Smith Center.

Since the conversion, the center has undergone several renovation and expansion efforts. In 2004, the players' lounge was improved, and the locker room and auditorium areas followed in 2005. A $1.5 million expansion of the weight room—with a lead gift of $500,000 from Alex Smith—brought about the Alex Smith Strength and Conditioning Facility, an 11,000-square-foot weight room that increased its size by about 50 percent. In 2004, the Spence Eccles Field House—an indoor practice facility that replaced an outdated and often-deflated bubble—was built next to the Smith Center.

Utah residents may remember the Smith name from the chain of grocery stores started by Dee's father, Lorenzo, in 1932. After Dee joined the business, he expanded throughout the Rocky Mountains and today operates 132 stores in seven states. Dee Glen Smith died in 1984, with his contributions to collegiate sports in the state not limited to the U—the Utah State basketball teams play in the Dee Glen Smith Spectrum in Logan.

96 Mike Giddings

Mike Giddings knows football, even though his 9–12 mark in two seasons at Utah is hardly the stuff of legends. When Ray Nagel left Utah for Iowa after the 1965 season, however, the 31-year-old Giddings was thrust into a role for which he was not prepared. And to Giddings' credit, he freely admits that his time at Utah was a disaster largely of his own making.

"Utah is not USC," said Giddings, who was defensive coordinator under John McKay at USC before landing his first head coaching job. "We recruited some good players, but I pushed my staff too hard. I really thought I knew it all."

How hard was Giddings on his staff? Reportedly after playing at Army with three games remaining in the 1967 season, five of his assistant coaches typed up their resignation letters and stuck them in an envelope and turned them in to athletic department officials with the instructions that they weren't to be opened until after the season.

His temper was also legendary. One time his wife called the student union to tell the cooks there that it was Mike's birthday

Mike Giddings

There are few people who are as qualified to speak accurately and frankly about Utah players in the NFL than Mike Giddings, whose Pro Scout Inc. service plays a key role in determining the salary structure in the pro ranks. They are the advocates of many NFL owners, and Giddings' word … err … "coloring books" are gospel in the front offices of several NFL franchises. Here's what Giddings had to say about some current and former Utah players.

Jamal and Mike Anderson: "They were interesting backs in that they were power backs, but most people figured out [after they played] you can't run these guys like you did in the past. They would make great committee backs, in my opinion. I don't know if they'd be any better, but I bet they would've gotten paid more. Their average yard per carry would be better."

Sean Smith: "The one thing about Smith that's very interesting is that he's the tallest cornerback in the league. His whole thing will be whether he can make big plays and change direction fast enough. If [Miami] moves him inside, he's got a chance. He's a very sure tackler. But we would not have drafted him as a corner with that height."

Kevin Dyson: When asked about Tennessee taking Dyson ahead of Randy Moss, "They missed on him. Part of it was his not staying well. As I recall, some of it was the difference in the NFL were the

and ask if they would mind baking him a cake. The cake was baked and brought to Giddings at the team dinner. He promptly threw it against the wall.

"Mike was the first to admit he had made plenty of mistakes at Utah. He shouldered full responsibility for the collapse of his football program," wrote John Mooney after Giddings' termination at the end of the 1967 season. But he was also "a much bigger man in his moment of greatest defeat than he ever approached in his triumphs."

"I met with Ike Armstrong at his home in Laguna Beach, where he was retired," Giddings said from his Orange County home where corners that can cover tight. Dyson was like a J.J. Stokes, so good at UCLA, and Mike Williams at USC. They can't get away from those feisty quick corners and they can't get open, and I think that's what happened to Kevin.

Chris and Ma'ake Kemoeatu: "Chris, he's been a project in the sense of knowing what to do. He is so aggressive, he can be too aggressive. There's a craftiness [that's lacking]. But he's become a solid starting lineman. When he knows who to hit, no one hits them like this guy. If Pittsburgh used the wishbone, he'd annihilate people. But he has trouble with speed rushers. His brother is one of the best first-and-10 run stuffers in the league. Ma'ake, his position is to get the ball to tirid-and-10 and give way to a speed rusher."

Alex Smith: "Smith's problem is he never mastered the footwork. You come up running the pistol or shotgun in college, you don't have the proper footwork to throw the routes that are necessary in the NFL. Routes take longer to get open. Bill Walsh, he always filmed his quarterback from the waist down. You have your 3-, 5- and 7-step drops in the NFL, but there's no dropback in the college offenses because they're running or they get the ball to someone that's open and they throw it to them. That doesn't work in the NFL. I hope nobody looks at him and sees he hasn't led San Francisco to a Super Bowl and because of that he's a lesser quarterback at Utah. He should be remembered as an all-timer."

he still runs Pro Scout Inc., a scouting service with whom he lists several NFL teams as clients. "I asked him if he could give me any advice and he told me, 'You're a California kid, a beach bum, and a Trojan. Make friends slowly up there.' I didn't listen to him, and I never saw Ike again, but when reflecting…man, was he right."

Giddings may have been able to endear himself to the program, bad temper and all, but he didn't win enough games. Especially critical was his 0–6 mark against Utah State, BYU, and Wyoming, teams Giddings knew he had to beat.

That didn't keep the Giddings era from getting off to a rousing start in 1966. Utah opened the season 5–1 with only a lopsided road loss to conference champion Wyoming. A four-game winning streak was capped with a road win against Arizona State.

"Frank Kush, he thinks [ASU] is so tough, but I said before that we might not even throw the ball against them," Giddings said. "We went down and threw something like four passes. That was one of my fondest memories at Utah."

That 21–6 loss ensured a non-winning season for the Sun Devils, a low they wouldn't attain for another 10 years.

After being fired from Utah, Giddings was concerned about his future in football. The reputation he built at Utah could have scared away teams interested in his services. So with his wife in tow, Giddings went down to the Virgin Islands to visit a friend. There he got an unexpected boost from a football legend.

"Tom Landry gave me a call and set me up with Dick Nolan in San Francisco," Giddings said. "I was very down when I got [the call], but a month later I was in the NFL."

Giddings was hired as defensive coordinator, but one of his first brushes with how the NFL operated gave him the inspiration to help change how NFL teams brought in new players.

"One of our linebackers had gone down with an Achilles' tendon injury," Giddings said. "He was done for the year. I went to Dick Nolan and said, 'How do we replace this guy?' and he said that was the front office's job. But their job was scouting college players, not pro players."

In effect, NFL teams didn't have the system in place to bring in existing pro players in the event of an injury. Giddings, being a college guy, was accustomed to having more than 100 players on the roster, so a lack of bodies was never a problem.

Nolan, realizing that Giddings was always looking for more to put on his plate, told him, "I'm going to put you in charge of scouting the league next year."

And with that, Giddings became a pioneer—the first director of pro personnel in the NFL. The title evolved later, but the job responsibilities were something that no pro team was forcing upon its organization. Giddings later coached in the World Football League, but he returned to the NFL with the Denver Broncos as a defensive assistant and pro scout. He lost his coaching job when Bronco ownership changed hands, but he kept the scouting job.

He's still scouting the NFL today for ProScout, although his son has a more significant role today. But Giddings remains influential in the game and loves his work grading and scouting interior linemen.

"Coaches used to get fired in the NFL for losing," Giddings said. "Now coaches are going to get fired for misspending the owner's money. We determine what a player is worth and what a team's needs are. If you don't fill your needs in the NFL, you lose."

97 Thomas Herrion

In one moment, Thomas Herrion was fighting for his team, playing left guard in a preseason game for the San Francisco 49ers as they were driving down the field for one last touchdown against Denver. The Broncos had already sewn up victory, but preseason wins and losses meant very little for those players in the game at that moment. Making an NFL roster was the only form of victory they could truly claim.

A few moments later, after San Francisco's last drive ended with a touchdown with two seconds left in a 26–21 loss, Herrion was fighting for his life.

This story does not provide a happy ending. After collapsing in the locker room following the team's postgame recital of the Lord's Prayer, team doctors rushed around in an attempt to save his life.

Unfortunately, Herrion was pronounced dead in the early morning hours of August 21, 2005.

"It kind of makes you stop and look at your own life," former Utah teammate Jesse Boone said of Herrion, noting at the time they were both just 23 years old.

Those who coached and played with Herrion look back on a life of smiles as wide as the lineman's 315-pound torso; he was a man who made a positive impression on everyone he met.

"What a neat guy. He lived life the right way," said Morgan Scalley, a teammate of Herrion's from 2002–03 and currently an assistant coach at the U. "That smiling and singing, I'm sure, is going on in the next world."

In just his third game as a Ute, Herrion quickly made an impression on his teammates, but that impression came from his actions in the locker room before the game rather than his play on the field.

Ron McBride asked Herrion to lead the team in a pregame prayer, and the invocation made an indelible impression on Boone.

"There was so much energy that Thomas put into it," Boone said. "That team prayer sticks out in my mind."

"We called him Ruben Studdard from *American Idol*," said Tommy Hackenbruck, who played with Herrion for two years at the University of Utah. "He just had an amazing voice and was always singing in the locker room. When he first got here and you saw him, this big guy with dreads hanging down, you didn't know what to expect from him. But after five minutes, you felt like you knew the guy, like you knew he was going to be a good teammate and friend."

And even as an unknown pro with long-shot hopes of making a roster, Herrion wasn't afraid to stand above the crowd. In a press conference the day after Herrion's death, 49ers coach Mike Nolan recounted an instance when quarterback Alex Smith—like

Herrion, also a rookie—was told by the team's veterans to stand up and sing his alma mater's fight song prior to an appearance by 49ers legend Steve Young.

Herrion quickly joined Smith to make a duo, and the assembled 49ers players went bonkers.

"Everybody began to hoot and holler," Nolan said. "At that time, [Herrion] came out of his shell. It was warming to see him like that."

Herrion had shown no signs of heart problems to team physicians with his previous teams, first at Utah, then with the Dallas and San Francisco practice squads in the 2004 season, followed by a season with the Hamburg Sea Devils in NFL Europe. Nolan said he didn't ever recall the big man becoming easily fatigued in conditioning drills. And blood and urine samples didn't come back positive for illicit drugs; doctors found only atrophine, a drug administered to him after he collapsed.

What killed Thomas Herrion? He had ischemic heart disease, as well as a high level of blockage in his right coronary that caused the death of his heart muscle. His heart was also slightly enlarged, and an autopsy revealed a small amount of scar tissue in Herrion's heart—a certain indicator he may have had a previous heart issue but wasn't aware of it.

At Utah, the 2005 Utes wore a round black decal on the back of their helmets with a white number 76—Herrion's number at Utah. There was also a moment of silence on his behalf prior to Utah's season-opener at Rice-Eccles Stadium against Arizona.

"It's an eye-opener," Coach Kyle Whittingham said as the Utes took to the practice field for the first time since Herrion's death. "It puts things in perspective real quick. It makes it very obvious that football is a very minor part of the big scheme of things."

98 Roy Jefferson

Roy Jefferson's dream as a budding football star in Compton, California, was to play for UCLA. That's not the only connection the Bruins had with Jefferson and ultimately a Utah squad that won the 1964 Liberty Bowl.

Utah's coach at the time was Ray Nagel, an all-conference quarterback under legendary coach Red Sanders, as well as an assistant in Westwood for three years before taking the head job at Utah. But it was another coach with UCLA roots that had the most impact on Jefferson while he was at Utah.

"Our defensive line coach, Bob Watson, came from Oregon State [after playing with Nagel at UCLA], and he was a really tough guy," Jefferson said. "I did not like him at all. He'd beat on me all the time. We'd do these 100-yard striders after practice—we were probably the best-conditioned team in college football. Well, whoever won the tenth one got to go. I'd take second or third, but on the tenth one I'd blow it out and win and be the first one out. So I'm running off the field and Watson goes, 'Jefferson! Where are you going!'"

Jefferson responded by saying he had done what the coach had said, and he was through running for the day.

"No, you've got to win all of yours, and if you don't, you're not going in," Watson responded.

"The thing was," Jefferson said, "I thought he was persecuting me. But at the end of the year he called me into his office and said, 'Roy, I want to apologize to you. I've been extremely tough on you. I just thought you were one of the most gifted athletes I ever coached, and I wanted you to get everything out of yourself.'

I broke down and cried, thinking here I was hating this man for being so tough on me, but basically he was doing me a favor. I really disliked myself for hating this man all through my junior and senior years and this guy was actively doing me a favor."

Jefferson made a name for himself in the NFL as a wide receiver. At first he played for the Pittsburgh Steelers, then after being traded to Baltimore in the 1970 preseason, he won a Super Bowl with the Colts. Two years later, he played on another Super Bowl team in Washington.

"We went from the outhouse to the penthouse in one year," Jefferson said of himself and fellow Steeler Ray May, both going from a team that went 1–13 in 1969 to one that defeated Dallas to win Super Bowl V.

But with Utah, which like the rest of the NCAA was still adjusting to unlimited substitution with players who were accustomed to playing on both sides of the ball, Jefferson's calling card was on defense.

Playing as a stand-up defensive end on the edge but with pass coverage responsibilities, Jefferson and his teammates made up the most dominant defense in program history after World War II, giving up just 68 points in 11 games. One would have to go back to 1938 to find a Utah stop unit that gave up fewer than the 6.2 points per game allowed in 1964.

Jefferson figures he led the team in sacks and had at least four interceptions. Teammate C.D. Lowery—one of only two Utah defenders not to go both ways—led the team with eight interceptions, a single-season mark that stands today at Utah. The team's 27 interceptions is one short of the 1947 school record.

On offense, Jefferson played split end and handled placekicking duties, kicking a pair of field goals in the Utes' 32–6 bowl win against West Virginia.

"That was unbelievable," Jefferson recalled of the days leading up to the game. "We come into town, and the papers had big, black bold headlines that said, 'Utah Who?' After we beat West Virginia, they knew who Utah was."

Jefferson earned All-American honors and was drafted by both Pittsburgh and the AFL's San Diego Chargers. Despite the proximity to home, Jefferson chose the more established league, even though the Steelers were a laughingstock at the time and the Chargers had just won the AFL title.

"The NFL was the place that I wanted to be in. It wasn't viable yet, the AFL," said Jefferson, who has been involved with numerous charitable movements and foundations during his retirement in the Washington D.C. area. "San Diego wanted me as a defensive back. Pittsburgh didn't know. They had no thought about which way I would play, and I didn't care if I played wide receiver or defensive back…that's how I thought back then."

99 Classic Finish V: 1972 Arizona

The fortunes of the two programs changed dramatically following Utah's record comeback against Arizona, which ended with Don Van Galder's quarterback sneak for a touchdown with 10 seconds to play and capped a Ute rally from a 27–0 deficit to start the fourth quarter. Until 2010, when Kansas rallied from 35 points down against Colorado, and trailing by only 28 to start the final 15 minutes, no team had ever come from as far back in the final quarter to win as Utah did.

The details of how this game affected the long-term fortunes of both programs will be described later. What must be explained first is how Utah staged its greatest comeback.

Arizona, with Coach Bob Weber facing increasing heat from all sides, looked to have turned a corner in his fourth year by getting off to a 3–0 start in Western Athletic Conference play, although losses in all four non-conference games to teams currently in BCS conferences had the Wildcats entering this game with a 3–4 mark.

Utah was marginally better at 4–3, having won a non-conference game but with a perfect WAC mark as well at 3–0.

For three quarters, Arizona appeared to be the clearly superior team. So superior that Salt Lake mayor Jake Garn, who would later serve three terms as a U.S. Senator, left the game early, along with his son Jake Jr.

"Dad, we don't want to sit through this," the younger Garn said. No point in making a child unhappier, the elder Garn thought, so they both left.

"But the torment of the day was too much," *Deseret News* sports editor Hack Miller said, reflecting on the mass exodus of fans from the stadium. "What a lousy team the Utes had suddenly come to be. You didn't have to take anyone's word for it—they were staging their drabbish drama right there on Bob Rice's front room."

Those who left were blindsided to realize Utah had won. Those who stayed out of the announced crowd of 19,236 got more than their money's worth. Arizona officials in attendance, among them the school president and athletic director, were whooping it up with "the fervor of freshmen" and now had to face the stark reality that a coaching change was needed.

Van Galder, who looked completely inept in throwing four interceptions, connected with Steve Odom on two long passes to get Utah within 27–14.

Still Arizona appeared to have the game in hand, marching to the Utah 36 with just more than four minutes to play before the Ute comeback received an unexpected boost. The Wildcats rushed for 357 yards, but quarterback Bill Demory audibled out of a fullback dive and threw a pass. Steve Marshall picked it off and ran 68 yards the other way for a score to get Utah within six points.

"Before the game Arizona officials were explicit and emphatic that all play would be directed from the bench with the quarterback as puppet. After that call it was said the quarterback changed the call at the line. Whoever did it deserved some time in the corner," Miller wrote.

The Utah defense, smelling blood in the water, forced a punt with 2:20 to play. Van Galder calmly marched Utah downfield and scored from four yards out. The extra point capped the improbable rally.

"Anybody who saw that game thinks I'm the greatest quarterback ever," Van Galder said, "but I had three plays in that game."

Weber was fired at season's end and his replacement, Jim Young, immediately led the Wildcats to a shared title the following year on the way to 26 wins in three seasons. Arizona's success under Young gave the program the belief it could compete in the Pac-8 Conference, so they joined the new Pac-10 in 1978 along with Arizona State.

Utah followed that victory by losing consecutive games to Utah State and BYU en route to a 6–5 finish. The following year, Arizona got revenge on Utah with 42–21 victory, but a Utah upset of Arizona State allowed the Utes to control its title hopes and a bid to the Fiesta Bowl. Unfortunately another loss to BYU derailed those hopes, and Utah entered a period of unprecedented failure on the field.

It's known as the Snafu of '72 at Arizona, but it paved the way for much greater things. However, Utah could never utilize the momentum from that game and turn it into bigger things.

100 Steve Marshall's Seven-Touchdown Game Against Colorado State

There has been a strong bond between Steve Marshall and football in the state of Utah for nearly 40 years. As a player, it was his interception return for a touchdown against Arizona that got Utah within six points, giving his team its first real belief it could come back from 27 points down entering the final quarter and win.

As a coach, Marshall has been a fixture on the sidelines at Skyline High for decades. Although never a head coach, he has been instrumental in the development of several players who went on to have successful careers at schools across the state—among them is Brandon Doman, BYU's current offensive coordinator and former quarterback who led the Cougars to consecutive heart-stopping Holy War victories in 2000–01.

As a father, he had two sons—Grady and Matt—who went on to play at Utah and BYU, respectively. Grady was a special teams demon on Utah's undefeated 2004 team, while Matt, a member of the Class of 2012, is a backup quarterback and holder on field goals and extra points.

And for one day—against Colorado State in a 62–36 victory in the 1972 season finale—Steve Marshall was the greatest quarterback in the 119-year history of Utah football, before or since. Against the Rams, Marshall accounted for seven touchdowns—four passing and three rushing. Marshall set three other single-game school records that could stand for another four decades—passing efficiency (253.78), rushing yards by a quarterback (160), and most 70-yard touchdown passes in the same game (two).

What in the name of Kurt Warner happened here? To understand how Marshall went from being an All-WAC defensive back in his junior year to making an assault on the Utah record book at the game's most demanding position, one has to know the events of the previous two weeks.

"Going into the Utah State game, our starting quarterback was Don Van Galder. Brownie, being Brownie, decided to run over a linebacker, and he broke his collarbone," Marshall said. "Going into the BYU game, we had a backup who transferred from Notre Dame, Dan Payne. We lost to BYU…and I think it cost us the Fiesta Bowl. Going into Colorado State, they called me in Sunday morning. I had played quarterback my freshman year and they said, 'Do you want to play quarterback this week?' We ran the Houston veer, and Dan was a bigger kid and wasn't as mobile. I said sure, I practiced three days, and I had a blast."

Helping matters was the presence of Marshall's roommate his first two years at Utah, wide receiver Steve Odom. "I could throw touchdown passes to him blindfolded," Marshall said.

Away from the field, Marshall had an event that justifiably took his mind away from game preparation and practice. On Thanksgiving Day, just two days before the game, his father had a heart attack and his initial prognosis was grim. After going to the hospital, Marshall rushed back to campus for practice and feared the worst.

"I was really late getting over, which I never was," Marshall said. "As I was running into the locker room, Coach [Bill] Meek was coming up the stairs and he was looking at me like, 'What the heck have you been doing?' I told him what happened and he said, 'Okay, go down to practice and tell Coach [Jim] LaRue that I'll be down there as quick as I can.'

"I didn't think much of it, and I told Coach LaRue what had happened. Well, Coach Meek had actually went to the hospital. That was pretty cool. He came back and told me things were going to be better than I thought they were, and I appreciated that."

Understandably, doctors said listening to a football game was out of the question for Mr. Marshall, but his wife slipped a transistor radio into the room.

At first glance, Marshall's performance seemed destined to make Van Galder the Wally Pipp to Marshall's Lou Gehrig. But Utah's coaching staff never thought about making a permanent switch, something Marshall knew even as he was having his record-breaking day.

"I had played really well on the defensive side and was a leader on the defense," Marshall said. "There wasn't any question I was going back to defense as soon as Brownie was healthy. It worked out great."

To show exactly why Marshall was needed on defense, in Utah's next game, the 1973 season opener against Texas Tech, Marshall tied Larry Stone's school record of 13 unassisted tackles. That mark has been since raised to 14 by Bill Gompf and Dave Revill, but it's a good bet Marshall's records at his "other" position will stand for quite some time.

General Sources

Disa and Data by John Mooney.

Official University of Utah website, www.utahutes.com

College Football Data Warehouse, www.cfbdatawarehouse.com

NCAA record book

NFL.com

Pro-football-reference.com

The Greatest Utah Football Games Ever website at http://utahfootball-countdown.blogspot.com/?zx=3871e2e79bf6e512 (invitation required)

Deseret News historical archives

1.

"ASU defeats Colorado at Folsom Field," *East Valley Tribune*, September 15, 2006.

"Utah officially accepts Pac-10 invitation," *Salt Lake Tribune*, Lya Wodraska, June 18, 2010.

"Utah athletic department to get $2 million from TV deal," by Dirk Facer, *Deseret News*, January 7, 2011.

"Pac-10 expansion: Revenue analysis for the 12-team league," by Jon Wilner, *San Jose Mercury News*, June 16, 2010 (blog).

2.

"Urban Meyer," by S.L. Price, *Sports Illustrated*, December 7, 2009.

"Meyer: I can't think of many schools that are better than Utah," by Kelly Whiteside, *USA Today*, January 13, 2009.

3.

"Who's No. 1? Utes feel like they've made their case," by Mike Sorenson, *Deseret News*, January 3, 2009.

"Perfect Utah Rolls Alabama in Sugar Bowl," by Ray Glier, *The New York Times*, January 3, 2009.

"Life of Reilly," Rick Reilly, *ESPN The Magazine*.

4.

"Utes could crash big-boys' party," by Pat Forde, ESPN.com, September 3, 2004.

"Utes say they can run the table," by Michael C. Lewis, *The Salt Lake Tribune*, July 25, 2004. http://newsnet.byu.edu/story.cfm/57500

5.

"First Intercollegiate Field Day," *Salt Lake Tribune*, May 19, 1895.

Bergera, Gary James, and Ronald Priddis, *Brigham Young University: A House of Faith*, Signature Books, 1985.

"Rivalry game needs a better title," by Dave Warby (letter to the editor), *The Daily Utah Chronicle*, November 30, 2010.

"Holy War is wrongly named—school spirit isn't about faith," by Jake Garfield, *The Daily Utah Chronicle*, November 27, 2010.

6.

"Red alert: Super-sharp Alex Smith, a Heisman candidate with smarts to match his skills, is leading Utah on a historic march," *The Sporting News*, November 22, 2004.

7.

Personal interview, Michael Rueckert.

"MUSS a key factor in U home success," by Dirk Facer, *Deseret News*, August 31, 2010.

"U impresses ESPN's GameDay," *Deseret News*, November 6, 2010.

8.

Personal interview, Chris Hill.

9.

Personal interview, Ron McBride.

"McBride firing, too, shall pass" by Brad Rock, *Deseret News*, November 27, 2002.

10.

"Utah 13, TCU 10," Associated Press, November 6, 2008.

11.

"Utes flying high, but with dignity," by Brad Rock, *Deseret News*, November 19, 1995.

12.

College Football Hall of Fame, www.collegefootball.org/famer_selected.
php?id=20100

13.

Personal interview, Chris Hill.

14.

My Cousin Vinny, directed by Jonathan Lynn, 1992, 20th Century Fox Film
Corp.

15.

Utah Outdoor Activities website, www.utahoutdooractivities.com
"Student volunteers paint the Block U," *Daily Utah Chronicle*, October 29,
2001.
"A new view for the Big U," *Salt Lake Tribune*, August 25, 2006.

16.

"Cards' Larry Wilson indicates he's tired," Associated Press, February 16,
1973.
"Wilson looms as Utah's choice," *Deseret News*, January 23, 1974.
"Wilson withdraws from Ute coach race," *Deseret News*, January 24, 1974.
"What made Larry leave?" *Deseret News*, January 25, 1974.
"Lovat gets Utah's grid post," *Deseret News*, January 26, 1974.

17.

Personal interview, Chris Yergensen.
"Utes give Provo whammy the boot," by Doug Robinson, *Deseret News*,
November 21, 1993.

18.

"Utah 37, Cal 27," Associated Press, December 23, 2009.

19.

"Weddle-Beck rivalry has developed into friendship," by Trent Toone,
Deseret News, November 23, 2010.

20.

Personal interview, Tom Barberi.

21.

Personal interview, Kyle Whittingham.

"U's Whittingham followed in his father's footsteps," by Doug Robinson, *Deseret News*, February 16, 2009.

22.

Personal interview, Bill Marcroft.

23.

Personal interview, Harold Lusk.

"When perfect Utes beat perfect Rams," by Mike Sorenson, *Deseret News*, September 24, 2003.

24.

"New Utah practice facility named for Eccles," by Mike Sorenson, *Deseret News,* August 18, 2004.

"U pleased to have its 'Bubble' burst," by Loren Jorgensen, *Deseret News*, June 18, 2004.

"Rice-Eccles Stadium," by Marjorie Cortez, *Deseret News*, July 29, 1998.

25.

Personal interview, Ron McBride.

Building a Winning Football Tradition at Brigham Young University by LaVell Edwards, as told to Lee Nelson, 1980.

"Rivalry Week: 'Red Blood, Blue Blood' documents the rivalry," by Natalie Barret, *The Daily Universe*, November 21, 2010.

26.

Personal interview, Bruce Woodbury.

Personal interview, Robert Gramse.

27.

Personal interview, Norm Chow.

Personal interview, Mike Giddings.

28.

Personal interview, Dick Rosetta.

29.

Personal interview, Bill Riley.

Personal interview, Bill Marcroft.

30.

"The Forever Fan," by Dale J. Neilson, *Continuum*, Spring 2009.

"Lifelong Ute: Scholarship established in Elder Wirthlin's name," by Jason Swensen, *The Church News*, December 27, 2008.

"Elder Wirthlin's goodness now a legacy at U," by Lee Benson, *Deseret News*, January 16, 2009.

31.

Personal interview, Gary Barker.

Personal interview, Ray Groth.

33.

"Letdown in Las Vegas for Utes," by Dirk Facer, *Deseret News*, September 23, 2007.

"Loss has Utes searching for answers," by Dirk Facer, *Deseret News*, September 24, 2007.

34.

"Afghanistan gives some perspective to rivalry," by Brad Rock, *Deseret News,* November 25, 2010.

"U. vs. BYU: Cheerleader's brawl lives on in rivalry lore," by Phil Miller, *Salt Lake Tribune*, November 14, 2001.

35.

Official website of The Pie at http://thepie.com.

"Pie Pizzeria picks South Jordan as site for largest outlet," by Debbie Taylor, *The Enterprise*, September 6, 2004.

37.

Personal interview

Tribute to George Seifert at http://home.earthlink.net/~seifertsite/seifert. html.

39.

"Rembrandt of the Rams," by Mark Mandernach, *Sports Illustrated*, September 5, 1994.

"The Life and Times of Fred Gehrke," by Peter Vischansky, *The Coffin Corner*, Vol 22, No. 3, 2000.

40.

Personal interview, Dick Rosetta.

41.

Personal interview, Brian Johnson.

"Pre-game comments motivate Utes," *The Birmingham News*, January 3, 2009.

42.

"The Utah Pass: 2003 team resurrects play popularized by U's 1957 champions," by Kurt Kragthorpe, *Salt Lake Tribune*, November 19, 2003.

43.

"Unique Game," by John Antonik, West Virginia University athletics website, June 22, 2005.

Official Liberty Bowl website at www.libertybowl.org.

45.

"Bob Rice – A great life well worth eulogizing," by Lee Benson, *Deseret News,* September 5, 2007.

"Robert Rice, Utah Man," *Deseret News*, September 1, 2007.

46.

"It's the season for tailgating at the U," by Tom Barberi, *Salt Lake Tribune*, October 8, 2010.

Personal interview, Greg Finch.

47.

Personal interview, Luther Elliss.

48.

"Utah takes out frustrations on Y, 57–28," by Brad Rock, *Deseret News*, November 20, 1988.

49.

"The Pride of Utah Marches On," by Alex Steele, *Daily Utah Chronicle*, September 26, 2006.

"Shake it Crazy Lady: Jackson is a Ute fan for life," *Daily Utah Chronicle*, September 11, 2009.

50.

"Just In Case You Missed It," by Kelli Anderson, *Sports Illustrated*, 1996 College Football Preview.

"Thank U, Love BYU: Down 21–7 Late in the Fourth, Utes Stage Miracle Rally," by Mike Sorenson, *Deseret News*, October 22, 1995.

51.

Personal interview, Mike Giddings.

52.

"Might have been better," by Hack Miller, *Deseret News,* September 24, 1964.

53.

"Champs!" by Brad Rock, *Deseret News*, November 23, 2003.

55.

Lumpy's Bar website at www.lumpysbar.com.

The Green Pig Pub website at www.thegreenpigpub.com.

The Fiddler's Elbow website at www.fiddlerselbowslc.com.

The Huddle website at www.huddle-sportsbar.com.

The Legends website at www.whylegends.com.

56.

Deseret News, December 28, 1994.

57.

"Utah 38, San Diego State 34," Associated Press, November 20, 2010.

"Utah 17, BYU 16," Associated Press, November 27, 2010.

58.

"Sakoda boots winning field goal to finish Utes comeback," Associated Press, October 2, 2008.

59.

"Polynesians in the Desert," by Ardis E. Parshall, August 16, 2008, via website at http://www.keepapitchinin.org/2008/08/16/polynesians-in-the-desert-utah-history/.

"Unfathomable becomes a reality for Appalachian State," by Jeff Ziglett, *USA Today*, September 4, 2007.

"Kaufusi family starting to resemble a football army," by Dick Harmon, *Deseret News*, April 15, 2009.

"McBride believes local boys are no ka oi," by Paul Arnett, *Honolulu Star-Bulletin*, July 30, 1997.

60.

"Just a game? Documentary reveals the true colors of Utah-BYU rivalry," by Brian Maffly, *Salt Lake Tribune*, November 18, 2010.

"Pride, paint and pranks," by Parker Williams, *The Daily Utah Chronicle*, November 20, 2007.

62.

Gastronomy website at www.ginc.com.

Red Iguana website at www.rediguana.com.

Hires Big H website at www.hiresbigh.com.

Trolley Square website at www.trolleysquare.com.

63.

"Pro day draft report: Alex Smith," by Charles Robinson, Yahoo.com, March 16, 2005.

65.

"That Clutch Raider Win; Frantic 14-Point Minute," by Bob Valli, *The Oakland Tribune*, November 18, 1968.

66.

"Fassel blitzes university at press conference," *Deseret News*, November 30, 1989.

"Revenge-minded BYU blasts Utah, 70–31," *Deseret News*, November 19, 1989.

68.

"White runs 95 and 57 yards and scores all CU points," *The Denver Post* via University of Colorado's athletics' website at http://www.cubuffs.com/fls/600/classic/content/events/fb_1937_white_utah.html

"Whizzer White: A pop-art icon of the Thirties," *College Football Historical Society Newsletter*, Vol. I, No. III, 1988.

69.

Personal interview, Steve Odom.

70.

Personal interview, Lavon Edwards.

71.

"Mitchell wears red, but his roots are blue," by Lee Benson, *Deseret News*, November 20, 1988.

72.

Personal interview, Bruce Woodbury.

73.

Personal interview, Don Van Galder.

74.

Personal interview, Louie Sakoda.

75.

Personal interview, Wayne Howard.
"Holy War rages on…in Utah," by John Henderson, *Denver Post*, November 21, 2008.

76.

"Livin' large," by Austin Murphy, *Sports Illustrated*, December 28, 1998.

77.

"This time Utes are stunned by Falcons," by Mike Sorenson, *Deseret News*, November 13, 1994.
"Utes can't hold lead, fall 23–21 to Lobos," by Mike Sorenson, *Deseret News*, November 6, 1994.

78.

"Hawaii deals Utes another heartbreaking loss," by Brad Rock, *Deseret News*, October 22, 1984.

"Opening salvos: First game surprises can make or break coaches," by Ron Higgins, *Memphis Commercial-Appeal*, September 3, 2010.

79.

Personal interview, Ron McBride.

81.

"Speedie turns home into a Hall," by Chris Foster, *Los Angeles Times*, September 12, 1991.
Personal interview, Mike Giddings.

82.

"Smith likes to stupefy defenders," by Brad Rock, *Deseret News*, October 24, 1999.
"Comeback Kid: No. 8 in a series," 623 Tries blog at http://sixtwothreetries.blogspot.com/2009/05/comeback-kid-8-in-series.html.

83.

"Remembering Pokey," BroncoCountry.com, August 23, 2009.
Evancho, Bob. "The Good Fight."

84.

"Harvey Holmes, Former Trojan Mentor, dies," *Los Angeles Times*, May 12, 1948.
"Joe Maddock may be induced to return to Crimson School," *Deseret News*, February 26, 1916.
"Fitzpatrick's name only one to come up before Regents," *Deseret News*, January 9, 1923.

85.

"Innovation gives Utah offense to quack about," by Jeff Browne, *Fort Lauderdale Sun-Sentinel*, September 23, 1987.
"Utah puts on a good show, loses 42–30," by Brad Rock, *Deseret News*, September 17, 1989.
"Utes paint Fort Collins red," by Mike Sorenson, *Deseret News*, October 23, 1994.
"WAC war an unbelievable masterpiece," by Doug Robinson, *Deseret News*, October 23, 1994.

86.
"The last roundup," by Lee Benson, *Deseret News*, October 17, 2010.
Watterson, John Sayle. *College Football: History, Spectacle, Controversy*, Johns Hopkins University Press, 2000.
"Cowboys steal victory from Utes," by Dick Rosetta, *Salt Lake Tribune*, September 30, 1984.

87.
"Utah, finishing 11–0, spells perfection B-C-S," by Vicki Michaelis, *USA Today*, November 21, 2004.
"Gomes famous remarks will never be forgotten," by Brad Rock, *Deseret News*, November 17, 2004.
"Collie calls reaction to his post-game comments 'ridiculous,'" by Dick Harmon, *Deseret News*, November 27, 2007.
"Mountain West reprimands Max Hall for 'I hate Utah' rant," by Michael David Smith, AOL News, December 1, 2009.

88.
Personal interview, Mike McCoy.

89.
"U unveils its athletic-academic center," by Mike Sorenson, *Deseret News*, February 28, 2001.
"Obituary: Kenneth Parry Burbidge," *Deseret News*, December 20, 1998.

91.
Personal interview, Tom Benjey.

93.
"Utah's Gross emerges as top offensive tackle," Jarrett Bell, *USA Today*, April 16, 2003.
"Gross donates $500K scholarship," by Dirk Facer, *Deseret News*, July 28, 2009.

94.
Personal interview, Morgan Scalley.

95.

University of Utah Fiscal Year 2012: Other Funds Capital Development
Project Request on website at www.higheredutah.org/pdfs/non-state-funded.pdf.
Projects being developed in 2011 on website at www.unews.utah.edu/
neighbors-pdf/2011%20Projects%20Being%20Developed.pdf.

96.

Personal interview, Mike Giddings.

97.

"Utah plans to honor Herrion," by Dirk Facer, *Deseret News*, August 23,
2005.
"Coroner says Herrion died of heart disease," Associated Press, September
6, 2005.
"Ex-Ute collapses, dies," by Dirk Facer, *Deseret News*, August 22, 2005.
"Death of lineman after game remains troubling mystery," by Clifton
Brown, *New York Times*, August 22, 2005.

98.

Personal interview, Roy Jefferson.

99.

Personal interview, Don Van Galder.
"Snafu of '72 comes to mind with Utah a conference foe once again," by
Javier Morales, *Tucson Citizen*, June 17, 2010.
"Impossible fourth quarter," by Hack Miller, *Deseret News*, November 6,
1972.

100.

Personal interview, Steve Marshall.